Roles and Contexts in Counselling Psychology

C000258274

Roles and Contexts in Counselling Psychology looks at the different contexts that counselling psychologists typically work within, offering a snapshot of the 'day job'.

The book provides insights into roles that reflect the human lifespan from birth to death, focusing upon specific mental health experiences and considering roles external to healthcare settings such as expert witness and independent practice. Each chapter is written by a counselling psychologist and offers an overview of their particular specialism and their experiences within it, bringing a unique transparency and personal insight. The book describes the skills that are required for the different roles and their challenges and rewards. It also discusses how the philosophy of counselling psychology is maintained and explores the associated ethical and legal considerations. Further, it takes note of the issues relating to leadership and diversity.

The book is an essential resource for undergraduate psychology and counselling students and trainee clinical or counselling psychologists, as well as qualified practitioners.

Daisy Best qualified as a counselling psychologist in 2008 and has worked therapeutically with clients for over twenty years within the NHS, third sector and currently within her own independent psychology practice. She taught on a doctorate in counselling psychology course for 12 years and is an active researcher.

Helen Nicholas is a registered practitioner psychologist and accredited EMDR therapist currently working in independent private practice. She taught in academia and was the (Interim) Head of the Department of Psychological Health, Trauma and Forensic Psychology at a UK university. Helen specialises in working with adults and older adults with trauma, adjustment disorders, depression, anxiety, phobias and work-related stress.

Mark Bradley is a registered practitioner psychologist working in independent private practice. He has worked with children and their families for 25 years and has substantial experience as an expert witness in family courts. His main area of expertise is in safeguarding and the effects of trauma on child development.

Roles and Contexts in Counselling Psychology

Professionals in Practice

Edited by
Daisy Best, Helen Nicholas and
Mark Bradley

Routledge
Taylor & Francis Group

LONDON AND NEW YORK

Cover image: © Getty Images

First published 2022
by Routledge
4 Park Square, Milton Park, Abingdon, Oxon OX14 4RN

and by Routledge
605 Third Avenue, New York, NY 10158

Routledge is an imprint of the Taylor & Francis Group, an informa business

British Library Cataloguing-in-Publication Data
A catalogue record for this book is available from the British Library

Library of Congress Cataloging-in-Publication Data
Names: Best, Daisy (Psychologist), editor. | Nicholas, Helen (Psychologist), editor. | Bradley, Mark (Psychologist), editor.
Title: Roles and contexts in counselling psychology : professionals in practice / edited by Daisy Best, Helen Nicholas and Mark Bradley.
Description: Milton Park, Abingdon, Oxon ; New York, NY : Routledge, 2022. | Includes bibliographical references and index. |
Identifiers: LCCN 2021053733 (print) | LCCN 2021053734 (ebook) | ISBN 9780367747442 (hardback) | ISBN 9780367747435 (paperback) | ISBN 9781003159339 (ebook)
Subjects: LCSH: Psychology--Vocational guidance.
Classification: LCC BF76 .R65 2022 (print) | LCC BF76 (ebook) | DDC 150.23--dc23/eng/20211109
LC record available at https://lccn.loc.gov/2021053733
LC ebook record available at https://lccn.loc.gov/2021053734

ISBN: 978-0-367-74744-2 (hbk)
ISBN: 978-0-367-74743-5 (pbk)
ISBN: 978-1-003-15933-9 (ebk)

DOI: 10.4324/9781003159339

Typeset in Times New Roman
by Taylor & Francis Books

Contents

Illustrations

Contributors

Lesley Armitage (South Tees Hospitals NHS Foundation Trust, England, UK) is a registered practitioner psychologist who has worked in physical healthcare settings since qualifying as a counselling psychologist in 2009. Her experience includes pain management, weight management, spinal cord injury rehabilitation and major physical trauma. She has a special interest in Compassion Focused Therapy as applied in physical healthcare.

Claire Arnold-Baker (New School of Psychotherapy and Counselling (NSPC), England, UK) is a counselling psychologist specialising in the perinatal period in her private practice. This is also where her research interests lie and the topic of her recently edited book, *The Existential Crisis of Motherhood*. She is also the Course Leader of the DCPsych programme and Academic Director at NSPC.

Daisy Best (North Yorkshire Psychological Therapies Ltd., England, UK) qualified as a counselling psychologist in 2008 and has worked therapeutically with clients for over twenty years within the NHS, third sector and currently within her own independent psychology practice. She taught on a doctorate in counselling psychology for 12 years and is an active researcher.

Mark Bradley (Bradley Psychological Service & Psychrep UK, England, UK) is a registered practitioner psychologist working in independent private practice. He has worked with children and their families for 25 years and has substantial experience as an expert witness in family courts. His main area of expertise is in safeguarding and the effects of trauma on child development.

Janice Brydon (Northumberland Tyne and Wear NHS Trust and Independent private practice, England, UK) qualified as a counselling psychologist in 2014 and has worked therapeutically with clients for over 25 years within the NHS, third sector and currently within her own independent psychology practice. A specialist in trauma, she is a supervisor for counselling psychology students and an active researcher in trauma recovery.

Philippa Capel (Herefordshire and Worcestershire Health and Care NHS Trust, England, UK) qualified as a counselling psychologist in 2006 and has worked within the NHS, MOD and private psychology organisations. She currently works within an Older Adult Service in the NHS with a special interest in trauma and trauma informed services. She has lectured at a range of universities and organisations.

Raymond Dempsey (TherapsGLA Consultants, Scotland, UK) qualified as a Counsellor in 1992 and a counselling psychologist in 2008. He has worked therapeutically in independent practice since 2003 and has extensive experience of consultancy in palliative care through bereavement service review and redesign; senior leadership development programmes; coaching; and facilitating practitioner reflective practice.

Andre Etchebarne (University of Manchester, England, UK) is a third-year trainee counselling psychologist. His interests are in pain management and the wellbeing consequences of racism and other forms of discrimination.

Charles Frost (Pennine Care NHS Foundation Trust, England, UK) qualified as a counselling psychologist in 2015 after twenty years working as a counsellor and counselling supervisor for ChildLine. He now works in a primary care mental health service in the NHS and has taught at both Liverpool John Moores University and the University of Manchester.

Terry Hanley (University of Manchester, England, UK) is a registered practitioner psychologist working as an academic in the Manchester Institute of Education. He has written widely about therapeutic work with children and young people, most specifically considering the importance of pluralistic provision and the development of web-based services for this age group.

Julia Ann Harrison (Psychology Services & Northumbria Healthcare NHS Foundation Trust, England, UK) is a registered practitioner psychologist and works within pain management. She has previously enjoyed a role in occupational health within a staff psychology service. Julia has a background in humanistic counselling and works in independent private practice.

Pam Jameson (Specialist Psychological Therapies Service, CNTW NHS Foundation Trust, England, UK) has worked in the NHS since qualifying as a counselling psychologist in 2007. Having worked predominantly in secondary care community teams, she has also worked in private practice, within a university setting, and has recently moved to a new NHS Trust to work within a specialist psychological therapies service.

Jessica McCarrick (Tees, Esk and Wear Valley NHS Foundation Trust, England, UK) qualified as a counselling psychologist in 2014 and has worked therapeutically with clients for over seven years within the NHS, third sector and independent sector. She taught on a doctorate in counselling psychology for three years and is an active researcher.

Helen Nicholas (HCN Psychology, England, UK) is a registered practitioner psychologist and accredited EMDR therapist currently working in independent private practice. She taught in academia and was the (Interim) Head of the Department of Psychological Health, Trauma and Forensic Psychology at a UK university. Helen specialises in working with adults and older adults with trauma, adjustment disorders, depression, anxiety, phobias, and work-related stress.

Stephen Ollis (Tees Esk Wear Valley NHS Foundation Trust, England, UK) qualified as a counselling psychologist in 2010 and has worked predominantly with adults with learning disabilities across the north east of England since then, with a particular interest in trauma-informed care. Stephen has also worked as a lecturer on the counselling psychology doctorate at the University of Teesside.

Joanna Omylinska-Thurston (Greater Manchester Mental Health NHS Foundation Trust, University of Salford, England, UK) has been working within NHS for the last twenty years, including eight years in IAPT. She integrates humanistic, cognitive-behavioural and psychodynamic approaches. Joanna has undertaken several research projects and she is currently co-leading a project exploring the use of creative methods in the treatment of depression.

Tony Ward (University of the West of England, England, UK) is an Associate Professor of counselling psychology at the University of the West of England, where he mainly teaches on the professional doctorate in counselling psychology. He is also a visiting lecturer at Paris 8 University in France and is active in private practice.

Gabriel Wynn (University of Manchester, England, UK) is a Lecturer in counselling psychology at University of Manchester. From 1994 she worked as a practitioner psychologist in hospital and community mental health settings in the USA. Following her move to UK in 2002 she has principally worked in third-sector service clinical and operational lead roles.

Introduction

Mark Bradley, Helen Nicholas and Daisy Best

We are very pleased to present this compilation of chapters that provide readers with a glimpse into the diverse range of counselling psychologists' roles. The chapters are written by practitioners and academics with significant expertise in and knowledge of the areas they describe. The book, although written by UK counselling psychologists and mainly from a UK perspective, is also relevant for an international audience. Counselling psychologists internationally, despite having different training routes into the profession, all have their foundation and roots within a person-centred philosophy. Although the work settings, regulatory and professional bodies, and training routes may vary between countries, all counselling psychologists share certain key recognisable features wherever they practise. For example, a recent survey of counselling psychologists covering eight countries identified the similarities within the profession, highlighting commonality in terms of core beliefs, foundations of the profession and the importance placed on the therapeutic relationship (Goodyear & Lichtenberg, 2019). It also illustrated the breadth and depth of our knowledge, experience and specialisms.

Many counselling psychologists work in private practice and academia. This is true in Canada, where the majority of counselling psychologists work in private practice or academia; in Australia, where nearly half work in private practice; and in New Zealand, where two thirds of counselling psychologists work in private practice or non-government-funded organisations. In addition to the chapters written about their own specialisms and areas of interest, international counselling psychologists may find chapters 16 and 17 of particular interest. The top three core values of counselling psychologists internationally are: 1) their attention to people's assets, strengths and resources, regardless of degree of distress; 2) a focus on diversity, as well as a consideration of sociocultural context and systemic barriers in making sense of and understanding people's experiences; and 3) a focus on person-environment interactions rather than exclusively on either person or the environment. All counselling psychologists will, at some point in their career, develop their interests, face challenges such as the changing job market and employability concerns, and think about their identity as a counselling psychologist and

DOI: 10.4324/9781003159339-1

what it means to them. We hold on to the uniqueness and the roots and values of counselling psychology as a profession and hope that this book provides the reader with a useful snapshot view. Each chapter highlights the many opportunities for personal and professional development within a particular area of mental health services, as well as identifying the potential challenges. Attention has been paid to the skills needed in each context, the personal reflections of the authors, and key ethical and legal considerations.

Section 1: Lifespan

Section 1 provides the reader with an overview of the various settings in which counselling psychologists work across the lifespan, from perinatal services to end-of-life care. Drawing on the experiences of counselling psychologists in practice, each chapter provides a detailed and personal account highlighting the many benefits and challenges of working in specific fields.

Chapter 1 highlights the complexity of *working in perinatal mental health* and how support for mothers has become part of the national picture. Pregnancy and the postnatal period is a time of transition that may involve major changes to a person's life. Consequently, it is a time of vulnerability for mothers, who can face challenges to their mental health. Perinatal mental health is a specialist area requiring knowledge of developmental and attachment theories and of family systems, as well as an understanding of physical health. Aspects of the role are described. In addition, the chapter looks at an existential framework to enable working in a holistic way. It also considers the key skills in containment and holding, mentalization and the perinatal frame of mind required for the role.

Issues around diversity – including ethnicity and culture and gender and neurodiversity – are highlighted, with particular attention paid to how discrimination can impact the mother's experience. The need for detailed risk assessment is emphasised, since maternal suicide is the fifth most common cause of women's deaths during pregnancy and its immediate aftermath. The chapter concludes by considering the challenges of the role as well as personal reflections on the rewards of working with this diverse client group.

Chapter 2 provides the reader with an insight into *working with children and adolescents* as a counselling psychologist. This is a particularly challenging and ever-changing area of practice. This chapter provides an overview of the core issues related to working in this area. It starts by highlighting the current context in which services have been developed and reflects upon the different settings in which individuals may work (e.g. within education, health or online). Following on from this, the chapter outlines how services, and therapy itself, might be tailored for these age groups. It briefly reflects upon differing modes of delivery and considers the nature of the child-adult therapeutic relationship. To end, the chapter outlines some of the additional activities that counselling psychologists might engage in when working with children and adolescents. These include service management tasks and being involved in research and training.

Chapter 3 then introduces the reader to the challenges and benefits of *working in Improving Access to Psychological Therapy (IAPT) services*, which has helped shape the way in which adult mental health services are delivered in the UK. The chapter is a personal and thought-provoking account of working in IAPT services as a counselling psychologist, based on the lived experiences of the authors and their colleagues. While it may not be representative of the experiences of all counselling psychologists operating in these services nationally, the chapter provides a unique insight into the work of counselling psychologists in some IAPT settings.

IAPT is the main provider of psychological therapy for adults within the National Health Service (NHS) in the UK. It was developed in 2008 as a way of organising a systematic delivery of evidence-based interventions for anxiety and depression. Counselling psychologists are usually employed within IAPT to work with clients with complex presentations. The skills required involve being able to undertake thorough assessments (including risk), prepare formulations and deliver a range of evidence-based therapies. Counselling psychologists have a range of roles within IAPT, including therapy, supervision and management. Roles within research and training are less common. Working within IAPT commonly requires counselling psychologists to consider risk and safeguarding issues, so BPS and HCPC ethical and legal guidelines are particularly relevant. Working in IAPT involves tight structures around client throughput, which is challenging in terms of counselling psychology's humanistic value base. However, counselling psychologists have an opportunity to work with a diverse group of clients within IAPT and connect with the social justice agenda, especially when working in deprived areas.

Chapter 4 then introduces the reader to the challenges and benefits of *working with older adults*. This chapter explores the causes of distress for older adults and the context of ageing in the UK. It highlights therapeutic considerations, differences, adaptations and challenges in working with the older population. The context defines older adults and their position within UK society, including life stage and changes in role, in addition to causes of distress.

The skills required include an ability to adapt therapeutic models. The chapter discusses factors related to psychometric measures and the assessment of risk with older adults, alongside helping the reader make sense of cognitive changes in relation to distress and therapeutic interventions. It outlines the challenges of building a therapeutic relationship with and relating to older people, and covers cohort differences and therapists' approaches and beliefs. The chapter looks at working with complexity related to physical health difficulties and operating within a larger system; it takes family, health and social care into account.

The chapter discusses the ethical considerations particular to older adults, including age discrimination, access to services, and information sharing in a complex system, and looks at the Capacity Act, the Mental Health Act and 'best interest'. It concludes with a reflection on the different roles a counselling psychologist can fill.

Finally, chapter 5 provides a unique insight into *working within the field of palliative care*. The author offers a thought-provoking account of their experience in the field, and outlines the challenges for and contributions of counselling psychologists. As the author points out, dying is inevitable: distress with dying is not. Responding therapeutically to the individual in their living-with-dying requires the counselling psychologist to understand the medical, psychological, social, spiritual and existential worldview of the one who is living-with-dying and their support network. The chapter promotes the spiritual/existential-biopsychosocial approach of the counselling psychologist – that is, honouring the subjective experience of the one with life-threatening or life-limiting illness and supporting the dignity of the individual in their care. Working through this 'dignity' lens, the chapter shows how the counselling psychologist supports individual difference, lifespan stage, cultural issues, spiritual/religious attunement, and far-ranging encounters in the trajectory of the individual's stable–unstable–deteriorating–dying progression through palliative care.

This chapter promotes the counselling psychologist working in end-of-life as a professional companion to the one who is living-with-dying; a support to their family and social network; and as an influencer to the multi-professional team enlisted as a professional care system.

Section 2: Condition Specific

Section 2 provides an overview of the experience of working with specific mental health and neurodevelopmental conditions through the lens of counselling psychologists. Each author has extensive experience of working in specialist services and introduces the reader to the opportunities, challenges and benefits of working as a counselling psychologist in a particular health setting.

Chapter 6 focuses on *working as a counselling psychologist in an adult learning disability team*. The chapter captures the author's experience of working as a counselling psychologist in an NHS adult learning disability team for over a decade. It outlines what a learning disability is before exploring the most critical current and historical contexts. Finally, it describes key aspects of the role and provides some personal reflections.

This chapter demonstrates the importance of the therapeutic relationship as an agent of change within therapy, as well as the different relationships that may impact on the life of the client. The chapter outlines how this ethos effectively fits in with both the client group and the discipline of counselling psychology.

Chapter 7, on *counselling psychology in medical and physical health settings*, explores the relationship between physical health conditions and psychological health. The author outlines the range of roles for counselling psychologists within physical health, the competencies required of applied psychologists in physical health settings, and the key features of these roles. The chapter includes an exploration of relevant models and clinical applications, including opportunities for counselling psychologists to expand their skills beyond therapy. Case examples and the author's personal reflections are used to indicate typical presentations and interventions.

The author discusses the challenges and opportunities for counselling psychologists in medical settings and explores whether the prevailing medical model is in opposition to the philosophy of counselling psychology. The chapter looks at how to cultivate an atmosphere of open, curious enquiry, valuing different perspectives on health and illness and thus making the most of both our similarities and our differences to the medical approach. The author suggests that counselling psychologists are uniquely placed to contribute to the evolving model of healthcare for physical conditions.

Chapter 8, on *working with neurological client groups*, explores the contexts in which counselling psychologists work with different neurological client groups. These include NHS neuropsychological services, stroke services, rehabilitation settings, services for older people and charities.

It briefly reviews the specialist knowledge and skills required for working in such settings, including knowledge of neuropsychology, brain anatomy and physiology, the nature of neurological conditions and their impact, and the principles of intervention and rehabilitation with such groups.

Neuropsychological assessment is an important part of the role in such settings. Key tests and principles are outlined, and suggestions made as to how counselling psychologists can develop their knowledge and practice in this area. The chapter describes recent developments that allow counselling psychologists to develop additional skills.

The focus of chapter 9 is *working with people with unusual experiences*. This chapter provides an introduction to psychosis, including the aetiology of psychosis and the development of the hearing voices movement. It includes a brief explanation of the setting, and explanations of the roles and skills that a psychologist in a secondary care community psychosis team would be expected to manage.

The challenges of the role, how to manage these and what can help are also explored. Challenges include maintaining integrity and professional identity, managing boundaries and expectations, and adapting the therapeutic frame of this client group. In addition, the chapter looks at the importance of the therapeutic relationship alongside formulation and progress within therapy.

The author describes her personal experience of working as a psychologist with this client group, together with some case examples, alongside reflections from service users about their experiences of psychological therapy or being part of a hearing voices group.

Working in secondary care adult mental health services is the focus of chapter 10. This is an interesting and challenging area of practice. The affective disorders service described by the author provides assessment and treatment for adults presenting with significant mental health problems associated with disorders of mood, emotion, behaviour and personality. There are services in other parts of the country that have similar delivery aims and are organised around psychosis and non-psychosis pathways; however, the structure is relatively unusual, with most mental health trusts tending to have more general community mental health teams.

The multidisciplinary service allows for a rich amalgamation of skills and understandings, brought together to develop detailed collaborative care plans. The role of a counselling psychologist within this service can be as diverse and interesting as the population it works with.

The chapter reflects upon the emotional, ethical and legal challenges of this role. It includes a case study to illustrate and contextualise the reflections and show what this approach can look like in practice.

Another complex and challenging area is *working with severe and enduring anorexia nervosa* (SE-AN), the focus of chapter 11. It explores why some people don't recover from anorexia nervosa (AN), summarises criteria for using the SE-AN label, and briefly reviews evidence-based SE-AN treatments. A rationale for counselling psychologists to develop socially informed formulations for SE-AN is discussed, along with alternatives to standard weight restoration treatment including reducing habituated behaviour and social isolation within a harm-minimisation framework.

Chapter 12 provides an overview of *working as a counselling psychologist in an NHS occupational health setting*. The occupational health service within an NHS Trust aims to promote and maintain health and prevent accidents and ill health caused at work, in line with the right of employees under the Human Rights Act (1998). Healthy working and wellbeing can raise staff morale, increasing the effectiveness of the organisation and reducing staff absence. The role of a counselling psychologist within this context is explored. Counselling psychologists work as part of diverse, multidisciplinary teams and demonstrate competency within a recognised therapeutic framework appropriate for time-limited, focused interventions.

The chapter considers counselling psychology philosophy within this context. It looks at individual therapy, clinical supervision, staff training, service development and clinical audit, all important roles for a counselling psychologist within NHS occupational health. The ability to work within professional ethics and trust policies and be cognisant of issues around equal opportunities and occupational health and safety is imperative for the counselling psychologist in this challenging yet highly rewarding position.

Working relationally with clients who have experienced a traumatic event or events is the focus of chapter 13. It looks at evidence-based therapies used by counselling psychologists in the treatment of trauma and complex trauma; these include eye-movement desensitisation and reprocessing and trauma-focused approaches. It points readers to psychometric and outcome measures that counselling psychologists use during the assessment and formulation process.

The chapter outlines the key skills counselling psychologists will need, as well as specific competencies required to work relationally with this client group. It looks at suggested 'beyond the therapy room' approaches and how counselling psychologists can incorporate body work into their therapy sessions. The variety the role offers, the opportunities it presents and the challenges that come with working with this client group are discussed. Attention is drawn to the importance of self-care in relation to vicarious trauma and compassion fatigue.

As this summary highlights, counselling psychologists have opportunities to work in a range of settings. Chapter 14 provides an overview of the author's experiences of *working in forensic settings as a counselling psychologist.*

Within a young person's medium secure setting, care and treatment is provided within a highly prescribed set of physical, relational and procedural security measures. The young person's care within this setting will be an individualised, multi-disciplinary and evidence-based treatment package, which is explored within this chapter alongside the challenges of this complex role. The secure environment and continual staff supervision enables the treatment of high risk and complex young people with serious mental health disorders. Counselling psychologists are working within the prescribed stringent levels of physical, relational and procedural security and clinicians have to adjust to a number of challenging situations.

The counselling psychologist's specific therapeutic skills need to be both broad and flexible as the range of influences on young people's lives mean that they are prone to periods of disengagement from interventions. It is through the quality of the relationship formed that real progress can be made in the prevention of future offending. This can be emotionally demanding and stressful. The chapter includes personal reflections on the integration of forensic and counselling psychology, as well as reference to the factors that lead to the detention of young people.

Section 3: Beyond Health Care

Finally, section 3 provides the reader with an interesting insight into areas of work beyond the health care setting. The three chapters have relevance for those wishing to work in independent private practice, in higher education or as an expert witness within the court arena. They highlight opportunities available to counselling psychologists who would like to develop skills and a career outside or alongside their work in health care settings.

First, chapter 15 draws on the author's experience to examine the role of *counselling psychologist as expert witness in the family courts.* As counselling psychologists, we can be called upon to give evidence in court as a professional witness and an expert witness. With this in mind, the chapter outlines the structure, process and formality of court proceedings, and the counselling psychologist's role within these.

It explores how counselling psychologists can assist the court in better understanding the social and human factors that can result in state intervention, with the aim of reducing the stigma and shame often experienced by vulnerable people moving through what is an adversarial process. With practical tips and advice, the chapter aims to share the author's personal experience of the court process and the importance of holding on to the core values that underpin our work as counselling psychologists.

Next, chapter 16 looks at opportunities to work in *independent private practice*. This chapter focuses on the potential career benefits of working in what is referred to throughout as 'private practice' as part of a portfolio career. It includes the development of a business idea and reflections on incorporating the 'businessperson' into our counselling psychology identity. There is discussion of the therapeutic setting and the challenges involved, in addition to legal and ethical considerations.

Based on the authors' clinical and business experience, they further highlight the importance of building and maintaining networking connections with colleagues, marketing consistently and appropriately and understanding the value of self-care, resilience and self-awareness.

Finally, chapter 17 explores *working as a counselling psychology lecturer in higher education*, with a particular focus on teaching a doctorate in counselling psychology. The chapter is informed by the author's 12 years of experience as a senior lecturer, including several years as the programme director for a doctorate in counselling psychology. The chapter considers the professional guidelines and standards, the many roles that a lecturer is likely to undertake, the relationships with stakeholders, including trainees, and opportunities for leadership.

The chapter outlines what makes an effective lecturer and what to take into account when contemplating a career in academia. Honest reflections based on the author's own experience provide insight into both the benefits and the challenges of the role.

In summary, each section provides the reader with information about the types of work and different careers chosen by counselling psychologists. Drawing together the experiences of counselling psychologists from around the UK, the book is an honest account of the challenges and opportunities within specific fields. As counselling psychologists, we are in the privileged position to help and empower the most vulnerable people in society. This book provides examples of how we do this, and how we continue to make a valuable contribution to improving the lives of others.

References

Goodyear, R. K. & Lichtenberg, J. W. (2019). *A Global Portrait of Counselling Psychology* (1st edition). Routledge.

Section 1

Lifespan

Chapter 1

Working in perinatal mental health as a counselling psychologist

Claire Arnold-Baker

The importance of maternal mental health during the peri and postnatal period has gained significance in recent years. With this increased awareness has come a recognition of the variety of ways in which pregnancy and the postpartum period is a vulnerable time for women or birthing people. The transition that women go through to become mothers – *matresence* or 'mother-becoming' (Raphael, 1975) – has been likened to adolescence: as women are confronted by changes to their bodies and hormones, social roles, identity, purpose and meaning in life, they can experience an existential crisis (Arnold-Baker, 2020). It is estimated that around one in five pregnant women will experience mental health problems either during pregnancy or within the first year after birth (Royal College of Psychiatrists, 2018). Recognition that motherhood can effect mothers' emotional experiences during the perinatal period is not a new concept, with Eastman coining the term 'baby blues' in 1940 to cover a myriad of emotional experiences. However, until recently mothers often felt there was a binary choice, having to describe their emotional experience of motherhood as either postnatal depression (PND) or 'baby blues' – a view that persisted despite literature such as Price's (1988) book *Motherhood: What It Does to Your Mind* that highlighted the emotional and psychological changes that can occur postpartum. Yet the reality of a woman's or birthing person's experience is far more complex than the restricted realm of depressive disorders and can result in issues around *matresence*, anxiety, eating disorders, obsessive compulsive disorder (OCD), phobias such as general health anxiety or tokophobia (fear of giving birth), birth trauma and post-traumatic stress disorder (PTSD), and psychosis. This chapter therefore aims to highlight the complexity of the perinatal period and considers the varied and important role counselling psychologists play in working with this diverse client group.

The intricacy of the perinatal period in terms of mental health is an area where counselling psychologists have much to offer. In fact, as greater awareness has been generated through campaigns or research – for example, by the Confidential Enquiry into Maternal and Child Health (CEMACH, 2007) – it has highlighted how perinatal mental health has become a

DOI: 10.4324/9781003159339-2

significant concern in terms of both economic costs and the cost to mothers' lives. It has been estimated that the impact of maternal mental health costs the UK approximately £8.1 billion per year (Bauer et al., 2014), which does not include the cost to people's lives. This compelling evidence has shifted policy within the NHS towards offering more support in the perinatal period, a much needed and important development.

Perinatal care is now part of the NHS Long-Term Plan, which aims to transform physical and mental health care provision. The plan gives a commitment to extend the period of time in which specialist help can be offered from one (the extent of the current provision) to two years postpartum, in recognition of the fact that mothers often delay seeking help or need more extensive help depending on the severity of their mental health problems. The Long-Term Plan is ambitious in its aim to offer help to 24,000 new mothers by 2023/4, which is in addition to the 30,000 women the NHS currently plans to help in the year 2020/21 (Psychological Professions Network, 2019). In order to meet these targets, new specialist perinatal psychology positions have been created within the NHS.

Psychologists working in the NHS will either be attached to a perinatal mental health team in a trust, or they may work in a mother and baby unit (MBU). The perinatal mental health team will normally work with moderate to severe mental health issues, which account for 5 in 100 women. These services are usually only accessed through referral and do not accept self-referrals from mothers or birthing people. The perinatal mental health team will often work closely with maternity services as well as with local community and in-patient mental health services, primary care services, social services and other third-sector organisations.

However, around 2–4 mothers per 1,000 will need more specialist in-patient care and will be referred on to a MBU (Royal College of Psychiatrists, 2018). These are important units as they keep the mother and baby together while giving the mother multidisciplinary support. The multidisciplinary team at a MBU will include psychiatrists, mental health nurses, nursery nurses, social workers, psychologists, health visitors, nursing assistants and administrators. However, this provision is limited, with only 19 MBUs in England, two in Scotland, one in Wales and none in Northern Ireland currently (Maternal Mental Health Alliance, 2019). This means that women may be unable to secure a place in a unit or they may be placed in a unit some distance from where they live.

The NHS is not the only setting where in which counselling psychologists can work within perinatal care; there are also opportunities to support mothers and birthing people in third-sector organisations. However, it is most likely that counselling psychologists will specialise in this area in their private practice. Working independently enables counselling psychologists to accept self-referrals and to work with mothers and birthing people past the first year, which is important as some mental health issues emerge later or it takes time for the individual to overcome any blocks which might have prevented them from seeking help sooner. Counselling psychologists work with a range of issues in private practice and are not restricted in the scope of this work by the severity of the presenting issue.

Day-to-day skills, roles and responsibilities

The main work of a perinatal counselling psychologist is to provide psychological therapy to clients who are suffering from mental health issues and distress during pregnancy and the first year postpartum, and beyond if working privately. Counselling psychologists will conduct assessment sessions and formulate treatment plans, often liaising with other members of a team. It is important that the perinatal counselling psychologist has a range of knowledge and understanding of not only mental health but also physical health care, particularly in maternity. Having a comprehension of the physical process and co-morbid health conditions related to the perinatal period will enable counselling psychologists to properly appreciate the struggles that women and birthing people go through during this time. It is a specialised area, and one where the counselling psychologist must be able to integrate and have an in-depth knowledge of not only maternal mental health but also infant mental health and developmental psychology, as matters pertaining to these areas often arise within the therapeutic work. Equally important is an understanding of family dynamics and how relationships with the partner and extended family may change during the perinatal period. Knowledge of these different disciplines makes this an interesting and rewarding area of work.

Working in private practice enables a greater scope of work. Most clients will self-refer, and many women and birthing people prefer the anonymous and confidential aspects of being supported by a therapist who is not connected to maternity or health visiting services, fearing what seeking help may communicate to health care professionals. There is still huge stigma for mothers around seeking help, and many mothers equate the need for additional support with having failed or not being a 'good' mother. For some there is also a fear that if they admit to not being able to cope their babies will be taken from them. It is therefore important that counselling psychologists are able to normalise experiences within the perinatal period to enable women to gain the help that they need.

Being a new and expanding field of counselling psychology there will be opportunities for counselling psychologists to play a role in service development; in addition to offering training, education and supervision to those working in maternal mental health that is informed by both practice-led and research-based knowledge. Furthermore, counselling psychologists can make a major contribution to understanding this complex area of mental health through their own research – indeed, there has been a rise in doctoral research from a variety of perspectives being produced by trainee counselling psychologists in recent years (Arnold-Baker, 2020; Smallwood, 2017).

For those counselling psychologists who are interested in social justice and policy development, there are a number of ways to be involved. Organisations such as the Maternal Mental Health Alliance campaign and lobby for better experiences for women and birthing people. The Division of Clinical Psychology's faculty of perinatal psychology is also involved in policy development, and counselling psychologists are eligible to join and take part in discussions, although we do not currently have voting rights.

Working relationally in the perinatal period

Pregnancy and the postpartum period are complex times, and they create a bio-psycho-social-spiritual phenomenon (Garland, 2020) for women and birthing people. It involves an intricate web of interconnecting dimensions which need to be understood, including their impact on the mother's or birthing person's experiences. It is worth considering an existential framework when conducting assessment sessions and devising formulations to take into account these different dimensions. While an understanding of each client's presenting issue is needed, their context and history are also important in understanding the impact they have on the mother. This will include an exploration of any previous mental health challenges or trauma, their physical experiences and symptoms, their social connections and support systems, how pregnancy and motherhood has affected their sense of self and how this has impacted on their values and beliefs. Table 1.1 highlights areas to explore within the therapeutic work.

The use of an existential framework to explore a mother's or birthing person's world ensures that a holistic view is created and there is proper recognition of how the different dimensions interact with each other. For example, expectations and values in the spiritual dimension connect with judgements of others in the social dimension, which then impacts the mothers' sense of self in the personal dimension.

As the perinatal period is a time of vulnerability for women and birthing people it is important to create a containing and holding therapeutic relationship. This requires the therapeutic relationship to be more positive and validating than other therapeutic relationships (Stern, 2004). Equally important is an understanding of the 'good enough mother' concept (Winnicott, 1989) and how it connects to attachment parenting, and also how the mother's initial sensitive responses to her baby lessen over time, which enables the infant to experience frustration and learn how to tolerate and cope with these moments. This is useful when counteracting the myth in Western cultures that women must be perfect mothers, which causes intense pressure to make the right choices at the right time without necessarily having the knowledge or experience to do this successfully. This in turn leads to feelings of stress, anxiety, guilt or depression. Challenging expectations around 'normal' or 'natural births', the ability to breast or chest feed and being a

Table 1.1

Dimension	Questions to consider during assessment
Physical	How do you • experience your body – pregnancy, birth and breastfeeding? • feel about your sexuality and your sexual body? • experience time and temporality? • manage lack of sleep and exhaustion? • experience the paradox of life and death, or health and illness? • experience any trauma or previous trauma that has been retriggered?
Social	How do you • feel supported by other people? • feel about your relationship with your partner? • feel about your relationship with your own mother? • feel about your friendships? A loss of old connections, or gaining new friendships? • feel about judgements of others/society, i.e. being a 'good mother'?
Personal	How do you • feel your sense of self has changed? • manage your new sense of responsibility? • feel emotionally, i.e. anxiety, depression, guilt, intense love, frustration, etc.?
Spiritual	How do you • feel your expectations matched your experience? • understand the values and beliefs you have around giving birth and caring for a baby? • feel about the myths and taboos you hold about the perinatal period and giving birth? • tolerate and cope with the 'unknown' and feeling 'out of control'?

'good mother' will help women and birthing people to normalise their experiences.

An essential part of understanding the mothers' experience is having an awareness of the impact of the transition to motherhood. Stern (1995) argues that motherhood cannot be seen as a developmental stage in its own right, as only birthing people undergo this transition. Yet he recognised that motherhood is a life-changing event involving a psychological transition from daughter to mother, in which women develop a new sense of identity, which is impacted by social discourse around the maternal role and the responsibility that mothers have for the survival of their babies. More recently Arnold-Baker (2020) elucidated how the transition to motherhood evokes an existential crisis in mothers as they experience change in all four dimensions of their existence. Mothers become more aware of the fundamentals: life and death; freedom, choice and responsibility; and time and temporality. Challenging expectations also result in a re-evaluation of values and beliefs, which ultimately creates new meaning and purpose in life.

When working with mothers and birthing people it is important to maintain the *perinatal frame of mind* which keeps both the needs of the mother and infant and the mother-infant relationship in mind. Counselling psychologists may use a combination of different therapeutic approaches when working with perinatal mental health. Those based on attachment theory, such as mentalisation and the circle of security, enable mothers to understand their own attachment styles so that they can form secure attachments with their babies, and parent-infant psychotherapy helps develop the relationship between parent and baby so that the parent can respond sensitively to them. Other approaches might include compassion-focused therapy, existential therapy, trauma-focused CBT and EMDR. The latter two are relevant as it is estimated that 1 in 25 women experience birth trauma (Svanberg, 2019), where mothers have felt out of control and trapped, not treated humanely, and have recurring nightmares of their childbirth experience, experience a rollercoaster of emotions and face disrupted relationships (Elmir et al., 2010).

Sensitivity to diversity and inclusion in perinatal mental health

An important but often overlooked area of perinatal mental health is the impact of diversity. Black mothers are four times more likely to die in pregnancy or in the first six weeks than white mothers, with Asian mothers twice as likely to die and other ethnicities three times as likely (MBRACE-UK, 2020). These inequalities may be accounted for by health conditions, as Knight et al. (2009) found, where non-white women were one and a half times more likely to suffer a severe maternal morbidity. However, they also intersect with other inequalities such as poverty. Additionally, women from different ethnicities have been found to be more likely to be affected by perinatal mental health problems and also face difficulties accessing mental health services. These challenges are often due to cultural stigma around mental health, but there are also practical issues around childcare and the transport needed to attend appointments (Womersley, Ripullone and Hirst, 2021). In addition, there is a general mistrust of maternity and mental health services which stems from wider issues of institutional racism (Horn, 2020).

Womersley et al. (2021) have highlighted how the screening tools used for the diagnosis of PND, for example, focus more on the psychological effects than the physical or somatic symptoms, which are more likely to be presented by other cultures and are therefore flawed for use in diverse populations. Perhaps more worrying, though, is the racial bias that can occur within the health care setting. Igwe (2020) describes how black mothers are often judged by their skin colour, resulting in health professionals withholding pain relief. Igwe attributes this to a cultural assumption that black women are particularly strong and are less sensitive to physical or emotional pain. There is also a misunderstanding about the way in which black women respond to pain, creating additional unconscious bias amongst the professionals involved. All this can result in distress for the mother and birthing person and lead them to experience their birth as traumatic.

Cultural sensitivity is therefore essential for perinatal counselling psychologists in order that they understand how the cultural context of mothers or birthing persons can impact their perinatal experience. For first or second-generation migrant mothers there may be issues around conflicting child care practices. Ofori (2020) highlighted how second-generation mothers often merge their two cultural identities to create a new sense of themselves. This process can be an unsettling time as mothers are confronted with often conflicting values and beliefs about childcare. However, other cultural issues may be present, such as issues around the gender of the baby, honour and shame. Likewise, first-generation migrant mothers have often experienced previous trauma, which may be reactivated during the birth and perinatal period and requires trauma-informed care (Fair et al., 2020).

You may have noted that throughout this chapter I have used the term birthing person as well as mother, to acknowledge that the person giving birth may not have the gender identity 'woman'. It is important to understand issues around gender identity and sexuality as babies are born into families constructed in many different ways. Much of the perinatal literature and research takes a heteronormative approach that excludes more diverse perinatal experiences, which may present in clients seeking support. Sensitivity and knowledge in this area is needed when working with perinatal clients.

Likewise, an understanding of the experiences and challenges of neurodiverse mothers is also important, as these mothers often find motherhood difficult. Neurodiverse mothers may struggle in their communication with health professionals and may also perceive their parenting skills negatively. This results in higher-than-average rates of postnatal depression being experienced by this population (Pohl et al., 2020).

Linked to this is the partner's perspective, which is often overlooked by health professionals. Sadly, many perinatal mental health teams are not able to cater for partners who experience mental health problems resulting from the birth of their baby. Yet there is a growing body of research (Walters, 2011; Darwin et al., 2017) that suggests that fathers and partners can be deeply affected by the birth of their baby. It is good practice to check how the partner is coping and to refer on if necessary.

The counselling psychologist's understanding of intersectionality and the Power, Threat, Meaning Framework (Johnstone and Boyle, 2018) means they are ideally placed to take the lead in promoting equality and inclusion in perinatal mental health. It is important that all health professionals working in maternity care are provided with appropriate education and training to ensure that they understand not only how different issues around diversity and inclusion can impact the experience of the perinatal period but also how the language people use can have a huge effect both positively and negatively on a person's experience. Counselling psychologists working within the NHS will be in a particularly good position to instigate this. But equally important is understanding issues around accessibility of services and how stigmas, created through social and cultural discourse, may prevent women or birthing people from accessing the support they need.

Ethical and legal considerations

MBRACE-UK (2020) found that suicide was the fifth most common cause of death for mothers during pregnancy and the first six weeks. However, it became the leading cause of death in the first year after the birth. This shockingly high statistic demonstrates the importance of supporting the birthing person's mental health in pregnancy and up to at least the first year of the baby's life. For the counselling psychologist this means ensuring a thorough risk assessment is done for each client due to their increased vulnerability at this time. But it also shows the importance of finding ways to reach those who are most at risk. A more integrated approach to maternity, one that includes the psychological and emotional aspects, would not only prepare women for the transition to motherhood but also, by placing an emphasis on the emotional experiences in the perinatal period, enable potential mental health issues to be highlighted.

Trauma is another area of risk during the perinatal period. Women and birthing people who have suffered previous trauma, especially if it has involved sexual abuse, may find the birth a retraumatising experience. Thankfully, this has now been recognised and specialist birthing centres have been set up for those who have suffered previous trauma but where they are not required to specify what has happened to them. Although this is an important development there is a need for all maternity care to be trauma informed.

Counselling psychologists may also be faced with potential ethical concerns relating to the safety or care of their client's baby or children as a result of their client's deteriorating mental health. Awareness of child protection and when disclosure and action may be necessary is therefore needed.

Challenges of the role

The main challenge, particularly for counselling psychologists working in the NHS, is that maternity has become a medicalised experience. This creates a tension between needing to work within a medical model that pathologises the experience of mothers or birthing persons and working on their difficulties using a more existential-humanistic or relational approach. While diagnoses are an important way of communicating between professionals, they can lead to labelling and create stigma that may be unhelpful in the therapeutic relationship. It is important to see each person's situation as unique and understand how the various aspects of the bio-psycho-social-spiritual combine to create difficulties and struggles for mothers and birthing people.

Personal reflections

I work in private practice specialising in perinatal mental health, which is varied and interesting. It is deeply rewarding to work with mothers, to hold a space for them in their distress and to see them emerge as more confident and more able to cope with the challenges that motherhood brings. The impact of the work is also far-reaching and effects the baby's as well as the partner's lives, making it particularly worthwhile. I have worked with a variety of presenting issues, from disturbing irrational thoughts to depression and crises of the self to birth trauma. From the despair of infertility to the joy of becoming pregnant after miscarriage. Each person brings a distress and a despair that is made more desperate due to the inadequacies they feel compared to others. Yet despite this, the overriding feeling is to take care of and be responsible for their baby, even when there are times when they feel unable to take care of themselves.

Many of the issues presented by mothers are exacerbated by the way in which society is structured. There are inadequate support structures in place, leaving women and birthing people feeling isolated. Societal discourses around birth, breastfeeding, weight loss after the birth, parenting, sleep and maternal instinct all serve to create a sense of failure in mothers. In addition, motherhood can feel chaotic and uncontrollable. Women move from a known world to one that is unknown and where they feel unskilled and lacking in experience. Being able to normalise clients' experiences can be helpful in creating space for them to acknowledge and work on what is troubling them, what they fear, what makes them anxious and overwhelmed. Acknowledging existential themes of responsibility, freedom and choice, mortality, anxiety and guilt can be useful when helping clients make sense of their experiences and the enormity of the changes that have occurred in their life. It is also important to encourage mothers to recognise how they can learn from their babies, when they feel deskilled and how mothering is about developing a relationship with, rather than something they 'do to', their baby. It is important to develop a trusting relationship where the client is able to talk openly about issues they feel unable to share elsewhere. Weekly sessions can act as a 'reset' (Arnold-Baker, 2020) that enables mothers to find the inner resources and courage to carry on and develop flexible ways of facing whatever is presented to them.

References

Arnold-Baker, C. (Ed.) (2020). *The Existential Crisis of Motherhood*. Palgrave Macmillan.

Bauer, A., Parsonage, M., Knapp, M., Lemmi, V. and Adelaja, B. (2014). Costs of perinatal mental health problems. LSE Personal Social Services Research Unit and Centre for Mental Health.

CEMACH (Confidential Enquiry into Maternal and Child Health) (2007). Saving mothers' lives: Reviewing maternal deaths to make motherhood safer. Retrieved from www.publichealth.hscni.net/sites/default/files/Saving%20Mothers%27%20Lives%202003-05%20.pdf.

Darwin, Z., Galdas, P. and Hinchliff, S. et al. (2017). Fathers' views and experiences of their own mental health during pregnancy and the first postnatal year: A qualitative interview study of men participating in the UK Born and Bred in Yorkshire (BaBY) cohort. *BMC Pregnancy Childbirth* 17, 45. https://doi.org/10.1186/s12884-017-1229-4.

Elmir, R., V., Schmied, L. Wilkes, and D. Jackson (2010). Women's perceptions and experiences of a traumatic birth: A meta-ethnography. *Journal of Advanced Nursing* 66(10), 2142–2153.

Fair, F., Raben, L., Watson, H., Vivilaki, V., van den Muijsenbergh, M., Soltani, H. et al. (2020). Migrant women's experiences of pregnancy, childbirth and maternity care in European countries: A systematic review. *PLoS ONE* 15(2), e0228378. https://doi.org/10.1371/journal.pone.0228378.

Garland, V. (2020). Existential responsibility of motherhood. In C. Arnold-Baker (Ed.), *The Existential Crisis of Motherhood*. Palgrave Macmillan.

Igwe, S. (2020). Being seen, being heard: Improving maternity care for Black women. *The Royal College of Midwives Opinion*, www.rcm.org.uk.

Johnstone, L. and Boyle, M. (2018). The Power Threat Meaning Framework: An alternative nondiagnostic conceptual system. *Journal of Humanistic Psychology*, August. https://doi.org/10.1177/0022167818793289.

Horn, A. (2020). Racism Matters: 'When people show you who they are, believe them': Why Black women mistrust maternity services. *The Practising Midwife*, 23(8).

Knight, M., Kurinczuk, J., Spark, P. and Brocklehurst, P. (2009). Inequalities in maternal health: National cohort study of ethnic variation in severe maternal morbidities. *British Medical Journal*, March. https://doi.org/10.1136/bmj.b542.

Maternal Mental Health Alliance (2019). Mother and Baby Units. www.maternalmentalhealthalliance.org/campaign/maps.

MBRACE-UK (2020). Saving lives, improving mothers' care: Lay summary. www.npeu.ox.ac.uk.

Ofori, J. (2020). Identity and mothering: The second generation of Ghanaian migrants. In C. Arnold-Baker (Ed.), *The Existential Crisis of Motherhood*. Palgrave Macmillan.

Pohl, A. L., Crockford, S. K., Blakemore, M., Allison, C. and Baron-Cohen, S. (2020). A comparative study of autistic and non-autistic women's experience of motherhood. *Molecular Autism* 11(3).

Price, J. (1988). *Motherhood: What It Does to Your Mind*. Rivers Oram Press/Pandora List.

Psychological Professions Network (2019). Implementing the NHS Long Term Plan: Maximising the impact of the psychological professions. www.ppn.nhs.uk.

Raphael, D. (1975). *Being Female: Reproduction, Power and Change.* De Gruyter Mouton.

Royal College of Psychiatrists (2015). Perinatal Mental Health Services: Recommendations for the provision of services for childbearing women. RCP Report.

Royal College of Psychiatrists (2018). Mother and Baby Units (MBUs). www.rcpsych.ac.uk/mental-health/treatments-and-wellbeing/mother-and-baby-units-(mbus).

Smallwood, S. (2017). Understanding the role of stigma in women's help-seeking behaviours for postpartum emotional difficulties: A grounded theory study. Doctoral thesis, London Metropolitan University. http://repository.londonmet.ac.uk/1246/.

Stern, D. (1995). *The Motherhood Constellation: A Unified View of Parent-infant Psychotherapy.* Karnac Books.

Stern, D. (2004). The motherhood constellation: Therapeutic approaches to early relational problems. In A. J. Sameroff, S. C. McDonough and K. L. Rosenblum (|Eds), *Treating Parent-infant Relationship Problems: Strategies for Intervention.* Guildford Press.

Svanberg, E. (2019). *Why Birth Trauma Matters.* Pinter & Martin.

Walters, J. (2011). *Working with Fathers.* Palgrave Macmillan.

Winnicott, D. W. (1989). *Playing and Reality.* Routledge.

Womersley, K., Ripullone, K. and Hirst, J. E. (2021). Tackling inequality in maternal health: Beyond the postpartum. *Future Healthcare Journal* 8(1), 31–35.

Chapter 2

Working with children and adolescents

Terry Hanley and Andre Etchebarne

Overview

This chapter provides an overview of the core issues related to working as a counselling psychologist with children and adolescents. It starts by highlighting the current context in which such services have been developed and reflects upon the different settings in which individuals may work (e.g., within education or health, or online). Following on from this, the chapter outlines how services, and therapy itself, might be tailored for these age groups. It briefly reflects upon different modes of delivery and considers the nature of the child-adult therapeutic relationship. To end, the chapter outlines some of the additional activities that counselling psychologists might engage in when working with children and adolescents. These include service management tasks and being involved in research and training.

Context and settings

Context

First, it is important to outline how we define the terms 'children' and 'adolescents' in this chapter. These terms, along with others such as 'young people' and 'young adults', are commonly used interchangeably in the literature. For the purposes here, we define 'children' as individuals younger than ten, and 'adolescents' and 'young people' as individuals between the ages of ten and 19. In our society, adolescence might be viewed as lasting beyond 19, with many believing that it extends to 25 (e.g., Sawyer et al., 2018). However, this chapter specifically focuses on those under 20, with discussions around working with those aged 20–25 potentially making more sense in other chapters of this book.

Young people experience profound changes to their cognitive, physical, emotional and social aspects of self. Individuals have to make sense of their bodies maturing and going through numerous growth spurts at the same time as their social lives start to extend from small family contexts to broader

DOI: 10.4324/9781003159339-3

community, school and online environments. These changes are experienced at a greater speed than any other stage across the lifespan, and the associated developments may be mediated by genetic factors, nutrition, socio-economic status and social relationships (Coleman, 2011). As such, childhood and adolescence are fraught with complex obstacles for individuals to navigate.

There are numerous reasons why children and young people access therapeutic services. They range from intrapersonal issues that relate to the individual starting to understand themselves and who they are to interpersonal issues that reflect how the individual relates to the people and systems they find themselves in (e.g., families, schools, communities). Common issues that young people attend therapy for support with include relationship issues between friends and family, issues around anger, significant bereavements, coping with bullying, and issues related to self-worth (Cooper, 2013). Such issues can range hugely in severity, with some individuals encountering extremely harmful events, such as physical or sexual abuse or neglect, on a daily basis. Such events are sometimes referred to as adverse childhood events (ACEs). Further, in contemporary society, the internet poses an additional challenge for individuals. In some instances, issues that have historically been confined to physical environments such as the school site can now extend into homes via digital devices. Issues such as cyberbullying can magnify face-to-face difficulties and lead to even more relentless pressures.

The wide variety of difficulties that young individuals encounter may help to explain why, as of 2020, 16% of 5–16-year-olds in England experience mental health difficulties. This figure represents an increase from 10.8% of 5–16-year-olds in the 2017 version of the same survey (NHS Digital, 2020). It highlights the large number of individuals who might benefit from additional support and has potentially significant implications for society. For example, it is argued that the onset of mental health and wellbeing difficulties in childhood increases the likelihood of individuals having difficulties that persist into adulthood (Caspi et al., 2020). Early interventions are thus viewed as critical for positive outcomes for both individuals and society. To put this into context, while the prevalence of physical health concerns tends to peak after the age of 50, half of all diagnosable mental health concerns are believed to develop before the age of 14 (Kessler et al., 2005). This view may actually underreport the prevalence of mental health concerns as many of the issues that bring a young person to therapy may not map neatly onto diagnostic manuals like the International Classification of Diseases (ICD-11) (World Health Organization, 2019) and the Diagnostic and Statistical Manual of Mental Disorders (DSM-5) (American Psychiatric Association, 2013).

Settings

Therapeutic interventions are offered in numerous environments. For instance, in 2017, 61% of schools offered some form of counselling service (Children's

Commissioner, 2020). Historically, however, the work that counselling psychologists provide to children and young people has been found in healthcare settings such as Child and Adolescent Mental Health Services (CAMHS). Additionally, Forensic Child and Adolescent Mental Health Services (FCAMHS) were rolled out in 2018, although it is also notable that in some areas of England and Scotland, FCAMHS were commissioned for some years prior to this. Counselling psychologists may therefore also work in inpatient settings where a significant risk to self, or others, has been identified for a young person. Finally, third sector and charitable organisations also provide a wide range of therapeutic services, often targeting particular groups (e.g., young men) or issues (e.g., parental bereavement) and frequently more flexible in the type of support offered.

There has been an increasing emphasis on providing online services to children and adolescents (Ersahin & Hanley, 2017). Some clinical guidelines now recommend using digital interventions for supporting young people with mental health and wellbeing difficulties (e.g., National Institute for Health and Care Excellence, 2019). Despite numerous challenges arising with the delivery of distance therapy, online and digital services offer the opportunity to address some of the power imbalances traditionally observed in face-to-face therapy services. Children and young people can access information through written articles and forum discussions with professionals and other young people. Alternatively, they may choose to engage directly with a therapist in structured online therapy (Hanley, Prescott & Ujhelyi Gomez, 2019). With online platforms, young people can thus potentially exert agency by tailoring the work they engage in. This may go some way in explaining why online services can be preferable for some individuals from this generation of 'digital natives' (Prensky, 2001).

Despite the range of services outlined above, there remains a need for increased funding and accessibility for child and adolescent services. Mental health services continue to receive limited funding compared to other areas of health care, with 10% of mental health spending going to young people, despite this age group accounting for 20% of the total population. More explicitly, for every £225 of NHS spending on adults, only £92 is spent on children (Children's Commissioner, 2020). It may not be surprising, therefore, that when surveyed, over a third of children and adolescents who required mental health services could not access support (Salaheddin & Mason, 2016), and the picture is likely to be much worse following the COVID-19 pandemic. It is also important to acknowledge that the provision for this age group is often quite patchy in nature. The funding, waiting times and types of interventions that are offered by services can vary substantially from region to region.

Before moving on to consider the specific skills and resources that counselling psychologists might need when working with young individuals, it is also important to note that therapeutic work can take different forms. For example, a counselling psychologist might find themselves working with a child or young person alongside their parents/primary care givers or broader family. Further, a counselling psychologist might also be asked to work with particular groups of young people. Such groups include those that support individuals to talk about specific difficulties alongside peers (e.g., eating distress) and those that facilitate dialogue between individuals with polarised viewpoints on topics within school (e.g., the place of immigration within society). Such work adds extra layers of complexity to therapeutic work and requires professionals to develop skills in facilitating groups that might involve difficult conversations.

Some key policy documents to be aware of when working with children and young people

Are we listening? (2019). A review of children's mental health services by the Care Quality Commission.

Transforming children and young people's mental health provision: A green paper (2017). A paper outlining the long-term plan for children and young people's mental health services.

Counselling in schools: A blueprint for the future (2015). A paper with guidance on setting up and providing counselling services in primary and secondary schools.

Future in mind (2015). A paper which outlined the government's ambitions for children's mental health services over the past five years.

Therapeutic skills and resources

Given the particular issues related to working with this client group noted above, it is important that counselling psychologists adopt ways of working that are responsive to individuals who fall within these age groups. However, it is important to note that counselling psychologists working with adult populations have skills that are transferable to work with children and adolescents. For instance, practitioners who primarily make use of psychodynamic, cognitive-behavioural or person-centred approaches will have plenty to offer younger individuals who seek support. The main points that we advocate in the sections below therefore relate to how these approaches are adapted to take into account the different developmental life stages and social situations that younger individuals are experiencing. In particular, we (i) reflect upon how services might align themselves to be youth friendly, (ii) consider how therapists might adapt their work for younger individuals, and (iii) outline some ethical and legal issues to be aware of when working with children and adolescents.

Therapy services always need to be tailored to the needs of the individuals seeking support. This is no different when working with children and adolescents, and services for these age groups need to be developed that are 'youth friendly'. Historically, services attempted to use adult service blue-prints as a basis for youth provision, with limited success (probably by doing something tokenistic like painting a picture of Winnie the Pooh on the wall). More recent developments, however, see services adopt more innovative ways of working and accept that being 'youth friendly' requires a more pervasive approach. Organisations have embraced new ways of offering therapy for children and adolescents that include expressive techniques (e.g., using art, drama or music) that can help engage individuals who may have limited vocabularies, systemic interventions that account for family relationships or social networks, and school-based or mediated therapies (e.g., online or tele-phone therapy) to meet individuals in familiar environments that feel safer to the individual. Such accommodations purposefully attempt to make therapy a more relevant and accessible activity for younger individuals – after all, as Castro-Blanco and Karver (2010) remind us when discussing the therapeutic alliance, 'even the best psychotherapeutic treatments in the world will not matter if there no one is there to receive them' (p. x). For this reason it is increasingly recommended that children and young people are actively involved in the development and oversight of services. Similarly, it is also important that young people have a voice in their own treatment plan and that they are an active participant in the decision-making process.

Working with young people (part 1)

Georgia, a 14-year-old, has been having difficulties maintaining healthy eating habits over the past year. Her parents became concerned about this and, after looking for additional support within Georgia's school, eventually met with their GP to seek out additional support.

The GP made a referral to a local CAMHS team, who met with Georgia to dis-cuss ways that they might work together to support her. Georgia was reluctant to meet with the CAMHS practitioner and in the assessment meeting decided that she did not want to return.

Respecting Georgia's wishes, she was discharged from the service.

When considering therapeutic work directly, counselling psychologists need to be mindful of issues related to power within the therapeutic relationship. The adult-child relationship is typically fraught with significant power imbalances, with the adult generally being in a position that holds much more power than the child. Given this, therapists need to pay careful attention to developing and managing facilitative therapeutic alliances with those seeking support. Such a task can prove complex, with some children expecting adult therapists to be very active in therapy, while others feel patronised by thera-pists that are too involved in directing the work. Further, the lives of children and adolescents can move very fast, with the issue they initially brought to therapy having sometimes changed shape completely by the next meeting. As a consequence, counselling psychologists need to be flexible and responsive to the needs and wants of the individuals engaging in therapy. The maturity of young clients needs to be carefully considered so as to navigate the work in a way that prizes the individual's agency but does not expect responses that lie beyond their developmental abilities.

To account for the challenges associated with navigating the child-adult therapeutic alliance, a pluralistic stance to therapy is advocated. Specifically, Cooper and McLeod's suggestion of a pluralistic framework (Cooper & McLeod, 2011) may be helpful for practitioners working with these age groups. This approach is further expanded for working with adolescents (Hanley et al., 2013) and advocates working collaboratively with young clients to identify the specific goals (e.g., be less anxious during exams or get on with family members better) and tasks of therapy (e.g., practising relaxation techniques or talking through what it means to feel anxious during exams), before considering what therapeutic methods (e.g., engaging in a conversation or structured problem solving activity) might be best employed to achieve them. This approach helps the individual and therapist identify the client's reason for attending therapy, rather than relying upon external sources that may be driven by different agendas. Further, it aims to bring to the fore conversations about the process of therapy itself. Such a process can be helpful in checking out the approach that is being adopted by the therapist. For instance, as young clients might choose to discontinue therapy if it doesn't meet their expectations (e.g., a person-centred therapist might be too silent or a cognitive behavioural therapist too directive), having a meta conversation about this process on occasions can be a useful way to maintain a healthy therapeutic relationship.

As therapy services commonly require therapists to make use of experience and outcome measures within their work, it is important that practitioners make use of the ones that are tailored towards younger client groups. These are often briefer and use less complex language but still encourage therapists to engage clients in a conversation about how they are experiencing therapy. The British Association for Counselling and Psychotherapy (BACP) and Child Outcomes Research Consortium (CORC) outline selections of relevant tools that professionals may wish to use to monitor their therapeutic work (BACP, 2013; CORC, 2021). These include goal-based outcome measures, brief experience measures, such as the Child Session Rating Scale, and short outcome measures, such as the CORE-YP. As well as soliciting feedback from young clients, counselling psychologists may also find themselves having to explain and manage the process alongside adult care givers (e.g., parents, carer, teachers). With this in mind, it can be important to contract at the outset of any therapeutic work how such relationships will be managed.

There are specific ethical and legal requirements related to working with children and young people that counselling psychologists should be aware of.

These differ from country to country and therapists should ensure that they are informed about local legislation. The British Psychological Society (BPS) notes, 'Safeguarding children remains the most fundamental responsibility of all psychologists whose work impinges on the lives of children either directly or indirectly' (British Psychological Society, 2014, p. 4). The work of psychologists thus needs to ensure that children are, first and foremost, safe from serious harm, factors that typically inform risk assessment processes and protocols for organisations working with these age groups. In addition to being up to date with national legislation, the issue of whether an individual has the competence to consent to attend therapy becomes important when working with younger individuals. Although a majority of children are likely to require parental or primary carer consent to enter into therapeutic relationships, some individuals under the age of 16 may be viewed as competent to make the decision themselves and thus receive confidential care without the permission of others. Such competence has precedents in support for sexual health for adolescents and is often referred to as Gillick competence, after a specific case which ruled that a young woman was deemed competent and sufficiently informed to receive medical care without the knowledge of her parents (Jenkins, 2007). Assessment of issues such as risk and competence should be discussed in clinical supervision and be managed in line with organisational policy, where relevant.

Working with young people (part 2)

Georgia had been finding home life difficult at the time her parents were seeking support. She knew that they wanted to support her, but she found it hard to share the difficulties she was facing with them. She often felt that they treated her like a young child rather than a young adult.

Without the knowledge of her parents, Georgia had contacted a number of online support services. This included using support forums that were moderated by professionals and occasionally meeting with a therapist. Within these therapy sessions, Georgia discussed her difficulties with communicating with her parents and even considered what she may say in her upcoming CAMHS appointment. The therapist supported her in exploring what she wanted and outlined the potential benefits of meeting with the CAMHS practitioner. Georgia felt strongly that, at this point in time, she did not want to engage with the CAMHS service, with her hope being to learn to be more assertive with her parents. Once again, Georgia explored these feelings with an online therapist and, once the work with CAMHS had ended, they agreed to meet for a series of appointments going forward. Two weeks into these sessions, Georgia found the confidence to tell her parents about the work that she was doing to support herself.

Beyond therapy

While the focus on therapy is understandable, counselling psychologists are well positioned to impact positively upon the lives of young people through different avenues. Here we consider four roles that sit alongside direct therapeutic work: (i) supervision, (ii) research, (iii) training and (iv) advocacy.

Counselling psychologists are well placed to provide supervision to trainees, psychologists and colleagues from other professions. Supervision plays an important role in managing the emotional labour associated with therapeutic work and safeguarding the best interests of the child or young person accessing support. Due to the emphasis upon reflexive practice within the profession (Hanley & Amos, 2018), counselling psychologists are often well equipped with the knowledge and skills to support others offering support to children and adolescents. They are informed about supervisory practices and models (Hawkins & Shohet, 2012) and, in many cases, knowledgeable about specific issues related to working with these age groups. For this reason, counselling psychologists might find themselves taking on supervisory roles for other practitioner psychologists or professionals such as teachers or nurses that work with this group (Hanley, 2017).

Researching issues relevant to children and adolescents can also contribute to developments in the care for the mental health and wellbeing of this group. Counselling psychologists often prize qualitative research that aims to bring to the fore the views of individuals that are not commonly heard (Ponterotto, 2005), as such counselling psychologists might be actively involved in conducting research with children and young people so that their views might be heard by service commissioners and managers. Further, the emphasis upon social justice that counselling psychology has (Winter & Hanley, 2015), might also see practitioners research issues that impact upon children and young people in other ways. For instance, systemic issues due to broader policies might be examined (Hanley, Winter & Burrell, 2019) or by challenging anti-discriminatory practices that relate to work with these age groups (Tribe & Bell, 2018).

Training others to engage with children and young people may also form part of the role of counselling psychologists. Training might directly focus upon disseminating skills to professionals working with young individuals or, alternatively, it may focus upon developing the skills of parents and carers too. For instance, training of primary carers can help a broad range of presenting difficulties for children and their parents (e.g., Sanders, 2008). Such interventions can increase parental agency, helping parents recognise that, with support, they can become skilled problem solvers. In keeping with the theme of this chapter, it is crucial that training is flexible and individualised to the specific needs of both child and parents.

Finally, many of the skills counselling psychologists are trained in are transferable to other settings. Some may consider using their skills and experience in ways that extend beyond therapeutic disciplines. For example, volunteering as a school governor may provide the opportunity to positively impact the lives of hundreds of children in their local community. Individuals could seek out opportunities such as restorative justice conferencing, which has its roots in challenging traditional western models of juvenile care for young victims and offenders. There may also be opportunities to support local youth projects, such as those involving music and the arts, that can positively improve wellbeing outside traditional therapeutic work domains. These are just a few suggestions of the possible routes where counselling psychologists' skills can be used outside of the therapy room.

Case example: Advocacy

Counselling psychologists might find themselves taking on advocacy roles with children and young people. Due to the power imbalance between children and adults, it can be helpful to support younger individuals in getting their opinions out into the world. For example, imagine a London-born ten-year-old of African descent placed into a residential care home hundreds of miles away in a small rural town. During therapy, the child shares concerns about his identity and how he fits in with the predominantly white staff and children. Staff express concerns about the child's increased challenging behaviour and disrupted sleep. In this case, advocacy may take the form of highlighting the need for cultural sensitivity and ensuring that the child's identity is considered in their care plan. Recognising that the child may not have the vocabulary to express this themselves, the counselling psychologist can potentially positively influence the child's environment.

Summing up

Counselling psychology is well positioned to contribute to the development of therapeutic work with children and adolescents. The foundation in humanistic psychology, which values the uniqueness and agency of those seeking support (Hanley et al., 2016), alongside the focus upon issues of power and social justice (Winter, 2019) can provide a helpful lens through which to view therapeutic work with these age groups. Childhood and adolescence are varied and complex periods in which individuals go through huge physical, psychological, social and spiritual changes. For this reason, psychologists working to support these individuals need to be creative in their response to the different issues that are brought to therapy. Although therapeutic work might prove very similar to work with older populations, at times it may require professionals to adopt proactive supportive approaches that are more involved than the way a therapist might typically see themselves working. For instance, counselling psychologists might choose to advocate for younger individuals by talking with parents or other professionals or adapt therapy so that it is more fitting to the developmental life stage of the individual. Further, they may be involved in overseeing services or research projects that specifically aim to support children and young people, feeding into the development of service development and delivery. Given the pluralistic nature of their training, counselling psychologists should therefore be well suited to working with these age groups and providing valuable support to younger generations.

References

American Psychiatric Association (2013). Diagnostic and statistical manual of mental disorders: DSM-V (5th ed.). APA. https://doi.org/10.1176/appi.books.9780890425596.

British Association for Counselling and Psychotherapy (2013). Children and Young People Practice Research Network (CYP PRN): A toolkit for collecting routine outcome measures. BACP.

British Psychological Society (2014). Safeguarding and promoting the welfare of children. Position Paper (2nd ed). BPS.

Caspi, A., Houts, R. M., Ambler, A., Danese, A., Elliott, M. L., Hariri, A., ... Moffitt, T. E. (2020). Longitudinal assessment of mental health disorders and comorbidities across four decades among participants in the Dunedin Birth Cohort Study. *JAMA Network Open*, 3(4), e203221. https://doi.org/10.1001/jamanetworkopen.2020.3221.

Castro-Blanco, D. & Karver, M. S. (2010). Elusive alliance: Treatment engagement strategies with high-risk adolescents. American Psychological Association. https://doi.org/10.1037/12139-000.

Care Quality Commission (2018). Are we listening? A review of children and young people's mental health services. CQC.

Children's Commissioner (2020). The state of children's mental health services. www.childrenscommissioner.gov.uk/wp-content/uploads/2020/01/cco-the-state-of-childrens-mental-health-services.pdf.

Coleman, J. C. (2011). *The Nature of Adolescence* (4th ed). Routledge.

Cooper, M. (2013). School-based counselling in UK secondary schools: A review and critical evaluation. University of Strathclyde.

Cooper, M. & McLeod, J. (2011). *Pluralistic Counselling and Psychotherapy*. Sage.

CORC (2021). Outcome and experience measures. www.corc.uk.net/outcome-experience-measures/.

Department for Education (2016). Counselling in schools: A blueprint for the future. Departmental advice for school leaders and counsellors. Department for Education.

Department of Health (2016). Future in mind. NHS.

Department of Health and Social Care (2017). Transforming children and young people's mental health provision: A green paper. NHS.

Ersahin, Z. & Hanley, T. (2017). Using text-based synchronous chat to offer therapeutic support to students: A systematic review of the research literature. *Health Education Journal*, 76(5), 531–543. https://doi.org/10.1177/0017896917704675.

Hanley, T. (2017). Supporting the emotional labour associated with teaching: Considering a pluralistic approach to group supervision. *Pastoral Care in Education*, 35(4), 253–266. https://doi.org/10.1080/02643944.2017.1358295.

Hanley, T., Prescott, J. & Ujhelyi Gomez, K. (2019). A systematic review exploring how young people use online forums for support around mental health issues. *Journal of Mental Health*, 28(5), 566–576. https://doi.org/10.1080/09638237.2019. 1630725.

Hanley, T., Williams, G. & Sefi, A. (2013). Pluralistic counselling for young people. In T. Hanley, N. Humphrey & C. Lennie (Eds), *Adolescent Counselling Psychology* (pp. 133–156). Routledge.

Hanley, T., Winter, L. A. & Burrell, K. (2019). Supporting emotional well-being in schools in the context of austerity: An ecologically informed humanistic perspective. *British Journal of Educational Psychology*, March. https://doi.org/10.1111/bjep. 12275.

Hanley, T. & Amos, I. (2018). The scientist-practitioner and the reflective-practitioner. In V. Galbraith (Ed.), *Topics in Applied Psychology: Counselling Psychology* (pp. 167– 182). Wiley.

Hanley, T. & Winter, L. A. (2016). Humanistic approaches and pluralism. In M. Cooper & W. Dryden (Eds), *The Handbook for Pluralistic Counselling and Psychotherapy* (pp. 95–107). Sage.

Hawkins, P. & Shohet, R. (2012). Supervision in the helping professions. In *Supervision in the Helping Professions* (4th ed). Oxford University Press.

Jenkins, P. (2007). *Counselling, Psychotherapy and the Law* (2nd ed). Sage.

Kessler, R. C., Berglund, P., Demler, O., Jin, R., Merikangas, K. R. & Walters, E. E. (2005). Lifetime Prevalence and Age-of-Onset Distributions of DSM-IV Disorders in the National Comorbidity Survey Replication. *Archives of General Psychiatry*, 62 (6), 593. https://doi.org/10.1001/archpsyc.62.6.593.

NHS Digital (2020). Mental health of children and young people in England, 2020: Wave 1 follow-up to the 2017 survey. https://digital.nhs.uk/data-and-information/p ublications/statistical/mental-health-of-children-and-young-people-in-england/2020- wave-1-follow-up.

National Institute for Health and Care Excellence (2019). Depression in children and young people: Identification and management. NICE Guideline No. 134. www.nice. org.uk/guidance/ng134.

Ponterotto, J. G. (2005). Qualitative research in counseling psychology: A primer on research paradigms and philosophy of science. *Journal of Counseling Psychology*, 52 (2), 126–136. https://doi.org/10.1037/0022-0167.52.2.126.

Prensky, M. (2001). Digital natives, digital immigrants, Part 1. *On the Horizon*, 9(3), 245–267. http://dx.doi.org/10.1108/10748120110424816.

Salaheddin, K. & Mason, B. (2016). Identifying barriers to mental health help-seeking among young adults in the UK: A cross-sectional survey. *British Journal of General Practice*, 66(651), e686–e692. https://doi.org/10.3399/bjgp16x687313.

Sanders, M. R. (2008). Triple P-Positive Parenting Program as a public health approach to strengthening parenting. *Journal of Family Psychology*, 22(4), 506–517. https://doi.org/10.1037/0893-3200.22.3.506.

Sawyer, S. M., Azzopardi, P. S., Wickremarathne, D. & Patton, G. C. (2018). The age of adolescence. *The Lancet Child & Adolescent Health*, 2(3), 223–228. https://doi. org/10.1016/S2352-4642(18)30022-1.

Tribe, R. & Bell, D. (2018). Social justice, diversity and leadership. *European Journal of Counselling Psychology*, 7(1), 11–125. https://doi.org/10.5964/ejcop.v7i1.145.

World Health Organization (2019). International statistical classification of diseases and related health problems (11th ed.). https://icd.who.int/.

Winter, L. A. & Hanley, T. (2015). 'Unless everyone's covert guerilla-like social justice practitioners…': A preliminary study exploring social justice in UK counselling psychology. *Counselling Psychology Review*, 30(2), 32–46.

Winter, L. A. (2019). Social justice and remembering 'the personal is political' in counselling and psychotherapy: So, what can therapists do? *Counselling and Psychotherapy Research*, 19(3). https://doi.org/10.1002/capr.12215.

Chapter 3

Working as a counselling psychologist in Improving Access to Psychological Therapy (IAPT) services

Joanna Omylinska-Thurston and Charles Frost

Introduction

Improving Access to Psychological Therapy (IAPT) services was introduced to the National Health Service (NHS) following the Layard report (2006). Layard argued for introducing a national mental health service offering National Institute for Health and Care Excellence (NICE) recommended treatments. He believed improving mental health in the population would lead to increased happiness and employment (Layard, 2005). He argued that this would pay for itself by decreasing unemployment and reducing state benefits. Layard's idea was developed into a national programme in 2008 and since then has been rolled out across England, with the aim of seeing more than a million clients per year (NHS England, 2021a). It is embedded in the NHS Long Term Plan and Five Year Forward View for Mental Health.

The British Psychological Society (BPS) criticised IAPT highlighting that people's mental health was affected by multiple issues, not only unemployment. Marzillier and Hall (2009) pointed out that unemployment was not a psychological issue per se, and Delgadillo, Asaria and Gilbody (2016) added that systemic issues such as socio-economic deprivation were at the root of many mental health problems. Other authors highlighted the limitations of cognitive behavioural therapy (CBT) as the main approach offered in IAPT (Omylinska-Thurston, Walton, McMeekin & Proctor, 2019). Lees (2016) and Jackson and Rizq (2019) discussed the impact of IAPT on wider society.

We have both worked within IAPT for a total of 13 years and have had mixed experiences. In preparation for this chapter we spoke to nine counselling psychologists with experience of working in IAPT. We recruited them via personal connections and Facebook and will share their experiences here.

The skills required for the day-to-day role

The skills identified ranged from basic therapy skills (e.g. empathy) and administrative skills (e.g. note taking) through to more personal skills for negotiating the workplace. Skills in risk management and safeguarding were

DOI: 10.4324/9781003159339-4

also considered essential. Practitioners said they required skills in evidence-based therapies needed for accreditation with bodies such as the BACP and BABCP to create 'a sense of credibility' in IAPT.

Many of the skills related to delivering therapy for clients with complex needs where IAPT steps 2 and 3 interventions failed but the criteria for secondary care were not met. Counselling psychologists (working at step 3 plus) often became the 'last chance' and worked between NICE-recommended therapies and integrative approaches tailored to the client's needs (Cooper & McLeod, 2010). Some practitioners felt able to blend approaches from third-wave CBT (e.g. compassion focused therapy) and cognitive analytic therapy, while others felt compelled to adhere to IAPT doctrine. Practitioners also discussed having skills for complex trauma work including addressing psychosocial needs, psychoeducation in relation to trauma and the body, dialectical behavioural therapy, eye movement desensitisation and reprocessing as well as psychodynamic psychotherapy.

Practitioners discussed needing determination in dealing with management and assertiveness in using clinical judgement. Some practitioners described having to 'watch your back' and dealing with power struggles with colleagues, including other psychologists. Being able to raise these issues and work collaboratively depended on the approach of managers and supervisors. Some practitioners coped by 'keeping your head down' and getting on with work to avoid conflict; others felt able to carve out their own role which helped them to feel valued.

All practitioners talked of the importance of assessment and formulation skills, particularly because of the short-term nature of interventions within IAPT. There is a need to quickly assess complexity, motivation and ability to engage with therapies offered. Sometimes therapy may not be appropriate as practitioners need to be realistic about what can be achieved in a short time. However, there is often a pressure to be 'all things to all people' due to the more challenging nature of client presentations at this level. There is also a need to be skilled in psychometrics, although this appears to conflict with counselling psychology's humanistic values (Van Scoyoc, 2020). Counselling psychologists can make a unique contribution to formulation by including family context and childhood experiences often missed in CBT's focus on the here and now. The shorter time frame available and the client's complexity requires also drawing on a plurality of approaches rather than using the medical model (Frost, 2012). Practitioners felt their training as counselling psychologists enabled them to identify the phenomenological themes in the client's diverse experiences in order to arrive at an integrated formulation, informed by the medical model but not distracted by it, which helped give a sense of coherence to the client's narrative (Johnstone & Dallos, 2013).

Additionally, caseload and time management skills were essential 'just to survive'. Consistent routines were important to keep on top of daily tasks as well as being able to prepare for clients' sessions. Thinking relationally in terms of client experience, teams and service dynamics was considered of value, as was supporting colleagues in supervision and consultation. Being able to identify training needs and provide training was considered helpful. Keeping abreast of research and being able to translate the findings in an accessible format was also useful.

Finally, the skills of self-care were considered vital. Being able to balance home and work life was necessary to survive the stressful IAPT environment. Not being focused on meeting targets as an indication of a practitioner's ability helped also with managing stress.

Challenges of the role

Counselling psychologists discussed high levels of stress resulting in anxiety, depression and consequently burnout, which echoes surveys undertaken by Rao et al. (2016) and Cotton (2019). Additionally, high staff turnover led to a sense of fragmentation within teams, resulting in a sense of isolation and lack of support.

High caseload was identified as one of the reasons for stress within IAPT. Full-time practitioners had to see 20 clients per week and provide seven assessments a month. They said they had no time allocated for admin and had to rely on clients who did not attend (DNA) appointments to do this. Frequent risk management and safeguarding issues were time consuming, but without specific time allocated to deal with them practitioners had to cancel other clients. Practitioners often worked above their allocated hours, leading to feeling exhausted. Rizq (2012) understood this high level of workload monitoring as a defense against anxiety related to human vulnerability. It can give an illusion that it is possible to deal with and recover from mental health issues and therefore return to work, which is the premise IAPT is based on.

Supervision was provided once a month, which was not enough for reflecting on clinical work. Because of the high caseload, clients often 'felt like numbers', which led to losing a sense of human connection with clients, essential in terms of building therapeutic relationships. Practitioners felt that because of lack of time, reflecting on client work happened on a superficial level, leading to difficulty in grasping clients' core issues. This was often compounded by the fact that most practitioners in IAPT were not trained in reflective practice so the environment in itself is not conducive to reflecting on clinical work. Without a proper reflective space, practitioners can feel that they are not addressing the key aspects of client problems, which can leave them feeling deskilled, undermining their sense of identity and leading to anxiety and depression.

Clients seen by psychologists within IAPT often have complex problems related to living in very deprived areas. Practitioners often felt like social workers, focusing on issues such as housing or benefits rather than psychological therapy. Others also commented that because of complexity they would be doing low-level work like behavioural activation and graded exposure as other types of therapy would not be possible. It would be also inappropriate to do trauma work with clients who don't feel safe enough due to regular violence and crime where they live. Practitioners also talked about having to work with clients they did not feel competent to work with because other services would not take them on due to their issues not being deemed 'complex enough'. Clients were often very distressed, which made it difficult to refuse them. Rizq (2013) talked also about clients in deprived areas being passed from service to service based on feelings of repulsion – services wanting to distance themselves from despair and vulnerability, which can be seen as too overwhelming. Practitioners said that at times they worked on the edge of competence (Health and Care Professions Council [HCPC], 2015) in terms of holding levels of risk, and focusing on safeguarding and psychosocial issues as they did not have any other service to refer their clients to. Although practitioners engaged in supervision and appropriate CPD, they said that sometimes providing safe and respectful therapeutic relationships was the only 'skill' they could offer when witnessing despair and vulnerability, which at times left them feeling really deskilled.

Practitioners felt distressed and also ethically challenged by clients who 'fall through the cracks' because their presentation was too severe for IAPT but not severe enough for secondary care. Practitioners spoke about having to reject referrals on the basis that a client was deemed unlikely to 'recover' (and meet IAPT performance indicators) but without being able to offer any other service. There was a sense that the service's needs were prioritised over clients' needs. Unfortunately, it was felt that the gaps between services have widened in recent years due to funding cuts. It should be the role of counselling psychologists to contribute to initiatives which address these gaps.

Our practitioners felt that IAPT structures can be rigid as there is insistence on adhering to NICE-recognised interventions only. Counselling psychologists are trained in building therapeutic relationships and providing interventions that relate to clients' needs, which often do not fit with NICE guidance. This can lead to either misrepresenting practice or losing integrity as counselling psychologists. Although managers are often supportive and understand clinical decision making, some practitioners spoke about pressure, micromanagement, not having any power and autonomy in their clinical judgement or time and flexibility to use different approaches and modalities. Additionally, counselling psychologists are trained for other roles besides therapy including being part of management, providing supervision, using psychometric assessments, developing staff training, conducting research and developing creative ways of engaging service users but it is unfortunate when these skills and training are not recognised or valued. Some practitioners spoke about being prevented from calling themselves counselling psychologists because they were employed as CBT or 'High Intensity' Therapists and some NHS Trusts didn't even list counselling psychology as a profession.

Professional development and leadership

When management is supportive, staff can develop and train in a variety of approaches. Counselling psychologists are suited to working in a range of IAPT therapeutic modalities (e.g. CBT, CfD, CTD, DIT, IPT, EMDR). However, some practitioners mentioned they were not allowed to train due to limited funding and service capacity. Other practitioners said they paid for training themselves and undertook it in their own time but resented that the organisation did not support them yet benefited from their skills.

Practitioners said that although there is scope for counselling psychology leadership, it requires practitioners to stand up for evidence-based practice and what is best for clients. Counselling psychologists have the ability to engage in compassionate and transformational leadership (Hall, 2020), but clinical psychologists are still more accepted for leadership roles.

Some practitioners commented on a long-standing rivalry between clinical and counselling psychologists that seemed present within IAPT. Although most practitioners said that both groups worked side by side, there were instances where clinical psychologists considered counselling psychologists as 'just counsellors', clearly not understanding that both groups are HCPC-registered practitioner psychologists (HCPC, 2015).

Some counselling psychologists felt that IAPT leadership is too hierarchical, detached and not clinically relevant to frontline practice. Practitioners felt that they were not involved in decision making and that they never met senior managers. Most of the practitioners felt that they were not able to express their leadership skills and move into leadership/management positions including higher pay bands. Practitioners commented that they did not know of any consultant counselling psychologists within IAPT and that these positions were usually occupied by clinical psychologists.

Although there is an assumption within the NHS that psychologists will go into leadership eventually, there are practitioners who actually prefer staying in clinical roles. Even though some counselling psychologists were able to progress into clinical leadership, a lot of IAPT leadership constituted management roles, which few of our practitioners were interested in.

Issues of diversity

Practitioners working in large cities worked with diverse client and staff groups, which was a very rewarding part of their job. One practitioner said that the reason they survived in the job was because it was exciting to work with people from different cultural backgrounds. However, practitioners working in more rural areas said that their client base was less diverse, which was reflected in service limitations, e.g. poorer access to interpreters and culturally sensitive services.

Race is an issue that is present and cannot be ignored (Msebele & Brown, 2011). Our practitioners of colour talked about experiencing racist comments, microaggressions from clients and colleagues that felt hurtful. Systemic racism in IAPT, where managers and supervisors did not challenge racism even though they saw the hurt and injustice, was also discussed. Although these experiences were mentioned in the context of IAPT, they reflect wider attitudes within the NHS (Iacobucci, 2020). The limited racial diversity within the counselling psychologists who chose to write this chapter was also glaringly obvious to us as the (white) authors.

One of our participants mentioned the impact of the rise of Black Lives Matter in 2020 and how this prompted them to reflect more on their practice. It made them realise racism was something not only on a therapist-client level, but something they could challenge at an organisational level to ensure more is done to make services accessible for BAME clients in a culturally sensitive way. Black Lives Matter seems to be shifting the perception amongst white people from the relatively passive stance of being 'non-racist' to the more active stance of being 'anti-racist' (Kendi, 2019).

Even though NHS England (2021b) seems to actively promote LGBTQI+ staff networks aiming to create a safe, inclusive and diverse working environment recognising differences between sexual orientation and gender identity, we had very limited representation from the LGBTQI+ community within our counselling psychology practitioners, and none of them mentioned LGBTQI+ issues as a consideration.

Ethical and legal considerations

In terms of legal considerations, our practitioners stressed the importance of having liability insurance, the difficulties of what to record and what not to record in the client's notes and the importance of being a member of the relevant regulatory bodies.

A lot more was said about the ethical considerations of IAPT. Some stated that they weren't sure how ethical IAPT was due to its restricted way of working. Some practitioners took issue with what is defined as 'evidence-based therapy', often seen as being used to 'sell' IAPT rather than to help clients. Some thought that promoting IAPT as an evidence-based service with a 50% recovery rate was ethically challenging. This is because session reporting can be hit and miss, over 50% of patients drop out of IAPT (NHS Digital, 2019) and the recovery rate in deprived areas can be 37% or lower (NHS Digital, 2016). The presence of a step '3 plus' within the service was also questioned due to its assumption that those clients can't recover and are therefore selected out of the statistics. Some felt that clients were being treated as numbers, making an IAPT service more like a factory production line. Indeed, payment by results based on targets such as waiting times and recovery can result in services being led by financial constraints rather than what is best for the client (Overington, 2020).

Some saw a conflict between what the client needs and what the service would allow them to do, including having to type up patient notes in the language of CBT in order to portray compliance with the IAPT model. There were also ethical concerns around client DNAs being used to discharge them and get to the next client on the waiting list rather than having an opportunity to address the cause of the client's DNA as part of their therapy. Some also objected to having to cancel client appointments in order to have time to deal with safeguarding issues or rely on DNAs in order to complete their admin work.

Conversely, there were concerns about the ethics of treating someone who doesn't want therapy but is told they have to come if they want to regain custody of their children, or those who need a letter confirming they are attending therapy as evidence for a benefits claim.

Finally, there were concerns about IAPT's ethics in terms of pressure on its workforce to meet targets. The high level of burnout results in people practising in a detached way to protect themselves, particularly if individuals are blamed for their burnout – i.e. 'not coping' – rather than the high workload structure being made responsible.

How the philosophy of counselling psychology is maintained

Many of our practitioners struggled to articulate what the philosophy of counselling psychology is, saying they always struggled with it during training. Counselling psychology is underpinned by humanistic values and brings together science and psychology with the therapeutic relationship of counselling and psychotherapy (Boshoff, 2020). It is rooted in viewing reality as a subjective interpretation. However, there is little opportunity to consider this when practising according to NICE guidelines based on randomised controlled trials with strict eligibility criteria, which rarely match the realities of clinical settings (Frost, 2012). Working in the NHS means working with the medical model of distress, which sets up a tension with counselling psychology's subjective and intersubjective view of distress (Boshoff, 2020).

Our practitioners felt that it is difficult to maintain counselling psychology philosophy when working in IAPT due to its roots in a strategy aimed at helping the economy by getting people back into work. Some felt it was not possible to develop a therapeutic relationship when seeing so many clients. Others felt it was not always possible to maintain a therapeutic alliance due to complex presenting issues such as alcohol use, EUPD and the prescribed and time-limited nature of the service. This resulted in practitioners having to work with the problem rather than the person. Also, medicalising distress can reduce an individual's belief in their own ability to change fundamental for therapeutic work (Strawbridge & Woolfe, 2010). IAPT also fails to capture the social justice aspect of counselling psychology's philosophy by not recognising that poverty and discrimination can be a cause of mental health problems (Millennium Cohort Studies, 2017), making it difficult for people to engage in therapy until those issues are resolved. It was felt that IAPT only suits people who are high functioning and are ready to engage.

Our counselling psychologists disagreed with being positioned in opposition to psychiatry. They felt there needs to be collaboration, recognising that all professionals have something to offer. Some felt that all they needed to do to maintain the counselling psychology philosophy was to ensure they work collaboratively with their clients in order to reduce the power differential by helping people understand their own expertise. In this way they can value the individual experience and approach their clients holistically.

The range of roles (supervision, research and training)

One of the practitioners said that roles within supervision, research, training or leadership depended on what practitioners wanted to do. She encouraged counselling psychologists to actively pursue roles they wanted and not wait for others to allocate them.

Practitioners commented that they provided supervision to staff, but this was not easy to establish and they supervised mostly CBT practitioners. They said they wanted to supervise other counselling psychologists but there weren't many within the service. They also wanted to be supervised by counselling psychologists, but this was not always possible. Practitioners valued arranging counselling psychology placements, even though they were difficult to set up, because it was important to contribute to developing the next generation of counselling psychologists.

Regarding training, CBT, IPT, DIT, etc. training was available but practitioners were not able to access non-IAPT-approved training. If practitioners felt their clients needed something different, they had to fund the training themselves. Practitioners said that they were only allowed limited days for training (four days for a full-timer) and funding (£100) towards the training. There was also not much opportunity to deliver training, although in some services this was arranged through peer meetings, which were poorly attended due to time limitations.

None of the interviewed practitioners discussed undertaking research within IAPT. Roles mostly focused on clinical work and supervision and there was no time for research. However, the first author of this article (Joanna) has experience of getting management approval, applying for funding and undertaking research within IAPT, although in her own time (Omylinska-Thurston et al., 2019; Karkou & Omylinska-Thurston, in preparation).

Conclusions

At the time of writing, most IAPT services have moved to deliver their service remotely due to the COVID-19 pandemic. They have adjusted well to this change and counselling psychologists are well placed to work flexibly with these changes. However, many services work in deprived areas of the UK and the engagement with clients within these areas has been difficult prior to the pandemic. It is possible that some clients will struggle with remote engagement due to lack of equipment, internet access or computer skills. The NHS Long Term Plan and Five Year Forward View for Mental Health identified digital therapy as a way forward for IAPT, so the current situation will highlight the potential issues related to this.

A lot of client problems in deprived areas are related to poverty and psychosocial issues. More funding is needed in these areas in the wake of ten years of austerity, and unless this is provided counselling psychologists are likely to struggle with feeling deskilled and focusing on psychosocial interventions and risk management. There seems to be a need for a properly funded bridging service between IAPT and secondary care psychological services. Counselling psychologists would be well placed to work within such a service and lead it. This would help prevent clients falling through the gap and allow counselling psychologists to make full use of their skills. This also fits well with the Five Year Forward View for Mental Health and NHS Long Term Plan.

CBT is still the main approach offered within IAPT. The current drop-out rate in IAPT is over 50% (NHS Digital, 2019), suggesting that clients' needs are not fully met and a diversity of approaches is needed (Omylinska-Thurston et al., 2019; Omylinska-Thurston et al., 2020). Counselling psychologists are ideal to draw on the evidence base to work flexibly with clients, focusing on their individual goals and preferences and not rigidly adhering to CBT structures.

Counselling psychologists are also able to deliver supervision and training. They make good researchers, and it would be beneficial if these skills could be utilised within IAPT to expand on what is included in the evidence base.

Finally, the levels of stress and burnout with IAPT practitioners need to be taken seriously and not seen as an individual's inability to cope. The practitioner is the primary tool for therapeutic change and will break if not properly maintained through appropriate support, adequate time for tasks and reasonable caseloads.

References

Boshoff, A. (2020). The philosophical bases of counselling psychology. *Counselling Psychology Review*, 35(1), 49–60.

Cooper, M. & McLeod, J. (2020). *Pluralistic Counselling and Psychotherapy*. London: Sage.

Cotton, E. (2019). It's time to talk about IAPT. *Surviving Work*. Retrieved 13. 11. 2019, from www.survivingwork.org.

Delgadillo, J., Asaria, M., Ali, S. & Gilbody, S. (2016). On poverty, politics and psychology: The socioeconomic gradient of mental healthcare utilisation and outcomes. *British Journal of Psychiatry*, 209(5), 429–430.

Frost, C. (2012). Humanism vs the medical model: Can pluralism bridge the divide for counselling psychologists? *Counselling Psychology Review*, 27(1), 53–61.

Hall, A. (2020). On leadership and counselling psychology. *Counselling Psychology Review*, 35(1), 38–42.

HCPC (Health and Care Professions Council) (2015). Standards of Proficiency for Practitioner Psychologists. HCPC. www.hcpc-uk.org/standards/standards-of-profi ciency/practitioner-psychologists/.

Iacobucci, G. (2020) The BMJ interview: Victor Adebowale on systemic racism in the NHS. *BMJ*, 371. doi:10.1136/bmj.m4111.

Jackson, C. & Rizq, R. (2019) *The Industrialisation of Care*. PCCS Books.

Johnstone, L. & Dallos, R. (eds). (2013). *Formulation in Psychology and Psychotherapy: Making Sense of People's Problems* (2nd ed.). Routledge.

Karkou, V. & Omylinska-Thurston, J. (In preparation). Arts for the blues: A new creative evidence-based psychological intervention for depression in IAPT.

Kendi, I. X. (2019). *How to be Antiracist*. The Bodley Head.

Layard, R. (2005). *Happiness: Lessons from New Science*. Penguin.

Layard, R. (2006). Depression report: A new deal for depression and anxiety disorders. London School of Economics.

Lees, J. (2016). *The Future of Psychological Therapy*. Routledge.

Marzillier, J. & Hall, J. (2009). The challenge of the Layard initiative. *The Psychologist*, 22, 396–399.

Millennium Cohort Studies (2017). Children's mental health and wellbeing. University College London.

Msebele, N. & Brown, H. (2011). Racism in the consulting room: myth or reality? *Psychoanalytic Review*, 98(4), 451–492.

NHS Digital (2016). Psychological therapies: Annual report on the use of IAPT services. Health and Social Care Information Centre. https://digital.nhs.uk/data-and-in formation/publications/statistical/psychological-therapies-annual-reports-on-the-use-of-iapt-services/annual-report-2016-17.

NHS Digital (2019). Psychological therapies: Annual report on the use of IAPT services. England 2019–20. https://digital.nhs.uk/data-and-information/publications/sta tistical/psychological-therapies-annual-reports-on-the-use-of-iapt-services/annual-rep ort-2019-20.

NHS England (2021a). Improving access to psychological therapieswww.england.nhs. uk/mental-health/adults/iapt/.

NHS England (2021b). Lesbian, Gay, Bisexual and Trans (LGBT+) network. www. england.nhs.uk/about/working-for/staff-networks/lgbt/.

Omylinska-Thurston, J., Karkou, V., Parsons, A. S., Nair, K., Lewis, J., Dubrow-Marshall, L., Thurston, S., Dudley-Swarbrick, I. & Sharma, S. (2020). Arts for the blues: the development of a new evidence-based creative group psychotherapy for depression. *Counselling and Psychotherapy Research*. https://doi.org/10.1002/capr.12373.

Omylinska-Thurston, J., Walton, P., McMeekin, A. & Proctor, G. (2019). Client perceptions of unhelpful aspects of CBT within IAPT serving an inner city/deprived area. *Counselling and Psychotherapy Research*, 19(4), 455–464.

Overington, C. (2020). Organisational structural and situational contexts in counselling psychology. *Counselling Psychology Review*, 35(1), 61–67.

Rao, A., Bhutani, G., Clarke, J., Dosanjh, N. & Parhar, S. (2016). The case for a charter for psychological wellbeing and resilience in the NHS. A discussion paper from the Wellbeing Project working group joint initiative between the BPS and New Savoy Conference. BPS.

Rizq, R. (2012). The ghost in the machine: IAPT and organizational melancholia. *British Journal of Psychotherapy*, 28, 319–335.

Rizq, R. (2013). States of abjection. *Organization Studies*, 34, 1277–1297.

Strawbridge, S. & Woolfe, R. (2010). Counselling psychology: Origins, developments and challenges. In R. Woolfe, S. Strawbridge, B. Douglas & W. Dryden (eds), *Handbook of Counselling Psychology* (3rd ed.). Sage.

Van Scoyoc, S. (2020). Psychometrics. *Counselling Psychology Review*, 35(1), 33–37.

Chapter 4

Older Adults' Psychology

Philippa Capel

Introduction

There are specific age-related differences that make working with older adults an important specialty for counselling psychologists. Different opportunities and challenges arise with ageing. These changes occur within our lives, families and selves – for example, retirement, change of role within the family and society plus changes in physical and cognitive abilities. Another key difference is the wealth of knowledge and wisdom one gains throughout life, for example about how to manage emotions, negotiate challenges and relate to people.

It is important to have an understanding of what we mean when we say 'an older adult'. Historically, an older adult was defined as someone above the age of 65, with many services being offered using this as a central criterion. However, this view has been challenged as an arbitrary age divide, *'not logical and now probably unlawful in the UK'* (Royal College of Psychiatry, 2015, p. 1, emphasis added) due to age discrimination. The thinking has progressed to consider categorising services by age-related difficulties, as follows:

Criteria

1   People of any age with a primary dementia.
2   People with mental disorder and physical illness or frailty that contributes to, or complicates, the management of their mental illness. This may include people under 65 years of age.
3   People with psychological or social difficulties related to the ageing process, or end-of-life issues, or who feel their needs may be best met by a service for older people. This would normally include people over 70 years of age.

(Royal College of Psychiatry, 2015, p. 1)

In this chapter I will follow these criteria and refer to older adults as people who have difficulties that are predominately seen in later life, but not necessarily limited to being aged 65 and above.

DOI: 10.4324/9781003159339-5

The chapter will provide an overview of the common causes for presenting issues, both mental health and neurodegenerative-related difficulties, highlighting how within the older adult life stage there can be significant variations in presentation and therefore an increased need for detailed formulation. The different causes may lead to offering a range of adapted interventions to support recovery, therefore the skills and adaptations required of the counselling psychologist will be outlined.

Older adults may present to counselling psychologists in a variety of settings. I will explore some of the different settings and roles for counselling psychologists, as well as acknowledge some of the challenges of working with older adults in the UK.

Context of Ageing in the UK

To set the scene for working with older adults in the UK, we first need to consider the population. The figures from the Office for National Statistics (ONS, 2016) showed that while the general population is projected to grow 12.7% from 2016 to 2046, the population aged 65 and over is forecast to grow by 55.1%, and the number of people aged 75 or over is expected to double. The increase is more marked in the 85 and over age group, with a daily increase of 200 people. This growth in the population highlights the increasing importance of considering the needs of older adults, which will be aligned with an increase in demand on services to support their wellbeing. It is therefore important that all psychologists are prepared to work with this population in order to meet the predicted increase in need.

In 2018, the Royal College of Psychiatrists published a report which highlights that ageism and age discrimination remain a major problem in the National Health Service (NHS) and that ageist attitudes are widespread. There is evidence to suggest that older adults are less likely to be given the correct diagnosis and treatment for mental health difficulties in comparison with younger people (Swift et al., 2016). Institutional ageism therefore presents a concern, as without equitable provision of service the needs of older adults will not be adequately met.

The UK government is considering the ageing population and their needs and role in UK society. A key publication considers the needs of the ageing population and outlines several important changes to the way the NHS should work to support patients and their carers (NHS, 2019). Improving care for older adults living with frailty or multiple long-term conditions is one of its priorities; however, it does not focus specifically on the mental health needs of older adults. With the government looking to consider the needs of older adults in planning for the future, it is hoped this begins to influence some of the challenges, myths and inequalities associated with ageing and therefore strengthen mental wellbeing.

Myths, Assumptions and Beliefs About Ageing

Take a moment to reflect

Who or what characteristics do you think about when you think of an older adult?

Older adults are a very diverse group. Many of us may have stereotypical notions of what it means to be an older person. This highlights a need to be aware of our own beliefs, prejudices and assumptions about ageing, which is important for counselling psychology in practice. For example, a survey by the Royal Society for Public Health (RSPH, 2018) reported a quarter of 18–34-year-olds believed that it is normal to be unhappy and depressed when you are old. Such individual and societal myths can have an effect on wellbeing and willingness to seek help as we age; potentially leading older adults to not access or be offered a service due to a belief that nothing will help.

Laidlaw et al. (2016) identified factors of normal ageing, and mental health and ageing, challenging some of the common myths about ageing and older adults' engagement in therapy. For example, they highlighted Blazer (2010; cited in Laidlaw et al., 2016), who reported that older adults have lower rates of depression than working age adults, therefore challenging the myth that depression is a result of ageing. They also cited Carstensen et al. (2011; Laidlaw et al. 2016), who reported older adults have high levels of wellbeing and emotional stability, despite the challenges associated with ageing. Laidlaw et al. (2016) acknowledged that later life is a time of growth and personal acceptance, and that when older adults look back on their lives they tend to have a positive bias during recall of past events.

Laidlaw et al. (2016) present older adults' views of therapy and accessing psychological services as positive. Cuijpers et al. (2009; cited in Laidlaw et al., 2016) reported that, when offered a course of CBT, older adults do as well as working-age adults, with no difference in treatment outcome. Older adults are less likely to drop out early and therefore, as they are more likely to complete the therapy, may even be better candidates for therapy than working-age adults (NHS Digital, 2017). In summary, older adults prefer 'talking treatments' over pharmacological treatments, and hold positive attitudes towards help-seeking, challenging some of the common myths that older adults are unsuited for psychological therapy (Collins & Corna, 2018).

Cohort factors and generational experiences can affect our beliefs, including about ageing. For example, people who were born in the 1920s are currently in their nineties and people born in the 1950s are currently in their sixties. Putting this into context, people in their nineties were born between the two world wars. Being born during this time would have had a particular impact on childhood and early adult experiences, different to being born in the 1950s. Additionally, the UK has seen huge changes over the years, including in health care. For example, in 1948 the NHS was born, with free universal healthcare changing early experiences of, and potentially influencing beliefs about, care. There are other multiple and variable factors – for example, your location within the UK and the world, and cultural background.

Presenting Issues

Some of the distress presented by older adults is displayed in similar ways to other life stages, however, the reasons for the distress can be quite different. There is also a greater chance of cognitive impairment, including the possibility of dementia, which adds to the complexity of working with this population. Common challenges associated with ageing are around loss of purpose and role, the value of a retired person and financial difficulties (Age UK, 2019). In the UK, the state retirement age is currently 66 years; however, many retire younger. Retirement itself can have a range of different impacts, including on identity, purpose and role in life. Beliefs about retirement and the impact it has on life can have a direct impact on mental wellbeing.

There can be an increase in social exclusion. This could be due to mobility difficulties that preclude access to certain situations, but also our changing role and purpose in the community as a result of retirement. This can decrease opportunities for social interactions, which is a common factor in older adults' mental distress (Age UK, 2018). A change in our purpose and social interactions can potentially lead to a variety of types of distress being experienced, including the possibility of an emergence of attachment-related distress.

Changes in physical health and physical abilities can have a negative impact on our view of ourselves, our future and our ability to engage with life in the same way as in the past. Physical health difficulties can form an increasingly complex and multifaceted stressor for many people, especially when the number of experienced difficulties and the impact on their lives increases. For example, a physical health difficulty may often include an increase in pain and an increase in dependence on others. A change in our ability to be independent can lead to an emergence of attachment-related distress as it affects the way we interact with others. Additionally, physical health can affect mental wellbeing directly and have an impact on cognitive functioning. I have highlighted some of the common reversible causes of cognitive impairment later in the section. Fear of cognitive impairment and dementia, either with or without structural change, can be the cause of increased psychological distress and individuals may need therapy to support psychological adjustment or manage health anxiety.

Physical changes can result in a sense of loss compounded by other age-related losses, including the loss of loved ones and friends. Grief is a common presenting difficulty as people age, alongside distress triggered by concerns about the finite nature of existence (Yalom, 2011).

Trauma and older adults is often not considered in the same detail as trauma at other life stages. However, trauma can remain a very significant cause of distress, especially as previous mechanisms for coping, for example work and remaining busy, are less easy to maintain with the changes and physical limits often involved as we age. Additionally, as our cognitive abilities change, our ability to cognitively manage trauma memories may become harder (Gielkens et al., 2018).

Assessment, Formulation and Treatment

Older adults' psychological needs can be met by a range of different services. At a primary care level, increasing access to psychological therapy (IAPT) services have access criteria that are often ageless and therefore meet the needs of some older adults. However, given the complexity of older adults' difficulties, other services may be more appropriate. This includes older adults community mental health teams (OA CMHT), which usually offer a specialist service to people with complex mental health difficulties, often in conjunction with a neurodegenerative difficulty. The role of the counselling psychologist within the team can include providing individual and group therapy, differential diagnosis of dementia, carer and family interventions, supervision and consultation, in addition to service development and leadership roles. For older adults who present with heightened distress and risk, there are older adults' inpatient wards, which offer specialist care to this population. The role of a psychologist on a ward covers a similar range of activities as in the community, but generally more weighted towards formulation, consultation and team interventions. Ross & Dexter-Smith (2017) have developed a document for working on wards.

Assessment can take the same format as in other life stages, but with an increased focus and awareness on physical health, assessing the whole life history and considering the presence and role of cognitive impairment. It is also important to include assessment of the family dynamics and, where appropriate, involve family members, close friends or carers to gain an overview of the older adult's history and cognitive changes from their perspective. Assessment and initial phases of therapy may therefore need to take longer.

Risk is important to assess and consider. The ONS (2018) reports that suicide rates tend to increase in the oldest age groups for both males and females. They indicate that many factors contribute to this widely seen phenomenon such as psychiatric illness, deterioration of physical health and functioning, and social factors, with men's risk of suicide being especially high and increasing significantly when they pass their mid-seventies.

Laidlaw et al. (2004) developed a useful CBT formulation framework to include common factors that impact on older adults' wellbeing: the comprehensive conceptualisation framework (CCF). It includes intergenerational linkages (networks, supports, tensions), sociocultural context (identity, culture, class, politics), transitions in role (e.g. retirement, bereavement), cohort beliefs (how one views ageing, psychological problems, interventions, services), health status and the older adult's understanding of this. These additions to the CBT formulation framework allow for the common challenges of ageing to be explored and formulated, leading to better informed collaborative interventions.

When formulating and planning interventions, it is also important to consider that older adults have gathered a wealth of knowledge during the course of their lives. This knowledge can be integrated in order to enhance therapy rather than relying only on new learning. An additional factor in planning therapy is pacing. As people age there is often a style change more towards storytelling, which may slow the pace. The adaptations for psychological work with older adults include considerations around how to build a therapeutic working alliance, which is essential for growth and important to the practice of counselling psychologists. James (2010) articulated specific strategies for enhancing the therapeutic relationship, which may be especially important when working with older adults. They include clarifying how the client wishes to be addressed and how they wish to address you. Also, remembering important details of the individual's life history, being open to and eliciting feedback, and being willing to gently confront any issues in the therapeutic relationship. Finally, giving clients credit for specific accomplishments but avoiding generic compliments can enhance the therapeutic relationship.

Other adaptions include allowing time to explore the breadth and depth of the person's life story and experience, and considerations about expected pace of change, especially when adapting to the normal age-related decline in cognitive functioning and physical health. There are adaptations to therapy that can be considered to address physical and cognitive changes. They are relevant for both mental health and neurodegenerative work and I will therefore include them in a separate section below.

Cognitive Impairment and Dementia

A common fear for older adults is that as they age, they will develop dementia. This fear can be a reason for increased distress, as can the cognitive decline or dementia itself. I will provide an overview of the causes of cognitive decline: normal age-related cognitive decline, common reversible causes of cognitive loss and – briefly described – the different types of dementia.

Normal age-related cognitive decline is cognitive decline related to ageing, not dementia. It can be seen from as early as our thirties, and although cognitive decline is different for each individual, there have been norms identified. Minimal age-associated decline is seen in some mental functions, such as verbal ability, some numerical abilities and general knowledge, but other mental capabilities decline from middle age onwards, or even earlier. The latter include aspects of memory, executive functions, processing speed and reasoning (Deary et al., 2009; Hedden & Gabrieli, 2004).

Significant cognitive loss can be caused by treatable conditions or reversible causes of cognitive decline. These conditions include depression, vitamin B12 deficiency, thyroid problems, alcohol abuse, dehydration, infections, pain and side effects of medication. Having an awareness of the treatable conditions, which may have an impact on cognitive abilities, is important when working with older adults due to the increased likelihood of complex coexisting physical health difficulties. Understanding, formulation and addressing the causes of reversible cognitive impairment is important as this may impact on the client's presentation. Unawareness of this would make it hard to conduct a valid and reliable cognitive assessment that informs diagnosis and would potentially lead to inappropriate or unhelpful psychological intervention.

As we age there is an increased likelihood of developing dementia. Having dementia can cause distress for the individual and their family systems. The Alzheimer's Society (2021) defines the word 'dementia' as 'describing a set of symptoms that may include memory loss and/or difficulties with thinking, problem-solving or language, and that the changes often start small and progress over time'. Dementias are caused when the brain is damaged by a progressive neurodegenerative disease. There are five common causes for dementia, with Alzheimer's disease (AD) being the most common, often first noticed as a deterioration in day-to-day memory. The second most common cause is vascular dementia (VAD), associated with a reduction in oxygen supply to the brain. Dementia with Lewy bodies, which some now believe is the second most common form, is often first noticed in varying alertness and hallucinations and is closely related to Parkinson's disease. A less common disease is mixed dementia, when someone has more than one type of dementia (often AD and VAD), and frontotemporal dementia, often first noticed in changes in personality, social conduct and behaviour. Each type of dementia tends to have different initial symptoms and a different pattern of deterioration depending on which parts of the brain are affected. The way in which dementia manifests is also influenced by the person's psychology, and their environment (i.e. those around them). As dementias progress there is an increase in global impairment across all areas of ability. In the later stages of dementia, the person will need more and more support to carry out everyday tasks; however, many people with dementia can live well for years after their diagnosis (Department of Health, 2009).

The role of a counselling psychologist in supporting people with cognitive impairment can include neuropsychological assessment to inform differential diagnosis of dementia. It can also include assessing and offering interventions to decrease distress caused by the cognitive decline, and/or pre-existing psychological disorders, and also to offer support for carers and care homes. Skills in neuropsychological assessment and testing are important to be able to formulate individuals' difficulties and reasons for distress. A widely used dementia screening tool is the Addenbrookes Cognitive Examination III

(ACE-III, 2012). This screening tool can give you an insight into possible areas of impairment, which may even begin to form a pattern indicating a specific type of dementia, and can guide further, detailed neuropsychological assessments.

Depending on the stage of dementia there are different challenges to the work. For example, it is helpful to have an early diagnosis of dementia; however, when a person has mild cognitive impairment (MCI), it is difficult to predict how and if it will progress, therefore additional assessment at a later date may need to be completed. Cognitive Stimulation Therapy (CST) groups are designed to support maintenance of skills at early stages of dementia (Spector et al., 2006) and may be set up and coordinated by counselling psychologists or occupational therapists but are often facilitated by others. Additionally, for some people, acceptance of cognitive decline or a diagnosis of dementia can be difficult, and can lead to non-engagement with assessment or therapy. As dementia progresses, individuals become less able to function and communicate their needs verbally. Their distress may relate to unmet needs, which they may communicate via their emotions or behaviours. These behaviours may challenge those around them to meet their needs and may be difficult to understand. It can then become more useful to work with the care system, rather than the individual alone, to understand and decrease the distress. James and Gibbons (2019) developed Communication and Interaction Training (CAIT) to support effective care, which helps to reduce levels of agitation in people with dementia by increasing the care team's understanding of the individual and their distress, and therefore how to change their approach to decrease the distress.

As the number of people involved in someone's care increases, it becomes important to frequently consider confidentiality. As with all psychological work, the British Psychological Society (BPS) Practice Guidelines (2017), BPS Code of Ethics and Conduct (2018) and Health & Care Professions Council Standards of Conduct, Performance and Ethics (2016) are an essential resource to support decision making. Additionally, individuals' mental capacity and ability to give informed consent is likely to decrease as dementia progresses. It is therefore essential to assess mental capacity to make a particular decision in line with the Mental Capacity Act (Department of Health, 2005), make a 'best interest' decision and follow the Deprivation of Liberty Safeguards (DoLs), which are both part of the Mental Capacity Act.

Services designed to support people with dementia are varied and a counselling psychologist may work in a memory assessment service, care home in-reach team, inpatient wards or directly with care homes. They may also offer support and interventions via third sector organisations, for example Age UK and the Alzheimer's Society. Experts by experience, people who are living with, or are caring for someone with dementia, are often involved in dementia services and are increasingly seen as essential in the provision and development of all services.

Adaptations for Working with People with Cognitive and Physical Impairment

Older adults may have sensory impairments, including those of hearing and sight, in addition to mobility difficulties. This means that when considering offering therapy, you will need to consider if any of the above will indicate a need for adaptations – for example, home visits or visual aids. In addition to considering the psychological impact of the client's physical health difficulties, it is useful to consider the impact on therapy – for example, the length and frequency of the work and the need for breaks.

James (2010) has articulated a range of adaptions that could be considered. For concentration difficulties it can be helpful to reduce complexity, have fewer topics, give more feedback and have a slower pace. Using breaks, short meaningful agendas and diagrams and avoiding distractions can also be helpful. Linking with this, for problem-solving difficulties, breaking down goals, scaffolding and behavioural experiments could be considered, as well as the counselling psychologist bringing their knowledge to aid problem solving. When considering adaptations for memory problems, pacing, repetition and facilitating recall are useful strategies, as is using a folder for therapy. Inter-personal difficulties may affect alliance and homework tasks. Recognising the signs and preparing for the difficulties in session may be useful. There may be a lack of motivation associated with the interpersonal difficulties. This could be supported by the use of meaningful tasks, acknowledging small gains and making expectations explicit. Finally, emotional regulation may be compromised and a lack of awareness of any changes in executive functioning ability or behaviour may occur. Conceptualising this as part of cognitive impairment and using explanations for the changes may be useful, as both can cause self-criticism and negative comparisons with their former self.

As technology becomes an increasingly important part of our lives, it can offer both opportunities and challenges for therapeutic work for older adults. It can aid engagement via the use of different communication modalities, such as video conferencing, which can decrease the need to travel if mobility is impaired. However, it can also be a barrier to engagement and building a therapeutic relationship as some may find new learning difficult and daunting and may not have the technological resources. There is increasing evidence for the use of neuropsychological assessment via online platforms – for example, Q-global by Pearson (Pearson, 2020) – however, currently this is not thought to be as con-sistently reliable as face-to-face assessment, relating to the user's technological skills, level of impairment and reliability of broadband (Marra et al., 2020).

Summary

Working with older adults and people with difficulties associated with ageing can be both rewarding and challenging. There are high levels of complexity in individual formulations and the systems around the person. This heightens the need for the counselling psychologist to be a reflective practitioner drawing on multiple theoretical models, adapting to meet the individual needs, while holding the client in the centre of the work.

During the time that I have worked with older adults, my own internal beliefs about older adults and ageing have been challenged and I have grown. However, at times I still notice myself making assumptions based on my own experience of ageing and loss, and not the client's individual experience. It can be harder to keep a distance from many of the challenges seen in ageing because we all age. This can add to the development of a therapeutic relationship but also has the potential to form a barrier to understanding the individual client need.

References

Age UK (2019). Struggling on: Experiences of financial hardship in later life. www.ageuk.org.uk/globalassets/age-uk/documents/reports-and-publications/reports-and-briefings/money-matters/lr-6064-age-uk-financial-hardship-final_v1.pdf.

Age UK (2018). All the lonely people: Loneliness in later life. www.ageuk.org.uk/globalassets/age-uk/documents/reports-and-publications/reports-and-briefings/loneliness/loneliness-report.pdf.

Alzheimer's Society (2021). What is dementia?www.alzheimers.org.uk/about-dementia/types-dementia/what-dementia.

British Psychological Society (2017). Practice guidelines (3rd ed.). www.bps.org.uk/sites/bps.org.uk/files/Policy/Policy%20-%20Files/BPS%20Practice%20Guidelines%20(Third%20Edition).pdf.

British Psychological Society (2018). Code of Ethics and Conduct. www.bps.org.uk/sites/bps.org.uk/files/Policy/Policy%20-%20Files/BPS%20Code%20of%20Ethics%20and%20Conduct%20%28Updated%20July%202018%29.pdf.

Collins, N. & Corna, L. (2018). General practitioner referral of older patients to Improving Access to Psychological Therapies (IAPT): An exploratory qualitative study. *British Journal of Psychiatry Bulletin*, 42(3): 115–118.

Deary, I. J., Corley, J., Gow, A. J., Harris, S. E., Houlihan, L. M., Marioni, R. E., Penke, L., Rafnsson, S. B. & Starr, J. M. (2009). Age-associated cognitive decline. *British Medical Bulletin*, 92: 135–152. https://doi:10.1093/bmb/ldp033.

Department of Health (2005). *Mental Capacity Act*. London: HMSO.

Department of Health (2009). *Living Well With Dementia: A National Dementia Strategy*. London: HMSO.

Gielkens, E., Vink, M., Sobczak, S., Rosowsky, E. & Van Alphen, B. (2018). EMDR in older adults with posttraumatic stress disorder. *Journal of EMDR Practice and Research*, 12(3). https://doi: 10.1891/1933–3196.12.3.132.

Health & Care Professions Council (2016). Standards of conduct, performance and ethics. www.hcpc-uk.org/globalassets/resources/standards/standards-of-conduct-performance-and-ethics.pdf.

Hedden, T. & Gabrieli, J. D. (2004). Insights into the ageing mind: A view from cognitive neuroscience. *Nature Reviews. Neuroscience*, 5(2): 87–96. https://doi:10.1038/nrn1323.

James, I. A. (2010). *Cognitive Behavioural Therapy with Older People: Interventions for Those With and Without Dementia*. Jessica Kingsley Publishers.

James, I. A. & Gibbons, L. (2019). *Communication Skills for Effective Dementia Care: A Practical Guide to Communication and Interaction Training (CAIT)* (1st ed.). Jessica Kingsley Publishers.

Laidlaw, K., Thompson, L., & Gallagher-Thompson, D. (2004). Comprehensive conceptualization of cognitive behaviour therapy for late life depression. *Behavioural and Cognitive Psychotherapy*, 32(4): 389–399. https://doi:10.1017/S1352465804001584.

Laidlaw, K., Kishita, N. & Chellingsworth, M. (2016). A clinician's guide to: CBT with older people. University of East Anglia. www.uea.ac.uk/documents/746480/2855738/CBT_BOOKLET_FINAL_FEB2016(7).pdf.

Marra, D. E., Hamlet, K. M., Bauer, R. M. & Bowers, D. (2020). Validity of teleneuropsychology for older adults in response to COVID-19: A systematic and critical review. *The Clinical Neuropsychologist*. https://doi: 10.1080/13854046.2020.1769192.

National Health Service (2019). NHS Long Term Plan. www.longtermplan.nhs.uk/wp-content/uploads/2019/08/nhs-long-term-plan-version-1.2.pdf.

NHS Digital (2017). Psychological therapies: Annual report on the use of IAPT services 2016–17. https://files.digital.nhs.uk/publication/q/1/psyc-ther-ann-rep-2016-17.pdf.

ONS (Office for National Statistics) (2016). National Population Projections: 2016-based Statistical Bulletin. ONS. www.ons.gov.uk/peoplepopulationandcommunity/populationandmigration/populationprojections/bulletins/nationalpopulationprojections/2016basedstatisticalbulletin.

ONS (Office for National Statistics) (2018). Suicides in the UK: 2018 registrations. ONS. www.ons.gov.uk/peoplepopulationandcommunity/birthsdeathsandmarriages/deaths/bulletins/suicidesintheunitedkingdom/2018registrations#:~:text=1.-,Main%20points,the%20first%20increase%20since%202013.

Pearson (2021). Q-global UK. Pearson. Retrieved from www.pearsonclinical.co.uk/q-global/q-global.aspx.

Ross, K., & Dexter-Smith, S. (2017). Psychological best practice in inpatient services for older people. *Faculty of the psychology of Older People, British Psychological Society*. https://shop.bps.org.uk/psychological-best-practice-in-inpatient-services-for-older-people.

Royal College of Psychiatrists (2015). Criteria for old age psychiatry services in the UK. Faculty Report. www.rcpsych.ac.uk/docs/default-source/members/faculties/old-age/old-age-challenging-ageless-services-criteria-for-old-age.pdf?sfvrsn=1e602061_4.

Royal College of Psychiatrists (2018). Suffering in silence: Age inequality in older people's mental health care CR22. College Report. www.rcpsych.ac.uk/docs/default-source/improving-care/better-mh-policy/college-reports/college-report-cr221.pdf?sfvrsn=bef8f65d_2.

RSPH (Royal Society for Public Health) (2018). That age old question: How attitudes to ageing affect our health and wellbeing. www.rsph.org.uk/static/uploaded/a01e3aa7-9356-40bc-99c81b14dd904a41.pdf.

Spector, A., Thorgrimsen, L., Woods, B. & Orrell, M. (2006). *Making a Difference: An Evidence-based Group Programme to Offer Cognitive Stimulation Therapy (CST) to People with Dementia*. Hawker Publications.

Swift, H. J., Abrams, D., Drury, L. & Lamont, R. A. (2016). The Perception of Aging and Age Discrimination. Briefing Paper. British Medical Association. www.resea

rchgate.net/profile/Hannah-Swift-4/publication/308970782_The_perception_of_ageing_
and_age_discrimination/links/57fbb2ec08ae6ce92eb2acaa/The-perception-of-ageing-
and-age-discrimination.pdf.

Yalom, I. (2011). *Staring at The Sun: Being at Peace with Your Own Mortality:
Overcoming the Dread of Death*. Piatkus.

Chapter 5

Counselling psychology and end-of-life care

Raymond Dempsey

Introduction

Dying is inevitable: distress with dying is not. Responding therapeutically to the individual in their living-with-dying requires the counselling psychologist to understand the medical, psychological, social, spiritual and existential world-view of the one who is dying and their support network. This chapter promotes the spiritual/existential-biopsychosocial attitude of the counselling psychologist honouring the subjective experience of the one with life-threatening or life-limiting illness and supports dignity of the individual in their care. In doing so, this chapter endorses the values, competencies and proficiencies of counselling psychology within the field of palliative care.

Working through this dignity lens, the counselling psychologist supports individual difference; lifespan stage; cultural issues; spiritual/religious attunement; and far ranging encounters with 'uncertain reprieve' (McWilliams, 2015, p. 546) in the trajectory of the individual's *stable-unstable-deteriorating-dying* progression through palliative care.

The counselling psychologist working in end-of-life is a professional companion to the one who is living-with-dying, a support to their family and social network, and an influencer to the multi-professional team enlisted as a professional care system.

Palliative and end-of-life care

The literature on defining palliative and end-of-life care is immense (Van Mechelen et al., 2012; WHO, 2013). That said, while there is variety in definition, there is consistency within these definitions of palliative care in key respects: expertise in medical, psychological, psychosocial and spiritual support that encompasses diagnosis to death and through to bereavement care. As such, this expertise in care has highlighted the requirement to develop competencies, monitoring and evaluation of service provision, training and development of staff appropriate to each 'stage' of the process to promote best positive outcome in interventions.

DOI: 10.4324/9781003159339-6

From this framework, palliative care is seen as involving both philosophy and systems of care. The philosophy of care is met in the holistic, person-centred focus that relieves distress and improves quality of life for patient and support network. This underpinning philosophy of care is realised through systems of care that are multi-professional. Such professionals have a valuable role in identifying patients with palliative need, helping the patient to clarify their goals for care, reducing hospitalisation rates, and introducing conversations to consider potential treatments for end-of-life (Thoosen et al., 2015). Initially the domain of adult services, palliative care is increasingly available for younger patients: neonatal, baby and infant, children and young persons (CHAS, 2020; Jindal-Snape et al., 2019; NICE, 2016; Wolfe et al., 2011).

Counselling psychologists across all therapeutic contexts operate from evidence-based practice through assessment-formulation-intervention-evaluation of intervention with clients (BPS, 2017). This is framed inclusive of age, difference and abilities; and works to promote resilience and support to individuals/family/support systems to help them regain/find their strengths. Hence, counselling psychologists have much to offer the field of palliative care. To date, there is no accredited curriculum for training as an applied (counselling) psychologist in palliative care. This has been considered by Jünger et al., (2010) building on the differential tier model of psychological support in palliative care recommended by NICE (2004). These authors argue for the introduction of an internationally recognised core curriculum for psychologists working in palliative care, to be endorsed to ensure seamless care across all services that can rapidly respond to changing health needs in the patient and is in alignment with the preferred choices and wishes of the dying. In 2018, the National Coalition for Hospice and Palliative Care (USA) presented eight areas that may suggest such a core curriculum: 1) Organisational structure/Process; 2) Physical; 3) Psychological/Psychiatric; 4) Social; 5) Spiritual, Religious, and Existential; 6) Cultural; 7) Patient care at the end of life; and 8) Ethical and legal aspects of care.

Palliative and end-of-life care, while used interchangeably in this chapter, are distinct, though subtly interlinked, phases in the movement from curative intervention to quality-of-life practices to support the dying individual and offer bereavement care to those grieving. Palliative care can often be misunderstood as being for the 'terminally ill'. A more accurate understanding of palliative care is that the individual is experiencing life-limiting or life-threatening illness, and in this sense palliative care is an umbrella concept inclusive of: advance care planning; active intervention; life-limiting/life-threatening illness; symptom management; quality of life; end-of-life; and bereavement. The earlier the transition to palliative care, the smoother the process from patienthood to personhood. That is, in palliative care the intention is to consider not the illness that has the person, but the person who has the illness.

The root of the English word palliative is found in the Latin *palliare* (to cloak) or *pallium* (a cloak). What is used as 'a cloak' for the dying individual identifies how we see the individual: From a medical model, in the curative stages of illness, symptomology is 'cloaked' with active intervention; from a counselling psychology model the experience of dying is 'cloaked' with intimacy and immediacy of relationship, acceptance and uncertainty, loss and hope. This positions all professionals involved with the dying to bring their own specific expertise to work together as one 'cloak'.

This approach, expertly presented by Chochinov (2007), provides the A, B, C, D model of competencies that I would recommend to counselling psychologists practising in palliative care:

> Attitude: Our approach towards the dying individual is shaped by how we conceptualise their situation. Thus, our levels of resilience and non-defensive engagement attend to the dying individual through our empirical evidence-based practice and our reflective-based practice (Hanley & Amos, 2018). Scientist and reflective practitioner align.
>
> Behaviour: This interconnects with attitude as it is an externalisation of inner values. Thus, person-centred care planning (Kitwood, 1997) focusing on respect, dignity, need, authority, and agency of the individual is presented as timely, sensitive and with the professional flexibility of the counselling psychologist's therapeutic activity. Creativity and mobility in therapeutic model are key. No one size fits all.
>
> Compassion: This is gained over time and through understanding, practice and reflection. Compassion leads the counselling psychologist to appreciate the immediacy of ambiguity and the confusion of uncertainty in the dying individual; the perplexed appearance of family members; and the hope-filled commitment of the healthcare professionals around.
>
> Dialogue: This is central in the professional relationship and therapeutic interventions with the dying individual. It is here that a spiritual/existential-biopsychosocial approach is key. It is the whole person who is dying and so the whole person needs attending. Empathy and unconditional positive is the investment that secures a compassionate attitude and meaningful effective therapeutic practice in end-of-life. Relationship is key.

These noted four competencies will promote best practice as outlined by the British Psychological Society (2017) and according to standards of proficiency upheld by the Health and Care Professions Council (2015).

The training of counselling psychologists influences their approach to intervening, beginning with our assessments, formulations, interventions and evaluations/reflections and how we communicate these. Formulation in counselling psychology has received copious attention in the literature (Challoner & Papayianni, 2018). At the same time, emotional unrest does not happen in a vacuum, so the counselling psychologist must also include in any formulation issues relating to changes in medical intervention, perceived identity, social/familial role and social isolation.

Because counselling psychologists are often one of the 'non-medical' members of a multi-professional team, they offer the opportunity to 'de-medicalise' the dying process and thereby challenge any pathologising of typical human distress while not minimising its importance or meaning. The starting point is one of person-centred care and remains the prerequisite for any application of psychological knowledge; therapeutic orientation; and best practice expertise. Practical concerns and existential issues (for example, the 'meaning of life', 'unfinished business', spiritual concerns) thus come to the surface, requiring attention. All of which can initiate a life review; regrets about plans/hopes not achieved; questions about the unfairness of life; questions of religious faith and doubt; memories, good and not so good, and so much more.

Challenges of the role and personal reflections

Living-with-dying is both universal and intimate: we all will die, and yet we each will live our dying our own way. This brings with it an entire array of issues and difficulties, as well as approaches to resolve them. Rando (1984) provides a masterful overview of many of these difficulties. Her book provides both the theoretical knowledge and the practical interventions helpful in working with those who are bereaved or dying.

The day-to-day routine and stressors as a family member of the one who is living-with-dying and members of their support network is comprehensively presented in the literature (Doyle et al., 2005). However, working within this field of end-of-life care brings challenges specific to the provenance of counselling psychology. For the purpose of this chapter these may be captured in three interconnected areas: 1) the dying individual; 2) their family/social networks; and 3) the counselling psychologist themselves.

The encounter with human distress is common in those who are living-with-dying. Interventions appropriate to their stage in this process may de-escalate, contextualise and regulate emotional distress. Indeed, effective intervention at this point may ease family bereavement when it arrives (Kissane et al., 1998). Assessment and intervention of emotional distress is promoted, at this point, by the efficient use of a formulation that distinguishes between typical experience(s) of adaptation/accommodation in living-with-dying and those that may suggest underlying presence of co-existing psychologically problematic issues.

Caring for a family member who is terminally ill is a complex procedure that requires constant attention and mobilisation of physical and emotional energy, not to mention the critical aspect of (limited) time. The issues of time-sensitive involvement, emotional energy and physical commitment requirements that are placed on the family members of the one living-with-dying is often referred to as the 'caregiver burden'. Family members may be in employment, and may have health issues themselves. Within this context they are also the providers of some 'direct care' in symptom management, emotional support, observing/monitoring change in their loved one, medication administration, comfort care and assistance with the activities of daily living. In addition, some 'indirect care' may also be needed: obtaining prescriptions; transporting to appointments; dealing with finances; 'negotiating' titration of care with healthcare professionals. This list is not exclusive, but even so it can be appreciated that family members, in exercising their daily routines, inclusive of caring, also experience emotional and psychological issues: relationship stress; role confusion; anxiety around 'doing things right'; fear of uncertainty; mood disorders; spiritual crises; and existential concerns (Given et al., 2001; Hudson & Payne, 2011).

Emotional burden is not only experienced by the individual who is living-with-dying and their family; it is also often experienced by those who work with those who are living-with-dying. For healthcare professionals, the emotional burden may have a variety of sources, including: the life experiences of the professional; their personal encounter with death in the family/social network; a sense of powerlessness and communication difficulties within the health system; 'death overload' from working with too many individuals dying in a (brief) space of time; frustration at not being able to offer the level of care they consider desirable due to late referral/system management issues; and over-investment in care for the living-with-dying without appropriate time for reflection and restoration.

It is critical to include reflection and restoration time/activities in the professional life of those working with individuals living-with-dying. There is evidence that activities that simply distract and allow little time for reflection are ineffective for building resilience and preventing burnout. In contrast, restorative activities, those that engage attention, appear to provide time for reflection, growth and change (Herbst & Cetti, 2001; Howard, 2008).

Reflective practice, clinical supervision, in all its modes, provides nurturance to all involved in living-with-dying. For the professional it refines, consolidates and renews their knowledge, expertise and practice; for the family/social network it supports their meaningful and purposeful engagement; and, most importantly, for the one living-with-dying it promotes best practice, effective care and quality of life. As Hawkins & Shohet (2012) eloquently conclude: 'The practice of supervision will become increasingly essential if humanity is going to preserve and develop its caring for the most vulnerable members of society, in a time when resources will be stretched and challenges increasing' (p. 255).

Therapeutic practice in end-of-life care

Counselling psychologists working in end-of-life care with patients and families report using several therapeutic strategies, selected to respond appropriately to client need.

- Family-centred approaches have been found to be helpful in working to facilitate family conversations (Kasl-Godfrey et al., 2014).
- Interventions involving psychoeducation, problem solving and cognitive restructuring have all shown discernible effects on carer well-being (Hudson et al., 2005; McMillan et al., 2006).
- A number of group work interventions, working both with family (Hudson et al., 2008) and with groups of carers (Hudson et al,. 2009; Milberg et al., 2005), report beneficial effects and a reduction in unmet carer needs.
- Different approaches effectively target different relevant outcomes for carers. Hudson et al. (2009) and Eagar et al. (2007) suggest that interventions based on an individual approach are more likely to have significant effects on caregiver burden and well-being while group approaches work well for building carer confidence.

Counselling psychologists are therefore expertly positioned to understand the tensions in caring within end-of-life care, as well as the rewards. This understanding can provide a useful framework for supporting carers (including professionals), which explains both the cost and the rewards of such caring as well as the psychological mechanisms involved (McWilliams, 2004).

Welcomed into the context of end-of-life psychology since 2002 is the emerging theory and practice of dignity therapy (https://dignityincare.ca/en/). Dignity therapy is presented by Martinez et al. (2017) as

> a brief, individualized psychotherapy and aims to relieve psycho-emotional and existential distress and to improve the experiences of patients whose lives are threatened by illness. This therapy offers patients an opportunity to reflect on issues that are important to them or other things that they would like to recall or transmit to others.
>
> (p. 493)

The findings of the first clinical trial of dignity therapy were presented in the *Journal of Clinical Oncology* (Chochinov et al., 2005). With strong evidence of effectiveness, a second study designed as a randomised control trial (RCT) was conducted in three countries (Chochinov et al., 2011). Participants were assigned to one of three interventions: dignity therapy, client-centred care, or standard palliative care. Three hundred and twenty-six participants took part. Participants reported that dignity therapy was more likely than the other two interventions to: improve quality of life; increase a sense of personal dignity; change how families perceived the dying individual; and support family needs. Dignity therapy emerged as significantly superior to client-centred care in improving spiritual well-being; and significantly superior to standard palliative care in remediating symptom of sadness and low mood.

Issues relating to leadership and diversity

The Practice Guidelines (BPS, 2017, p. 32) state: 'It is expected that all psychologists will have the necessary skills and abilities to work with all sections of the community.' This declaration has its locus in the document as working with culture and diversity. It promotes the appreciation that every individual is a cultural being with identifiable sociopolitical and spaciotemporal domains. In brief, we do not exist in a vacuum. Thus, the guideline recognises the importance of honouring, respecting and valuing the overt and covert meetings with culture (systems of attitudes, beliefs, assumptions) and the encounters with the intimacies of diversity (age, disability, gender reassignment, marriage and civil partnership, pregnancy and maternity, race, religion or belief, sex, sexual orientation). By following such guidance, the counselling psychologist in palliative care is empowered to offer individualised care.

The above endorses the leadership of the counselling psychologist, appreciating that their effectiveness is the result of their engagement with others (patient, family and organisations) and their collaboration in coaching/mentoring/training others involved, to the benefit of patients and families. Awareness and inclusion of culture and diversity is imperative for accurate and effective assessment, formulation and treatment planning (Sue & Sue, 2013). Advancing this, Comas-Diaz (2014) presented the competencies when working within a multicultural frame as reflexivity, empowerment and pluralism.

Ethical and legal considerations

It goes without saying that all counselling psychologists who work within palliative settings must adhere to the British Psychological Society Code of ethics and conduct (2018) and 'Practice Guidelines' (2017) and the Health and Care Professions Council Standards of proficiency (2015) and Standards of conduct, performance, and ethics (2016).

Palliative care is a context with constant challenges. It is an environment of rapid change, with frequently conflicting value-based conversations and decision-making that have impact on both life and death itself. Courage, candour and clarity are essentials for the counselling psychologist working with the one who is living-with-dying, their family and the healthcare team, as well as systems and policymakers. This means that counselling psychologists in such settings need to reflect on their work and their application of ethics and standards within the specific needs and demands of palliative involvement (Werth & Kleespies, 2006). In addition, it is essential that counselling psychologists in palliative settings have a strong understanding of current legislation as it relates to this setting. Further, it is essential that when working in a palliative setting the counselling psychologist needs command of the essentials of both biomedical ethics and their therapeutic application in assessing of capacity, as well as expertise in conversations relating to advance care planning; preferences regarding place of care (and dying); and withdrawing of intervention.

Significant to the efficacy of this work is that the counselling psychologist working in a palliative setting is mindful that they are not solo practitioners. They are one specialist member of the multi-professional team around the palliative individual and family.

A framework to support the counselling psychologist in such palliative care endeavours is found in the ethical principles of respect, competence, responsibility and integrity (BPS, 2018):

> Respect: This value underpins all others and is mutually facilitated to enhance the relationship. It is centred on rights of privacy and confidentiality. Effective palliative care involves intimacy and immediacy in multi-professional team working, so transparency in role(s) and responsibility are imperative.
>
> Competence: While palliative psychology remains an evolving specialism, specific codes or best practice guidelines are not readily available. That said, the need to be continually updating knowledge, skill, and practice in the field is paramount. Of itself, it is this ethical principle that notes the need for a curriculum, outlining competencies, and best practice guideline specific to the context of psychology in palliative care.
>
> Responsibility: The ethos of multi-professional working requires strong professional identity alongside a strong commitment to trusting relationships with professional colleagues. This demands commitment to teamworking and not self-aggrandisement as the 'key-player' to palliative intervention. Multi-professional working is egalitarian, honouring the unique specialism of each member of the team.
>
> Integrity: The above is inextricably linked to integrity. Integrity is evidenced in open, clear, and respectful conversations and necessary functions within all aspects of palliative settings. Integrity is about challenge-making through a dignified, collaborative, and cooperative attitude.

The above are the essentials for efficient navigation of challenging, perhaps even difficult, conversations within the palliative trajectory.

Legal considerations in palliative decision-making

It needs to be noted that the diagnosed individual, their family and even healthcare professionals are often hesitant to discuss options for the kind of care and intervention that may be hoped for at the end-of-life. However, without such conversations the dying may not have their wishes known (realised). It is true that such conversations are difficult. That said, they are not impossible. Opening the conversation on wishes for end-of-life care/intervention as early as is possible in the palliative trajectory will establish a shared understanding of the way forward in practical terms and offer invaluable information to the multi-professional team regarding the values of the one who is dying and those closest to them. This lays a sound foundation for the intimacy of encounter, the rapid-changing condition of the one who is dying, the evolving roles and duties of all involved, and above all the selection of interventions for patient care.

Advance care planning is, simply put, a generic term for the process whereby the patient's wishes and values in relation to their end-of-life care are made clear and documented (with regular updates). It is best done as a series of conversations. This can be an emotional process, so sensitivity and empathy are needed. Such conversations, and their documentation, are helpful in many ways: they report how the one living-with-dying would like to be cared for at the end of life; they relieve family members from the potential burden of difficult decision-making at a time of difficult emotions; and they guide professional care. This puts the patient at the centre of care and secures their autonomy, dignity and values.

This document becomes truly effective if/when the patient lacks capacity and is unable to make informed decisions with regard to their own end-of-life health-care. It is often a bridge for the patient to consider, and have legally prepared, a power of attorney document. This document sets out what a dying individual wants a named person to do for them in the future should they lack capacity.

Conclusion

While it is hoped that this chapter will be of interest to all professionals involved in palliative care, it is written particularly for counselling psychologists interested in this work and/or to support counselling psychologists currently in the field. First, it has presented an overview of significant professional issues counselling psychologists experience working in palliative care; second, to add support to the recognition that counselling psychology in palliative care be considered a specialism requiring defined proficiencies.

My experience to date in both adult and children's palliative care has taught me that all those who are living-with-dying, as well as their family/support networks, have psychological needs. The specialised knowledge and skills, the assessment and interventions of the counselling psychologist can contribute to the remediation, if not resolution, of the experience of human distress in palliative care. Applying the competencies and values that express our identity as counselling psychologists can promote well-being, support meaningful acceptance and facilitate growth and change for *all* living-with-dying.

References

BPS (British Psychological Society) (2017). Practice Guidelines (3rd edition). www.bps. org.uk/news-and-policy/practice-guidelines.

BPS (British Psychological Society) (2018). Code of ethics and conduct. www.bps.org. uk/sites/bps.org.uk/files/Policy%20-%20Files/BPS%20Code%20of%20Ethics%20and %20Conduct%20%28Updated%20July%202018%29.pdf.

Challoner, H. & Papayianni, F. (2018). Evaluating the role of formulation in counselling psychology: A systematic literature review. *European Journal of Counselling Psychology*, 7(1), 47–68. https://doi.org/10.5964/ejcop.v7i1.146.

CHAS (Children's Hospices Across Scotland) (2020). Children in Scotland requiring Palliative Care (ChiSP) 3. www.chas.org.uk/about-us/our-vision/our-publications.

Chochinov, H. M. (2007). Dignity and the essence of medicine: The A, B, C, & D of dignity-conserving care. *British Medical Journal*, 335, 184–187. https://doi: 10.1136/bmj.39244.650926.47

Chochinov, H. M., Hack, T., Hassard, T., Kristjanson, L. J., McClement, S. & Harlos, M. (2005). Dignity therapy: A novel psychotherapeutic intervention for patients near the end-of-life. *Journal of Clinical Oncology*, 23(24), 5520–5525. https://doi: 10.1200/JCO.2005.08.391

Chochinov, H. M., Kristjanson L. J., Breitbart, W., McClement, S., Hack, T. F., Hassard, T. & Harlos, M. (2011). Effect of dignity therapy on distress and end-of-life experience in terminally ill patients: A randomised controlled trial. *Lancet Oncology*, 12, 753–762. https://doi: 10.1016/S1470-2045(11)70153-X.

Chochinov, H. M., McClement S., Hack T., Thompson G., Dufault B. & Harlos M. (2015). Eliciting personhood within clinical practice: Effects on patients, families, and health care providers. *Journal of Pain Symptom Management*, 49(6), 974–980. https://doi: 10.1016/j.jpainsymman.2014.11.291

Comas-Diaz, L. (2014). Multicultural psychotherapy. In F. T. L. Leong (ed.), *APA Handbook of Multicultural Psychology: Applications and Training* (vol. 2, pp. 419–442). Washington, DC: American Psychological Association.

Doyle, D., Hanks, G., Cherny, N. and Calman, K. (2005). *Oxford Textbook of Palliative Medicine* (3rd edition). Oxford: Oxford University Press.

Eagar, K., Owen, A., Williams, K., Westera, A., Marosszeky, N., England, R. & Morris, D. (2007). Effective caring: A synthesis of the international evidence on carer needs and interventions. Centre for Health Service Development, University of Wollongong. https://ro.uow.edu.au/chsd/27.

Given, B. A., Given, C. W. and Kozachik, S. (2001). Family support in advanced cancer. *CA: A Cancer Journal for Clinicians* 51, 13–31. https://doi.org/10.3322/canjclin.51.4.213.

Hanley, T. & Amos, I. A. (2018). The scientist-practitioner and the reflective practitioner. In V. Galbraith (ed.), *Counselling Psychology* (pp. 167–183). London: Routledge.

Hawkins, P. & Shohet, R. (2012). *Supervision in the Helping Professions* (4th edition). Maidenhead, UK: Open University Press.

Health and Care Professions Council (2015). Standards of proficiency: Practitioner psychologists. www.hcpc-uk.org/resources/standards/standards-of-proficiency-practitioner-psychologists.

Health and Care Professions Council (2016). Standards of conduct, performance and ethics. www.hcpc-uk.org/standards/standards-of-conduct-performance-and-ethics/.

Herbst, L. H. & Cetti, J. (2001). Management strategies for palliative care: Promoting quality, growth, and opportunity. *American Journal of Hospice and Palliative Care*, 18, 327–333. https://doi.org/10.1177/104990910101800508.

Howard, F. (2008). Managing stress or enhancing wellbeing? Positive psychology's contribution to clinical supervision. *Australian Psychologist*, 43, 105–113. https://doi.org/10.1080/00050060801978647.

Hudson, P. L, Aranda, S. & Hayman-White, K. (2005). A psycho-educational intervention for family caregivers of patients receiving palliative care: A randomized control trial. *Journal of Pain and Symptom Management*, 30(4), 329–341. https://doi.org/ 10.1016/j.jpainsymman.2005.04.006

Hudson, P. & Payne, S. (2011). Family caregivers and palliative care: Current status and agenda for the future. *Journal of Palliative Medicine*, 14(7), 864–869. https://doi.org/10.1089/jpm.2010.0413.

Hudson, P., Thomas, K., Quinn, K., Cockayne, M. & Braithwaite, M. (2009). Teaching family carers about home-based palliative care: Final results from a group education program. *Journal of Pain and Symptom Management*, 38(2), 299–308. https://doi: 10.1016/j.jpainsymman.2008.08.010

Hudson, P., Quinn, K., O'Hanlon, B. & Aranda, S. (2008). Family meetings in palliative care: Multidisciplinary clinical practice guidelines. *BMC Palliative Care*, 7 (12). https://doi: 10.1186/1472-684X-7-12.

Jindal-Snape, D., Johnston, B., Pringle, J., Kelly T. B., Scott, R., Libby Gold, L. & Dempsey, R. (2019). Multiple and multidimensional life transitions in the context of life-limiting health conditions: Longitudinal study focussing on perspectives of young adults, families and professionals. *BMC Palliative Care*, 18(30). https://doi.org/10.1186/s12904-019-0414-9.

Jünger, S., Payne, S. A., Costantini, A., Kalus, C. & Werth, J. L., Jr. (2010). EAPC Task Force on Education for Psychologists in Palliative Care. *European Journal of Palliative Care*, 17(2). www.researchgate.net/publication/277190808_The_EAPC_TASK_Force_on_education_for_psychologists_in_palliative_care.

Kasl-Godfrey, J. E., King, D. A. & Quill, T. E. (2014). Opportunities for psychologists in palliative care: Working with patients and families across the disease continuum. *American Psychologist*, 69(4), 364–375. https://doi.org/10.1037/a0036735.

Kissane, D. W., Bloch S., McKenzie M., McDowell, A. C. & Nitzan, R. (1998). Family Grief Therapy: A preliminary account of a new model to promote healthy family functioning during palliative care and bereavement. *Psycho-Oncology*, 7, 14–25. https://ogg.osu.edu/media/documents/sunset/FamilyGriefTherapy_Kissane_David_W.pdf.

Kitwood, T. (1997). *Dementia Reconsidered: The Person Comes First*. Philadelphia, PA: Open University Press.

Martínez, M., Arantzamendi, M., Belar, A., Carraso J. M., Carvajal, A., Rullán, M., Centeno, C. *Palliative Medicine*, 31(6), 492–509. https://doi.org/10.1177/0269216316665562.

McMillan, S. C., Small, B. J., Weitzner, M., Schonwetter, R., Tittle, M., Moody, L. & Haley, W. E. (2006). Impact of coping skills intervention with family caregivers of hospice patients with cancer: A randomized control trial. *Cancer*, 106(1), 214–222. https://doi: 10.1002/cncr.21567.

McWilliams, E. (2004). Stress in palliative care. *Progress in Palliative Care*, 12(6), 293–301. https://doi.org/10.1080/09699260.2017.1395980.

McWilliams, E. (2015). A discourse around death. *The Psychologist*, 8(7). https://thepsychologist.bps.org.uk/discourse-around-death.

Milberg, A., Rydstrand, K., Helander, L. & Friedrichsen, M. (2005). Participants' experiences of a support group intervention for family caregivers during ongoing palliative home care. *Journal of Palliative Care*, 21(4), 277–284. www.diva-portal.org/smash/get/diva2:510425/FULLTEXT02.

National Coalition for Hospice and Palliative Care (2018). Clinical practice guidelines for quality palliative care (4th edition). www.nationalcoalitionhpc.org/ncp/.

NICE (National Institute for Clinical Excellence) (2004). *Improving Supportive and Palliative Care for Adults with Cancer: The Manual*. London: NICE. www.nice.org. uk/guidance/csg4/resources/improving-supportive-and-palliative-care-for-adults-with-cancer-pdf-773375005.

NICE (National Institute for Health and Care Excellence) (2016). End-of-life care for infants, children and young people with life-limiting conditions: Planning and management. http://nice.org.uk/guidance/ng61.

Rando, T. (1984). *Grief, Dying, and Death: Clinical Interventions for Caregivers*. Champaign, IL: Research Press.

Sue, D. W. & Sue, D. (2013). *Counselling the Culturally Diverse* (6th edition). Hoboken, NJ: John Wiley & Sons.

Thoosen, B., Vissers, K., Verhagen, S., Prins, J., Bor, H., van Weel, C., Groot, M. & Engels, Y. (2015). Training general practitioners in early identification and anticipatory palliative care planning: A randomised control trial. *BMC Family Practice*, 16(126). https://doi.org/10.1186/s12875-015-0342-6.

Van Mechelen, W., Aertgeerts, B., De Ceulaer, K., Thoonsen, B., Vermandere, M., Warmenhoven, F., Rijswijk, E. & De Lepeleire, J. (2012). Defining the palliative care patient: A systematic review. *Palliative Medicine*, 27. https://doi.org/10.1177/0269216311435268.

Werth, J. L. & Kleespies, P. M. (2006). Ethical considerations in providing psychological services in end-of-life care. In J. L. Werth & D. Blevin (eds), *Psychological Issues near the End-of-life: A Resource for Professional Care Providers*. Washington, DC: APA. https://doi.org/10.1037/11262-003.

WHO (World Health Organization) (2013). Definition of palliative care. www.who.int/cancer/palliative/definition/en.

Wolfe, J., Hinds, P. S. & Sourkes, B. M. (eds) (2011). *Textbook of Interdisciplinary Paediatric Palliative Care*. Philadelphia, PA: Elsevier.

Section 2

Condition specific

Working as a counselling psychologist in an adult learning disability team

Stephen Ollis

This chapter will attempt to capture my experience of working as a counselling psychologist in an NHS adult learning disability team over the last decade. It will outline what a learning disability is before exploring the most critical current and historical contexts. Finally, it will describe key aspects of the role and provide some personal reflections.

Learning disability

A learning disability (sometimes referred to as an intellectual disability) is defined in the United Kingdom as

- A significantly reduced ability to understand complex information or learn new skills.
- A reduced ability to cope independently.
- A condition which started before adulthood and has a lasting effect.

(Department of Health, 2001)

Diagnostic criteria for learning disability generally consist of 'significant' deficits in 'adaptive' and 'intellectual' functioning present from childhood. This would typically include people being assessed as having a measured 'Intelligence Quotient' (IQ) score below 70 and 'significant deficits' in adaptive functioning (NICE, 2015). Approximately 2.5% of people in the United Kingdom would meet the criteria for the diagnosis of learning disability, which amounts to around 1.5 million people overall (NHS, 2021). Around 10% of this number access full-time adult social care support (Public Health England, 2019).

People with diagnosed learning disabilities have a significantly lower life expectancy when compared to the wider population (University of Bristol Norah Fry Centre for Disability Studies, 2019). They are more likely to experience abuse, live in poverty and be given a mental health diagnosis (NICE, 2016). In the last decade, over 40% of people with learning disabilities report having reductions in care and support provided to them (Forrester-

DOI: 10.4324/9781003159339-7

Jones et al., 2020). In the recent global pandemic, the death rate from COVID-19 of people with a learning disability was estimated to be three to four times the average rate in the general population (Public Health England, 2020).

Historical context

Prior to the 20th century, the use of a label to differentiate people (often far more unpleasant than the term 'learning disability') was arguably more motivated by the idea of 'protecting' the 'public' (see Digby & Wright, 1996 and Jarrett, 2020 for a broader history of the treatment of people with learning disabilities). Over time this attitude has, in theory at least, shifted towards being more about protecting potentially vulnerable people from harm, maintaining their human rights and improving their quality of life.

Since the turn of the last century, people that may now be labelled as having a learning disability often lived in large institutional settings (Butler & Drakeford, 2005). The advent of 'Care in the Community' during the late 1970s saw some of those people move to being supported in the community by teams of health professionals.

In 2001 the Department of Health and Social Care published the policy paper 'Valuing People: A New Strategy for Learning Disability for the 21st Century'. This said that people with learning disabilities must no longer be marginalised or excluded. It identified areas where people with learning disabilities and their carers suffered poorer outcomes in relation to health, employment and human rights. It also identified that health and social care services needed to work more closely together in the future.

In 2012, horrifying abuse at the Winterbourne View private care home for people with learning disabilities was broadcast by the BBC Panorama programme. This is recognised as serving as a prompt for the NHS England 'Transforming Care' agenda, which identified that around 3,500 adults were still living in hospital-style settings or assessment and treatment units (ATUs). The goal was ultimately to close all of these facilities and move people into homes in their local communities. This was not achieved, however – for example, as of November 2020, at least 2,075 people remained in ATUs (NHS Digital, 2020). Furthermore, around 4,000 uses of restraint were being reported monthly at this time, including physical restraint, use of medication as restraint and sometimes illegal use of seclusion and isolation (NHS Digital, 2020). A second, alarmingly similar Panorama programme in 2019 exposed further abuse at another site in County Durham, Whorlton Hall.

While how we treat the most vulnerable members of our society has to an extent changed for the better over time, themes of abuse and marginalisation remain prominent. It is critical that anybody coming to work in this area is aware of the traumatic past and disempowered present for people with learning disabilities.

The work setting

At present, adults with learning disabilities in the United Kingdom typically receive support from specialist NHS community health teams, social care teams, private providers and charitable organisations (usually a combination of these). Services are configured in different ways – for example, some areas will integrate health and social care professionals who share the same goals. In other areas, social care and health teams work separately. Community services can often include additional specialist teams such as Assertive Outreach (which attempt to reduce hospital admissions), Health Facilitation (reducing the impact of health inequalities) and enhanced crisis teams.

Counselling psychologists may be employed alongside a range of different professionals in both NHS, charitable and private settings. Other professional disciplines that work alongside counselling psychologists in this field include specialist nurses, support workers, occupational therapists, speech and language therapists, specialist social workers, physiotherapists and psychiatrists. Some may work just with adults in the community whereas others may work across the lifespan, exclusively with children, within hospital settings or exclusively with adults who are at risk of offending.

The role of the counselling psychologist

The role of the counselling psychologist within both this community team set-up and the wider health and social care system is multifaceted. While there is now an expectation that they will take on leadership, management and service development-related work, clinical interventions with the overall goal of supporting the client still make up most of the workload. The clinical work can be broadly divided into direct and indirect approaches. Direct approaches encompass therapeutic or educational interventions with clients as well as supportive or instructional interventions with the people who support them such as parents/family or teams of professional paid carers. The 'behavioural' theoretical paradigm still underpins some of the more common 'indirect' approaches; however, being able to integrate different theoretical paradigms is helpful in this type of work. Regardless of preferred theoretical orientation, counselling psychologists would usually play some part in what is often a multi-disciplinary approach to care. Taking on a range of roles including, observational assessment, formulation, care planning, staff training and supervision. Sometimes they may be asked to provide assessment of 'eligibility' for service or diagnosis of neurological conditions such as autism or dementia. Assessment roles may also include determining whether a client legally has the mental capacity to make a specific life-impacting decision, assessing levels of general risk to inform care plans or sexual/relationship knowledge. Sometimes counselling psychologists will be asked to write reports for court in relation to issues such as mental capacity or act as expert witnesses.

Direct therapeutic approaches

A small however growing evidence base for psychological therapy for adults with learning disabilities has gradually emerged (NICE, 2016). Some examples of making adaptions to established models of therapy include cognitive analytical therapy (Lloyd & Clayton, 2013), compassion focused therapy (Cowles, Randle-Phillips & Medley, 2020), psychodynamic therapy (Frankish, 2016), cognitive behavioural therapy (Kroese, Dagnan & Loumidis, 1997) and systemic family approaches (Baum & Lynggaard, 2006).

Clients can present for therapy for a range of different reasons. Most referrals will come via other professionals such as GPs or social workers. Sometimes referrals come from members of your own team; very occasionally a client may self-refer or, more likely, be referred by family members. In my experience, what is described on the referral doesn't always match what the client or family may see as their most problematic issue. Sometimes, what the psychologist may perceive as being psychologically related distress may be labelled as something different such as a physical health problem or simply attributed to their learning disability (called diagnostic overshadowing). Counselling psychologists are well placed to position the person at the centre of any assessment process and guide other professionals to prioritise this in order to make sure they receive the right help for the right difficulty. This can often be a tricky thing to navigate!

Historically, people with learning disabilities were not considered capable of engaging and benefitting from psychological therapy (Hollins & Sinason, 2000). Sadly, I still see these attitudes amongst some professionals and carers, both within and more commonly from outside of this field. Thus, professionals often need to identify when a person may benefit from a psychology referral and actively suggest this.

In most (but not all) cases the counselling psychologist needs to adapt their trained approaches to the needs of the client. It is worth seeking post-doctoral training in areas where 'mainstream' therapies have been adapted. In general, adapting talking therapy can include (not an exhaustive list) changing the length of sessions, making communication simpler, reflecting on language used to communicate, using pictures, generally going at a slower pace and involving carers more (with the client's consent). It is also crucial that psychologists give the client a space to talk alone and extra time to develop a therapeutic relationship as often they are not used to being afforded these conditions. The other allied health professionals in the team are often extremely helpful in thinking about how to meet the client's communication and sensory needs, which can be critical to successful therapy outcomes.

A learning disability should never prevent somebody from being able to benefit from a therapeutic relationship with another person. The counselling psychologist's ethos that the therapeutic relationship is the key aspect of any intervention and the most effective way to help a person in distress makes them well placed to promote this attitude. Frankish (2016) helpfully describes how to think about a person's stage of emotional development in order to determine how to appropriately tailor your intervention as well as describing ways of working with less verbal clients. Therapies can be adapted effectively while retaining their validity; however, clients with greater degrees of cognitive impairment may be more likely to benefit from approaches that rely less on verbal communication. Examples of these include 'intensive interaction' or the use of 'talking mats', but the fundamentals of the relationship should remain intact.

Trauma-informed care and the therapeutic relationship

People with a diagnosis of learning disability are more likely to have experienced a range of different types of trauma and adversity, and this is often not recognised (for a summary, see Hollins & Sinason, 2000). It is important to widen your consideration of what constitutes impactful traumatic experiences for people with learning disabilities. It has been argued that just the process of being perceived by others as 'different' is a significant trauma that can have multiple impacts on development and relationships (Sinason 1992). Although there may be a growing recognition of experiences such as abuse and neglect, consideration of identity and relational trauma is from my experience still underacknowledged and misunderstood when thinking about how people with learning disabilities present to services as adults.

In recent years, part of my role has been to attempt to introduce trauma-informed approaches to this field of work. Treisman (2021) offers a good summary of the values that underpin these approaches. These approaches can align well with the ethos of counselling psychology – for example, the focus on the relationship, being culturally sensitive, embedding reflective practice and the importance of recognising the client's own subjective meaning and experience.

Trauma-informed approaches encourage mental health difficulties (or what are sometimes labelled as 'behavioural issues' in this area) to be primarily understood within the context of 'what has happened?' rather than 'what is wrong?' This views a person's behaviour (what is wrong?) within the context of how a range of traumatic experiences have impacted on them (what has happened?). Working in this field, the relationship focus is often not prioritised or just seen from the narrow perspective of between client and therapist rather than the impact of all the relevant relationships on the client at a personal and system level.

These approaches also highlight the need to reflect on our practice to avoid iatrogenic harm and secondary trauma. Herman (1992) described how people who have suffered trauma are more likely to be disempowered and disconnected from others and therefore need to be empowered to create new connections as part of their process of recovery. This is highly relevant to the experiences of people with learning disabilities; however, it can be a real source of internal conflict for the professional trying to navigate various different systems which don't always consider the impact of trauma and their own impact of inadvertently creating more trauma.

When thinking about direct therapeutic work or assessment regardless of modality or approach, the focus on the therapeutic relationship within the ethos of counselling psychology is crucial for helping adults with learning disabilities to reduce psychological distress and improve their overall well-being. Basing any therapeutic approach around trying to develop the opposite conditions to being disempowered, controlled, feeling unsafe or disconnected is a critical starting point for any direct contact. Fostering feelings of control and safety are early building blocks of the therapeutic relationship, particularly when working with this client group.

As counselling psychologists, we are trained to recognise the importance of the person's own subjective experience, and this also sits comfortably within the ethos of trauma-informed approaches that stress the importance of a person making their own meaning about what has happened to them. Communication difficulties can make it hard for people with learning disabilities to use language to name their distress and find personal meaning this way. Furthermore, people with learning disabilities may not have been given enough opportunity in the past to develop their own narratives as to 'what happened to me', which often leads to difficulties in establishing a strong sense of identity. A common occurrence is a carer who may want to come into your session and a client who will passively agree with their opinions. Often the first and dominant narrative I will hear is the parent's or carer's, followed by a similar version by a possibly acquiescent client. The carer usually means well, but sometimes the professional's role is about helping a client to find their own voice and meaning to their distress. This can take time and an acknowledgement that talking therapy approaches alone will not achieve this.

Assessment-focused roles

The most common assessment role typically requested by the referrer is in relation to whether a client is 'eligible' to access services. While services may adopt different eligibility criteria, in simple terms the psychologist's role is to form an opinion in relation to whether a person has a learning disability or not as part of this process. The diagnosis of learning disability can also have future legal implications for that person, such as whether their capacity to make important decisions – for example, being able to stand trial for a criminal offence, engage in a sexual relationship or sign a tenancy agreement – can be questioned by others. Being able to access specialist services in terms of both health and social care could have a profound impact on that person's life, making this a potentially life-changing assessment. It therefore has to be handled with care, transparency and compassion.

As a clinician you are being asked to come to a binary decision around a social construct (learning disability) using psychometric tools that measure other constructs (such as 'intelligence' and 'adaptive functioning'). The validity and reliability of these tools have been queried particularly in relation to the assessment of intelligence at the lower end of the scale (Whitaker, 2008). Although the British Psychological Society guidelines recommend the use of standardised assessment tools such as the Weschler Adult Intelligence Scale, 4th edition (WAIS-IV) and the Adaptive Behaviour Assessment System, they conclude in their guidance that decisions should involve 'clinical judgement' (BPS, 2015, p. 4). Given the potential for iatrogenic harm during any assessment process, the counselling psychologist has to be highly reflective on the ethical issues that surround this, particularly in relation to the power they hold within this dynamic and the potential impact of any report they write both at the time and in the future. The reality is that the concept of 'eligibility' for service is an imperfect system that needs to be navigated with great care.

All assessments can also potentially be 'therapeutic' and should be approached with thoughts of, first, how can I help this person and how can I avoid harming this person? Although you are employed by a service and have contact with services that may have different interests in what you do, the client's wellbeing must always be your priority. Sometimes clients may be missing basic needs in their life such as feeling safe in their home or having friendships, sexual relationships or a job, and a psychologist can act as a powerful ally, in the first instance helping by raising these issues with the relevant people.

It is crucial that a client truly understands the purpose of any assessment or intervention, or if they do not (as may legitimately be the case if they lack capacity), that it is clearly being done in their best interests, with proper discussion with carers and the decisions documented. It is not unusual for clients or carers to arrive to your appointment without full knowledge of the reasons why they are there, and this can never be acceptable. As previously described, people with learning disabilities are more likely to be coming to see you with histories of significant trauma adversity and marginalisation in addition to their current distress. It is crucial to prepare a client to be safely asked about both what has happened to them and what their present difficulties are, and not presume this has been asked by somebody else.

Regardless of what I had been asked to do by a referrer, I would try my best to make sure that the client received support for any immediate quality of life issues, even if this means signposting to get needs met elsewhere. Often that broader, relational and more curious approach to assessment and the ability to develop a strong early rapport will lead to referrals initially designated as 'assessment' leading on to more therapeutic interventions and building a longer-standing relationship with the client.

Indirect interventions

Indirect interventions can be summarised as actions where you are trying to influence how carers and services think about and interact with their clients or family members, in order to improve the wellbeing of the client. This can take place alongside direct individual work with clients or on its own when this is not possible. It is crucial that clients are involved with this approach and consent to it as best as possible when able to. Clients may sometimes lack the capacity to do this, in which case carers and advocates should be involved to ensure the client's best interests are taken into consideration. This type of work can take many different forms and involve working alongside different professionals. A common multi-disciplinary team approach is using a psychological model to document a strategy or care plan that is designed to inform the carers about the best and most evidenced-based approach to work with a client. These approaches often can involve the production of written documents, subsequent related training with staff teams and further supervision or coaching.

In my experience this approach doesn't necessarily translate into meaningful or sustainable change in practice unless you focus on the different relationships and developing these. Interventions with carers and staff teams are more likely to be effective if you can spend time developing a good rapport with the carer or support team in the first instance and get to really understand what is happening for the client – for them and the system around them. Approaches such as positive behaviour support (PBS) are very popular but in my experience often do not pay enough attention to all the different relationships surrounding the client. Counselling psychologists are ideally placed to help in this circumstance, viewing it in the same way they would when doing typical individual work where the relationship comes before any meaningful change. I have observed that a lot of carers are poorly paid and placed in high-pressure situations with limited training and heavy workloads. In these circumstances, any kind of intervention is likely to fail, and it is partly the psychologist's responsibility to highlight this and take action. Additionally, carers may have their own experiences of trauma and be working in 'trauma-soaked' (Treisman, 2021) organisations. Evidence is also emerging that the carers' and families' experience of the care system can itself be traumatising and can in turn impact on the wellbeing of the client and their ability and motivation to engage with services (The Challenging Behaviour Foundation, 2020). These issues are critical to the success of interventions, and the work may be about dealing with this and modelling over a long period of time good practice that then becomes embedded in the carers' organisational culture.

Counselling psychologists are in a strong position to promote reflective practice, which is also important in this work. The 'low arousal' approach (McDonnell, 2019) places an emphasis on the role of the carer and their influence on the observed behaviour of the client. For example, focusing interventions on understanding and regulating the carer's own distress and how this may influence their interactions with a client. Cultural factors and attitudes can also impact on the success of these interventions. Some of the interventions can be challenging to carers' values, particularly approaches that are strictly non-punitive. Being able to reflect safely in group or individual supervision on how they influence the day-to-day behaviour of their clients can be crucial. Carers and health professionals commonly describe feeling frustrated and 'stuck' as well as experiencing sometimes overwhelming feelings of guilt and shame, and it helps to have time to process and understand these feelings in order to deliver care plans successfully.

In return the counselling psychologist must be able to reflect on their own role in this process, acknowledge the impact of the work and take care of themselves. My experience of working in this field after qualifying as a counselling psychologist was that I wanted to focus on offering one-to-one therapy as much as possible. As the years passed, I found myself working more with carers and staff teams and attempting to work with them more intensely and for longer periods. Whichever psychological approach used it was important to collaborate with carers and get them to view you as somebody who could help them and not judge them. It is vital that time is spent forming a relationship with carers and allowing time for a carer or staff team to feel listened too and validated. In these circumstances the counselling psychologist must be able to reflect on and acknowledge their own privilege and power within the wider system and be empathic and aware of the hardships, trauma and adversity that carers themselves have sometimes experienced. Having to balance this 'curious observer' stance with the role of being the 'expert' and taking on a clinical lead role can be challenging.

Additionally, you are often put into a position where (sometimes alone) you have to be an ally for the client and promote narratives about them that are more compassionate and trauma informed – for instance, trying to help carers understand the role that trauma and adversity (including the impact of their learning disability) has in influencing the client's behaviour. Changing the narrative from seeing behaviour as 'challenging' and located 'within' the client to thinking about it as an adaptive means of survival, or what McDonnell (2019) nicely describes as a client communicating distress about their immediate environment.

Supervision interventions need to also consider caring for the carers. A great deal of research supports the view that a carer's wellbeing and ability to manage their own distress impacts significantly on the distress experienced and expressed by the person they care for (Shah, Wadoo & Latoo, 2010). While I have never worked in a formal therapeutic relationship with a carer, there would certainly be times when supervision or conversations would feel a bit like this, and I am aware of psychologists working in this field who would offer more structured therapy directly to carers. More common is running sessions for carers to teach simple self-care techniques. Facilitating group sessions can help them reflect on, normalise and process feelings that were emerging at work and help avoid burnout and secondary trauma.

Final reflections

Among a range of strong feelings, the frustration and guilt voiced by carers in particular can also be experienced by professionals when they reflect on their own experiences of work. The frustration and 'stuck' feeling (particularly common amongst trainees) certainly mirrors often unvoiced feelings of clients that may be being communicated instead through observable behaviour. One of the most challenging parts of the job in the last decade has been witnessing the impact of financial cuts on services, leaving fewer clients having their basic needs –particularly their social and occupational needs – met. Being referred a client for therapy when their basic needs provision has been cut places a psychologist in a very difficult position, wanting to help but knowing that it will be extremely hard to make meaningful change until the client has their basic needs met. Professionals who work in this field can fall very quickly into a 'rescuer' role and burn out.

On a final, more positive note, working as a counselling psychologist in adult learning disability teams can mean that you have a measure of both ability and power to positively influence the lives of people who have been historically disenfranchised and disregarded by wider society. It can also bring great feelings of joy, moments of shared humour and certainly personal growth. The work requires heart, humility, courage, compassion, creativity and an ability to think on your feet.

References

Baum, S. & Lynggaard, H. (eds) (2006). *Intellectual Disabilities: A Systemic Approach* (1st ed.). Abingdon, UK: Routledge.

Butler, I. & Drakeford, M. (2005). *Scandal, Social Policy and Social Welfare*. Bristol: Policy Press.

Cowles, M., Randle-Phillips, C. & Medley, A. (2020). Compassion-focused therapy for trauma in people with intellectual disabilities: A conceptual review. *Journal of Intellectual Disabilities*, 24(2), 212–232. https://doi.org/10.1177/1744629518773843.

Department of Health (2001). Valuing people: A new strategy for learning disability the 21st century. https://assets.publishing.service.gov.uk/government/uploads/system/uploads/ attachment_data/file/250877/5086.pdf.

Digby, A. & Wright, D. (eds) (1996). *From Idiocy to Mental Deficiency: Historical Perspectives on People with Learning Disabilities*. Abingdon, UK: Routledge.

Esterhuyzen, A. & Hollins, S. (1997). Psychotherapy. In S. Read (ed.), *Psychiatry in Learning Disability* (pp. 332–349). London: W. B. Saunders.

Forrester-Jones, R., Beecham, J., Randall, A., Harrison, R., Malli, M., Sams, L. & Murphy, G. (2020). Becoming less eligible? Intellectual disability services in the age of austerity. National Institute for Health Research School for Social Care, 7 July. www.sscr.nihr.ac.uk/SSCR-research- findings_RF100.pdf.

Frankish, P. (2016). *Disability Psychotherapy: An Innovative Approach to Trauma Informed Care*. Abingdon, UK: Routledge.

Gore, N., McGill, P., Toogood, S., Allen, D., Hughes, J. I., Baker, P., Hastings, R., Noone, S. & Denne, L. (2013). Definition and scope for positive behaviour support. *International Journal of Positive Behavioural Support*, 3, 14–23.

Herman J. L (1992). *Trauma and Recovery*. New York: Basic.

Hollins, S. & Sinason, V. (2000). Psychotherapy, learning disabilities and trauma: New perspectives. *British Journal of Psychiatry*, 176(1), 32–36.

Jarrett, S. (2020). *Those They Call Idiots: The Idea of the Disabled Mind from 1700 to the Present Day*. London: Reaktion Books.

Kroese, B. S., Dagnan, D. & Loumidis, K. (1997). *Cognitive Behaviour Therapy for People with Learning Disabilities*. Abingdon, UK: Routledge.

Lloyd, J. & Clayton, P. (2013). *Cognitive Analytic Therapy for People with Learning Disabilities and Their Carers*. London: Jessica Kingsley Publishers.

McDonnell, A. (2019). *The Reflective Journey: A Practitioner's Guide to the Low Arousal Approach*. Studio 3.

NHS Digital (2020). Assuring Transformation data. https://digital.nhs.uk/data-and-information/data-collections-and-data-sets/data-collections/assuring- transformation/content.

NHS (National Health Service) (2021). Overview: Learning disabilities. www.nhs.uk/conditions/learning-disabilities/. Retrieved 16/06/2021.

NHS Digital (2020). Learning Disability Services monthly statistics (AT: September 2020, MHSDS: July 2020 Final). https://digital.nhs.uk/data-and-information/publica tions/statistical/learning-disability-services-statistics/learning-disability-services-m onthly-statistics-at-september-2020-mhsds-july-2019-final.

NICE (National Institute of Clinical Excellence) (2015). Challenging behaviour and learning disabilities: Prevention and interventions for people with learning dis-abilities whose behaviour challenges. www.nice.org.uk/guidance/ng11/resources/cha llenging-behaviour-and- learning-disabilities-prevention-and-interventions-for-peop le-with-learning- disabilities-whose-behaviour-challenges.

NICE (National Institute for Health and Care Excellence) (2016). Mental health pro-blems in people with learning disabilities: Prevention, assessment and management. www.nice.org.uk/guidance/ng54.

Office for National Statistics (2019). Estimates of the population for the UK, England and Wales, Scotland and Northern Ireland.

Public Health England (2019). People with learning disabilities in England: Updates of national statistics about people with learning disabilities in England and the services and support available to them and their families. www.gov.uk/government/publica tions/people-with-learning-disabilities-in-england.

Public Health England (2020). COVID 19 deaths of people identified as having learn-ing disabilities: Summary. www.gov.uk/government/publications/covid-19-dea ths-of-people-with-learning-disabilities.

Shah, A. J., Wadoo, O. & Latoo, J. (2010). Psychological distress in carers of people with mental disorders. *British Journal of Medical Practitioners*, 3(3), 18–25.

Sinason, V. (1992) *Mental Handicap and the Human Condition*. London: Free Asso-ciation Books.

The Challenging Behaviour Foundation (2020). www.challengingbehaviour.org.uk.

Treisman, K. (2021). *A Treasure Box for Creating Trauma-informed Organisations.* London: Jessica Kingsley Publishers.

University of Bristol Norah Fry Centre for Disability Studies (2019). The Learning Disabilities Mortality Review (LeDeR) programme: Annual report 2018. Health-care Improvement Quality Partnership. www.hqip.org.uk/resource/the-learning-disa bilities-mortality-review-annual-report-2018.

Whitaker, S. (2008). The stability of IQ in people with low intellectual ability. *Intellectual and Developmental Disabilities*, 46, 120–128.

Chapter 7

Opposites attract? Counselling psychology in medical and physical health settings

Lesley Armitage

Introduction

This chapter explores physical health conditions and their relationship to psychological health. It highlights the range of roles for counselling psychologists within physical health, outlining competencies and key features of these roles. It explores relevant models and clinical applications, including opportunities for counselling psychologists to expand their skills beyond therapy. It discusses the challenges and opportunities for counselling psychologists in medical settings, considering to what extent this area of work fits with the philosophy of counselling psychology. Case examples are used to illustrate typical presentations and interventions.

Approximately 30% of the population live with a long-term physical health condition (LTC) (Department of Health, 2011). Evidence suggests that integrating psychological and physical health care for people with LTCs would improve clinical and cost effectiveness (Chiles et al., 1999; Naylor et al., 2012; Prince et al., 2007; Psychological Professions Network, 2020; Steel et al., 2018). Research and NHS guidance suggest that LTC services should facilitate conversations about mental health, offer counselling and prioritise patients' individual values (National Voices, 2019; NHS, 2019; NICE, 2016). Counselling psychology's philosophy, training and core clinical skills promote patient-centred care and integrated perspectives on health and well-being. Therefore, counselling psychologists are ideally positioned to support people with physical health difficulties and the staff working with them.

Work settings for counselling psychologists in physical health

The terms clinical health psychology and medical psychology are commonly used to describe departments of psychologists (and other psychological professions) specialising in physical health. The term used throughout this chapter is 'applied health psychology'. Applied health psychologists may work with a range of conditions including persistent pain; diabetes; paediatric health psychology; stroke; HIV; cancer/oncology; cardiac rehabilitation;

DOI: 10.4324/9781003159339-8

spinal injuries; neurological conditions; medically unexplained symptoms; burns and plastics; critical care; major physical trauma; chronic fatigue; rheumatology; bariatrics/weight management; transplant; respiratory conditions; renal medicine; palliative care; and (more recently) long Covid. Applied health psychologists may work in the NHS, private healthcare organisations or independent practice. Some are generalists, seeing patients with a range of different conditions who have been referred by their GP or hospital consultants. Others specialise in one or more physical health areas. They may work on hospital wards, in outpatient clinics or in patients' own homes. Opportunities within applied health psychology are broad. Roles may involve assessment, therapy and group work, consultation, supervision and staff support/training.

At the time of writing, the NHS faces unprecedented demand. The COVID-19 pandemic has created a surge in demand for psychology services within hospitals to facilitate staff well-being, support acute services such as critical care and manage the impact of long Covid. Another recent development is the expansion of IAPT (Improving Access to Psychological Therapies) to include a long-term conditions pathway, providing psychological treatment for depression and anxiety comorbid with LTCs (NICE, 2018). In the future there is potential for psychological professions to become more involved in public health and prevention of illness (Psychological Professions Network, 2020).

Having spent most of my career working with long-term conditions, I have recently been working on inpatient settings as a psychologist on acute hospital wards. In counselling psychology training, we learn the importance of the therapeutic setting and boundaries. Prior to starting my current role, like most psychologists I had only conducted psychology assessments in a private room, with patients fully dressed and awake. However, an acute medical ward is vastly different to our comfortable therapy rooms. My assessments are often conducted standing next to the bedside, with only a curtain providing a degree of privacy from the busy, noisy ward. When I arrive, the patient may be asleep or busy with another healthcare professional. They may be half-dressed, with visible wounds, tubes and medical machines. It can be quite an assault on the senses and is certainly not for those of a squeamish disposition. Informed consent to assessment and treatment must be carefully considered when patients are bed-bound and cannot choose to miss their appointment. Inpatient work requires high levels of flexibility and resilience as the work is unpredictable and fast-paced. It is also exciting, challenging and rewarding. To bear witness, providing psychological first aid, when someone is physically at their most vulnerable is a privilege and a humbling experience. I have been struck by the capacity for post-traumatic growth following life-threatening injuries. For some who have come close to death and survived, a natural re-evaluation of life and re-alignment with their values can provide clarity and purpose, with renewed energy for living life to the full.

Another aspect of my role that I find particularly rewarding is developing and delivering psychological skills training for healthcare staff across the hospital trust. I am part of a dedicated psychology teaching and training team. Examples of our training include: motivational interviewing and health behaviour change; communication skills; self-care, psychological first aid; and mindfulness. This training role allows psychologists to enhance the psychological skills of the staff who provide patient care and influence the culture across the hospital to become more psychologically minded. The value of this has been articulated by the Psychological Professions Network (2020), highlighting the scarcity of psychological training in physical healthcare organisations.

Specialist competencies

Challenging the current training model for applied health psychologists, Larkin and Klonoff (2014) propose that psychologists in the USA in the future may first train to work in general health settings, and then specialise in clinical or counselling psychology. I see advantages and disadvantages to this proposed model. When I started working in physical health, I felt ill-prepared for a medically dominated world. While I would have benefited from more training in applied health psychology pre-qualification, I feel that my counselling psychology training created the person and psychologist I am today and is the foundation of my professional identity. In my opinion, a better model would be that proposed by the Psychological Professions Network (2020): that all pre-qualification psychological training should include some training in physical health and post-qualification training could be offered in specific health conditions. This would provide a robust grounding in physical health for all psychological professions, with the opportunity to specialise further.

Onyett (2007) suggests that applied health psychologists should be competent in facilitating self-management and lifestyle change, improving treatment adherence and coping skills. The Psychological Professions Network (2020) lists the competencies of psychological professionals working with physical health problems and give specific examples of these in practice. They include clinical skills, consultation, staff support, education and training, research and audit, leadership and management. Larkin and Klonoff (2014) highlight additional specific competencies such as biopsychosocial knowledge of health and disease; promotion of self-care in health care providers; understanding social and cultural factors, ethical and legal issues within health care settings. They emphasise the importance of developing a professional identity as a clinical health psychologist. This is something I have struggled with at times. When first qualified, I was still developing my identity as a counselling psychologist and could not manage another new identity. In my experience, some clinical health psychology departments are reluctant to employ counselling psychologists. However, I have worked alongside many clinical psychologists who have accepted me as equal. I have found it helpful to use the term 'applied health psychologist', which I feel accurately represents my professional role, alongside my identity as a counselling psychologist.

In applied health psychology, a 'client' may be the patient, their family, their healthcare workers and/or the wider healthcare system. A large part of our role is to facilitate the progression of patients through the healthcare system. Often, this requires systemic work, transcending the individual and interpersonal focus of many psychological models. There are two main aspects to this: the biopsychosocial approach (the patient's system) and inter-disciplinary working (the healthcare system).

The biopsychosocial approach

Engel (1977) developed the biopsychosocial model to expand the medical model, incorporating biological, psychological and social factors contributing to illness. Research supports a biopsychosocial understanding of illness (e.g., Bolton & Gillett, 2019; Prince et al., 2007), which is complex and multi-directional (Naylor et al., 2012; Psychological Professions Network, 2020). This complexity can create a sense of discomfort when contrasted with the certainty of the medical approach (Bolton & Gillett, 2019) and as a result, many healthcare practitioners struggle to hold a biopsychosocial perspective in practice (Psychological Professions Network, 2020). Counselling psychologists are trained to tolerate uncertainty, value curiosity, enquiry and experiential learning, rather than taking an expert role. In short, 'we attend to the person, not the body part' (Bolton & Gillett, 2019, p. 116). Counselling psychologists are therefore well placed to be able to develop modern medical healthcare services, leading and supporting teams to put the patient at the heart of the process.

Interdisciplinary working

Alongside colleagues from other disciplines, applied health psychologists design and deliver groups (e.g., pain management programmes). When embedded within multi-disciplinary teams (MDTs), we share psychological skills by modelling, managing group dynamics and providing supervision and consultation using the patient's formulation. This can help staff and patients to better understand and manage relationship dynamics with helping professionals. Psychologists may also assist with care coordination, goal setting, treatment planning and discharge planning.

Psychologists can influence team leadership, values and philosophy by facilitating compassionate reflection, promoting staff well-being and patient-centred care. For example, it can sometimes feel like a failure of the patient and/or healthcare professional when the patient has not been 'fixed'. We can help to reframe and manage setbacks by modelling acceptance and adjustment, encouraging colleagues to pause, reflect and support one another. Our 'therapeutic failures' then become opportunities for teams and individuals to develop professionally and personally.

Case example

Wendy (53) was admitted to hospital following a fall. Ward staff requested a psychology assessment because Wendy appeared withdrawn and resistant to treatment. During her psychology assessment, Wendy disclosed a previous trauma that had happened in hospital, leading her to mistrust hospital staff. When this understanding was shared with staff, it increased their compassion towards Wendy, and they were able to re-frame her 'challenging behaviour' as 'fear'. We developed a plan to help Wendy to feel safer on the ward. As a result, she began to allow staff to help her.

Working in physical healthcare provides opportunities for interdisciplinary research and service development. This may be small scale (e.g., designing and evaluating a new group programme) or larger scale (e.g., contributing to a hospital trust's strategic aims). Psychologists have the potential to influence organisational culture in acute hospital trusts, embedding psychological principles from the top down as well as from the bottom up.

Clinical example

The Medical Psychology team developed 'Wellbeing Coordinators': staff members from a range of roles and departments who provide peer support across the trust. Applied health psychologists provide training, supervision and resources to support the Wellbeing Coordinators in their roles. This work has a wide-ranging impact, providing staff support and training in core psychological skills, which in turn impacts on the quality of patient care and influences organisational culture.

Psychological assessment

Different roles within applied health psychology require different approaches to assessment. Some multi-disciplinary services conduct the initial biopsychosocial assessment as a team. Each practitioner has allocated time to ask questions and form an opinion; the team then develops a joint care plan. Advantages of this include avoiding repetition; reducing inappropriate referrals; learning from other disciplines; and more integrated working. Disadvantages include missing subtle psychological difficulties; patients may feel intimidated being faced with an interview panel; it can be challenging for staff as well! I initially felt nervous about colleagues watching me conduct assessments, until I realised how much they valued my input. We all learn from watching and listening to each other. This experience helped me to develop a stronger sense of the unique role of psychology and its value in physical health care.

Risk assessment is a priority for patients with severe pain and/or life changing physical symptoms, who may feel that life is not worth living and often have access to lethal drugs for pain relief. In acute hospital settings, we link with the Liaison Psychiatry team from our neighbouring mental health trust, who provide risk assessment and management for inpatients. Another purpose of assessment is to determine whether the person needs psychological intervention and who is best placed to provide that. Often, the role of the psychologist is to educate the referrer that distress is a normal reaction to ill-health and can be validated rather than pathologised. Undiagnosed mental health conditions or previous traumatic experiences may be preventing the person from successfully achieving adjustment or self-management, in which case referral may be required. A skilful assessment and formulation can help the patient see that there is more to their difficulties than just the physical aspect. Although painful, this understanding can facilitate acceptance, reduce self-blame, normalise grief, and create hope.

Case example

Lily was referred to weight management psychology to address overeating, which was affecting her health. We completed a formulation using the compassion-focused model (Goss, 2011), to understand how her life experiences impacted on her relationship with herself and food. We identified unresolved grief. As a child, she had been given food to comfort her when her mother died, instead of affection and compassion. She summed her formulation up: "I eat chocolate because I need a hug; I've never had one for 20 years and don't have anyone in my life to give me one." She was then able to begin grieving for her mother and learning to take care of herself, her emotional needs and her body. Gradually, she stopped comfort eating and reduced her weight.

On the major trauma wards, I assess patients soon after they are brought into hospital, to determine risk factors for post-traumatic stress and other mental health conditions. We offer information about common psychological responses to trauma and referral/signposting to other services. In bariatric services, psychologists assess for eating disorders, psychological barriers to coping, and need for psychological support (NICE, 2014). Ratcliffe et al. (2014) recommend that psychologists working in bariatric services should provide intervention rather than just assessment. They found that 68% of psychologists in bariatric services believed they were perceived as gatekeeper to surgery. A perceived 'gatekeeper' role may clash with the philosophy and values of counselling psychology because it positions the psychologist as 'expert' and may compromise person-centred values, creating a power imbalance.

Often in physical health, the hoped-for outcome is not an improvement in symptoms, but in coping or living well with symptoms. Psychometric measures are used to assess psychological adjustment, well-being, quality of life, self-efficacy and coping skills. It is particularly important in physical health that outcome measures reflect biopsychosocial treatment aims. Many symptoms of physical health problems (e.g., low energy and restlessness) overlap with symptoms of depression or anxiety. Specific tools have been developed for use in physical health settings, to take this into account. Some common outcome measures are:

- HADS – Hospital Anxiety and Depression Scale (Snaith, 2003)
- EQ-5D – Quality of life measure (Herdman et al., 2011)
- SF-36 – Quality of life measure (Ware & Sherbourne, 1992)

Therapy for physical health conditions

Therapeutically, applied health psychologists help the patient to identify and overcome psychological and social barriers to health. Referrers may ask for help with compliance, motivation or health behaviour change. As counselling psychologists, we recognise that the client must first feel safe, connected and valued. The therapeutic process begins with the core conditions (Rogers, 1961): presence, empathy and valuing the client's individual experience. Contrast this with the medical world, where a ten-minute consultation is the norm; consultants provide an expert opinion; psychological distress is often seen as inhibiting medical intervention. The psychologist has a responsibility to educate the patient and healthcare staff that acknowledging and expressing psychological distress is an important part of the work. Often, it *is* the work. As we saw with 'Lily' above, formulation can transform the way that patients see their condition and themselves; it can also transform the way that they are treated by the team and the wider healthcare system. It is arguably the most effective intervention that we have in our toolkit, and it differentiates our work as applied health psychologists from that of other disciplines (such as occupational therapy) that may utilise psychological skills.

Some patients may be suitable for psychological therapy within the physical health setting. Therapeutic goals typically include facilitating adjustment, self-efficacy and self-management. Cognitive-behavioural therapy (CBT) for physical health conditions addresses unhelpful thoughts (e.g., catastrophising) and promotes healthy behaviours, such as sleep hygiene and pacing (Edeleanu et al., 2013). Other relevant therapeutic models include motivational interviewing (Miller, Rollnick & Butler, 2008), mindfulness-based therapies (Burch & Penman, 2013; Kabat-Zinn, 2009), acceptance and commitment therapy (ACT, e.g., Dahl & Lundgren, 2006; Owen, 2014) and compassion-focused therapy (CFT, e.g., Armitage & Malpus, 2019; Goss, 2011). The integrative model of adjustment to chronic conditions (IMACC) (Hammond & Hirst-Winthrop, 2018; Hammond, Farrington & Kılınç, 2019) outlines a process model of psychological adjustment to physical ill-health, explaining factors influencing the adjustment process and how these can be blocked or facilitated. The IMACC is trans-theoretical and provides a useful framework to guide psychological assessment and intervention.

Grief is a common and understandable reaction to major ill-health (Eccleston, Morley & Williams, 2013; National Voices, 2019). A mental health diagnosis can be unhelpful and overwhelming when someone is struggling to come to terms with a life-changing physical condition. It is important to remember that most patients in physical health settings have not referred themselves to see a psychologist. They often feel that they have been 'sent to the shrink' because the doctor thinks it is 'all in their head'. The most important message we can give is that distress is normal and understandable when faced with serious ill-health. 'Being with' the patient in their suffering and not expecting anything in return can be very therapeutic. Reframing distress as grief and acknowledging losses (such as work, mobility, sexual intimacy, financial independence) gives the patient permission to mourn for the person they were, and to acknowledge the changes in their identity post-illness. It is imperative that we do not rush people through this process, as this may unintentionally reinforce unhelpful belief systems and behaviours.

Case example

Philip (aged 29) was referred to the pain management team after an accident at work, which left him disabled and unable to continue his career. Angry with himself and his employer, he withdrew from his wife and friends, becoming depressed. He felt his life was over and no longer felt like a man. When we normalised his emotions and behaviours as part of the grieving process, he was able to see the futility of his efforts to 'fight' pain and return to his previous life. For Philip, the most devastating part of his disability was the impact on his sexual identity and ability to be intimate with his wife, which he felt ashamed about. After acknowledging and grieving for his losses, he was able to begin to find acceptance. He chose to tell his story of adjustment through a series of tattoos on his body. It felt important for him to take control over his body, when so many of his bodily 'rights' had been taken away from him.

Conclusion and personal reflections

Central to my identity as a counselling psychologist is my grounding in humanistic philosophy (e.g., Rogers, 1961). When training as a counselling psychologist, I believed I would not work in the NHS because I did not want to be part of the medicalisation of psychological distress. Nonetheless, I applied for a role in primary care and was offered a post in pain management instead. Thanks to this happy accident, I have spent nearly 13 years in physical health settings.

During this time, I have noticed a gradual change in how I talk about my work. Somewhere along the line, clients became 'patients'; therapy became an 'intervention'; a therapeutic ending became a 'discharge'. The newly qualified version of me would have been shocked to hear me speaking about my work using medical terminology and would probably have thought I was compromising my core values. On reflection, I realise that I have not eroded my person-centred principles. In fact, paradoxically quite the opposite. My clients see themselves as 'patients': they have come expecting 'treatment' for physical health problems. To patients and colleagues, I am a medical professional – part of a wider team and hospital system. The biggest challenge for me has been learning to accept and adapt to the culture in which I have found myself. In this adaptation, there are parallel processes with the work that I engage in with clients/patients.

I have gradually moved from an either/or perspective, to both/and. I have learned that there is value in the 'medical model'. One perspective on health is not enough. We need complementary skills and knowledge. Over the years, my multidisciplinary colleagues have learned from me and have become more 'psychologically minded'. It is right that I, in turn, should become more 'medically minded'. Like any good relationship, over time each takes on characteristics of the other, without losing what makes them individual and special. Soth (2007) advocates a 'paradoxical integration' between the medical model and the humanistic philosophy of counselling [psychology]. Working with patients who are seriously unwell and may not recover is a demanding and stressful job. When we are stressed, it is natural to move into a competitive mindset (Gilbert, 2010) and position ourselves in opposition to those who are different (i.e., MDT colleagues). We can lose our psychological flexibility, and with it we lose opportunities to learn and develop. As with patients, my aim is to cultivate for myself and colleagues an attitude of openness and psychological flexibility, valuing different perspectives on health and illness and how these come together to provide a holistic approach for the patient. I find the best way to do this is from the inside out: I use mindfulness, compassion and acceptance to ground me and give me space. I aim to be reflective rather than reactive (most of the time!). I try to model this for colleagues and encourage them to do the same, reminding them that we are all just people, doing the best we can with what we have. So, perhaps we are not opposites at all: our common humanity and desire to help the patient, along with our specialist skills and knowledge, suggest we have more similarities than differences. We are like two eyes that each see things slightly differently. Working together, we have greater perspective, allowing us to successfully steer ourselves, each other and our patients to achieve our potential.

References

Armitage, L. and Malpus, Z. (2019). Compassion-focused therapy for strivers in pain. *Clinical Journal of Pain* 47, 6–11.

Bolton, D. & Gillett, G. (2019). *The Biopsychosocial Model of Health and Disease: New Philosophical and Scientific Developments.* Springer Nature. https://library.oap en.org/handle/20.500.12657/22889.

Burch, V. & Penman, D. (2013). *Mindfulness for Health (Enhanced Edition): A Practical Guide to Relieving Pain, Reducing Stress and Restoring Wellbeing.* Little, Brown Book Group.

Chiles, J. A., Lambert, M. J. & Hatch, A. L. (1999). The impact of psychological interventions on medical cost offset: A meta-analytic review. *Clinical Psychology: Science and Practice* 6(2), 204–220.

Dahl, J., Lundgren, T. (2006). *Living Beyond Your Pain: Using Acceptance and Commitment Therapy to Ease Chronic Pain.* New Harbinger Publications.

Department of Health (2011). Ten things you need to know about long-term conditions. www.dh.gov.uk/en/Healthcare/ Longtermconditions/tenthingsyouneedtoknow/index.htm.

Eccleston, C., Morley, S. J. & Williams, A. C. de C. (2013). Psychological approaches to chronic pain management: Evidence and challenges. *British Journal of Anaesthesia* 111(1), 59–63.

Edeleanu, A., Sowden, M., Chorlton, E. & Sage, N. (2013). *CBT for Chronic Illness and Palliative Care: A Workbook and Toolkit.* Wiley.

Engel, G. L. (1977). The need for a new medical model: A challenge for biomedicine. *Science* 196(4286), 129–136.

Gilbert, P. (2010). *Compassion Focused Therapy: Distinctive Features.* Taylor & Francis.

Goss, K. (2011). *The Compassionate Mind Approach to Beating Overeating.* Series editor, Paul Gilbert. Little, Brown Book Group.

Hammond, L. D. and Hirst-Winthrop, S. (2018). Proposal of an integrative model of adjustment to chronic conditions: An understanding of the process of psychosocial adjustment to living with type 2 diabetes. *Journal of Health Psychology* 23(8), 1063–1074. doi:10.1177/1359105316664131.

Hammond, L., Farrington, A., & Kılınç, S. (2019). Validation of the integrative model of adjustment to chronic conditions: Applicability to adult-onset epilepsy. *Health Psychology Open.* https://doi.org/10.1177/2055102919884293.

Herdman, M., Gudex, C., Lloyd, A., Janssen, M., Kind, P., Parkin, D., Bonsel, G. & Badia, X. (2011). Development and preliminary testing of the new five-level version of EQ-5D (EQ-5D-5L). *Quality of Life Research* 20(*10*), 1727–1736. doi:10.1007/s11136-011-9903-x.

Kabat-Zinn, J. (2009). *Full Catastrophe Living: How to Cope with Stress, Pain and Illness Using Mindfulness Meditation.* Piatkus.

Larkin, K. & Klonoff, E. (2014). *Speciality Competencies in Clinical Health Psychology.* Oxford University Press.

Miller, W. R., Rollnick, S. & Butler, C. C. (2008). *Motivational Interviewing in Health Care: Helping Patients Change Behavior.* Guilford Publications.

National Health Service (NHS) (2019). The NHS Long Term Plan. www.longtermpla n.nhs.uk.

National Voices (2019). Multiple long-term conditions: Exploring the priorities of people of working age workshop report. National Institute for Health Research. www.evidence.nhs.uk/document?id=2250615&returnUrl=search%3fpa%3d2%26q% 3dlong%2bterm%2bcondition%2bguidelines.

Naylor, C., Parsonage, M., McDaid, D., Knapp, M., Fossey, M. & Galea, A. (2012). Long-term conditions and mental health: The cost of co-morbidities. The King's Fund, London. www.nationalelfservice.net/cms/wp-content/uploads/2012/02/long-term-conditions-mental-health-chris-naylor-feb12.pdf.

NICE (National Institute for Health and Care Excellence) (2014). Obesity: Identification, assessment and management. NICE Clinical Guideline CG189. www.nice.org. uk/guidance/cg189/chapter/1-Recommendations#surgical-interventions.

NICE (National Institute for Health and Care Excellence) (2016). Multimorbidity: Clinical Assessment and Management. NICE Guideline [NG 56] www.nice.org.uk/ guidance/ng56.

NICE (National Institute for Health and Care Excellence) (2018). The Improving Access to Psychological Therapies (IAPT) pathway for people with long-term physical health conditions and medically unexplained symptoms. www.england.nhs.uk/ wp-content/uploads/2018/03/improving-access-to-psychological-therapies-long-term -conditions-pathway.pdf.

Onyett. S. (2007). New ways of working for applied psychologists in health and social care: Working psychologically in teams. British Psychological Society, Leicester.

Owen, R. (2014). *Living with the Enemy: Coping with the Stress of Chronic Illness Using CBT, Mindfulness and Acceptance.* Routledge.

Prince, M., Patel, V., Saxena, S., Maj, M., Maselko, J., Phillips, M. R. & Rahman, A. (2007). No health without mental health. *The Lancet* 370(9590), 859–877.

Psychological Professions Network (2020). Maximising the impact of psychological practice in physical healthcare. Discussion Paper. www.ppn.nhs.uk/resources/ppn-p ublications/34-maximising-the-impact-of-psychological-practice-in-physical-healthca re-discussion-paper/file.

Ratcliffe, D., Ali, R., Ellison, N. et al. (2014). Bariatric psychology in the UK National Health Service: Input across the patient pathway. *BMC Obesity* 1(20). https://doi.org/ 10.1186/s40608-014-0020-6.

Rogers, C. (1961). *On Becoming a Person: A Therapist's View of Psychotherapy.* Constable.

Snaith, R. P. (2003). The Hospital Anxiety and Depression Scale. *Health Quality Life Outcomes* 1(29). https://doi.org/10.1186/1477-7525-1-29.

Soth, M. (2007). Embracing the paradigm clash between the 'medical model' and counselling. *Therapy Today* 18(10), 4–6.

Steel, N., Ford, J., Newton, J., Davis, A., Vos, T., Naghavi, M. et al. (2018). Changes in health in the countries of the UK and 150 English local authority areas 1990–2016: A systematic analysis for the Global Burden of Disease Study 2016. *The Lancet* 392(10158), 1647–1661. https://doi.org/10.1016/S0140-6736(18)32207-4.

Ware, J. E., Jr., & Sherbourne, C. D. (1992). The MOS 36-item short-form health survey (SF-36). I. Conceptual framework and item selection. *Medical Care* 30(6), 473–483.

Chapter 8

Working with clients with neurological conditions

Tony Ward

Summary

This chapter presents an overview of working as a psychologist with neurological populations. It begins with a brief background to the area, and then goes on to outline the kinds of services that exist. The chapter then considers the impact on clients of neurological conditions. Given that the organ affected is the brain the impacts are often profound. The ways in which cognitive functions are affected is described and there is an outline of each of the major areas such as memory and attention. Examples of relevant assessments are given in each case. The chapter then identifies the psychological and emotional impact. It is suggested that counselling psychologists may be ideally placed to deal with the profound adjustment that confronts clients in these circumstances. Finally, the current developments are outlined which are allowing counselling psychologists to enter specialist training in this field.

Background

According to an online report, neurological conditions accounted for 3.5% of the NHS spend in 2012/13 (£3.5 billion) and 14% of the social care budget (NHS England, 2020). There are over 600 different types of recognised neurological condition, which can be summarised under four main headings:

- Stable long-term conditions such as cerebral palsy.
- Sudden onset conditions such as head injury or stroke.
- Intermittent and unpredictable conditions such as multiple sclerosis, ME, and epilepsy.
- Progressive conditions such as Huntington's disease, Parkinson's disease and various types of dementia such as Alzheimer's disease (note that in this chapter we will not discuss conditions which primarily affect older adults, as this is dealt with in another chapter).

Conditions which affect the brain are likely to have profound consequences for people and their families. All aspects of wellbeing are likely to be affected,

DOI: 10.4324/9781003159339-9

in terms of personal identity, emotional adjustment and cognitive function (Heilman & Valenstein, 2010). Depending on the nature and severity of the condition, a wide variety of different services may be involved. Such services may provide care as well as helping people to adapt and adjust. Counselling psychologists often have a key role to play in many of these services.

Services

The types of services available to people with neurological conditions vary enormously across the United Kingdom and will depend on the specific nature of the condition.

Where people have suspected progressive conditions which typically have a slow onset, they will initially be referred by their medical practitioner to neurological services. The initial screening might include short cognitive status assessments such as the Mini Mental Status Examination (MMSE – for recent stratified norms, see, for e.g., Crum et al., 1993). If screening scores indicate there may be an issue, they will undergo a variety of investigations, likely to include detailed brain scans using magnetic resonance imaging (MRI) as well as neuropsychological assessment to determine current cognitive status (Nestor, Scheltens & Hodges, 2004; Salmon & Bondi, 2009; Sepulcre et al., 2006). A neurologist will weigh up all the evidence and come to an initial view. In many cases, there may be follow-up over a period of months. Once a firm diagnosis is established, this may lead to referral to specialist services for ongoing treatment, assessment and support. Support may be available through third sector organisations, e.g. the MS Society or the Alzheimer's Society.

Conditions with a sudden onset such as head injury or stroke will usually result in people being admitted to hospital. In very mild cases this might be for a period of observation. In more serious cases, people may be treated and stabilised for some time on an acute medical ward, before eventually being moved to an acute rehabilitation unit. Such rehabilitation units will attempt to enable people to recover as much of their previous functioning as possible (Formisano et al., 2017). This is usually through a multi-disciplinary approach which may include psychology, physiotherapy, occupational therapy, speech and language therapy, music therapy as well as nursing and medical input as necessary. Once people have stabilised, they may be discharged home, with provision of community support services. In other cases, people may be referred on for ongoing intensive rehabilitation, where this is thought to be beneficial. In some cases – for example, where there are complex behavioural challenges – people may be referred to specialist units (Worthington et al., 2006). As in the case of progressive conditions, there are also third-sector organisations which offer support in these areas. The Headway organisation offers long-term support for adults with head injuries. In some areas it offers well-resourced day centres, which can include provision of health and rehabilitation activities. Similarly, the Stroke Association offers advice and support to people following stroke and their relatives.

All of these different services can include input from psychologists. The precise nature of their work will depend on the type of service and the neurological population being served. Increasingly, many counselling psychologists are working in these types of services. We will discuss at the end of this chapter the current state of play and how counselling psychologists can aspire to work in these services.

The impact of neurological conditions

Neurological conditions primarily impact on the brain. This is the organ of the body responsible for the essential aspects of the human condition, including personality, behaviour and thought processes. It is not surprising therefore that these conditions severely disrupt people's lives. We will look at the cognitive dimension, considering how the different mental processes can be disrupted. We will then go on to look at the psychological and emotional effects. In most conditions both of these aspects will be affected, and the relative impact of each can vary across conditions and between individuals.

Cognitive

The cognitive domain is concerned with the thought processes which underlie our day-to-day functioning. The processes involved can be evident from the problems which can be observed. For example, in Alzheimer's disease people might from an early stage begin to forget people's names and not recognise the faces of their loved ones (Nestor, Scheltens & Hodges, 2004). This is obviously an example of memory difficulty. In other cases, the person affected might change their behaviour – for example, becoming quite short-tempered and using profane language. It could appear that the persons personality has changed quite markedly. This kind of change is often observed after damage to the frontal parts of the brain (Strub, 1989). It is often thought to be underpinned by problems inhibiting behaviour, though this might not be obvious from the way the person's difficulties manifest in their day to day lives. Relatives are more likely to perceive this as the person becoming difficult or argumentative.

We will now go on to look briefly at the different aspects of cognitive function. Anyone aspiring to work with neurologic clients would do well to brush up on their knowledge of cognitive psychology. There are excellent textbooks which cover the area. For example, Eysenck and Keane (2020) is a comprehensive textbook of cognitive psychology. A classic text (Ellis & Young, 2013) is still to this day one of the best overviews of how the different aspects of cognitive function relate to each other in a modular fashion. A more recent account is given by Morgan and Ricker (2016). It is very useful to have such cognitive models in mind when thinking about and assessing the difficulties of patients with neurological conditions. To illustrate this a summary diagram of the overall human cognitive architecture is presented here. (For an account of how an overarching view of human cognitive function can be also be useful in psychotherapy, see Ward & Plagnol, 2019).

Figure 8.1 shows a summary of the human cognitive architecture as it relates to language processing. This is typical of the diagrams found in current texts on cognitive neuropsychology such as that by Ellis and Young (2013). In diagrams such as this, the boxes show processes which are thought to be discreet, while the arrows indicate the flow of information through the system. This diagram is illustrating how stimuli in the outside world such as spoken or written words are perceived and understood. These types of processes are involved in many cognitive assessments. For example, the vocabulary test in the Wechsler Adult Intelligence Scale (WAIS – Wechsler, 2008; see also Drozdick et al., 2012) requires clients to define given words. The words are presented in spoken form. So, for example, the client might be asked, 'What does the word "cat" mean?' To answer the question, the client needs first of all to be able to hear and process the sound stimulus. If the person is hard of hearing or their sound perception has been disrupted as a result of their brain damage, then they may not be able to proceed past this early stage. If they can perceive the sound, the next step is to compare it against all the word sounds that they know in their auditory lexicon. Mild problems at this early stage could lead to misidentification. For example, they might mishear the word 'cat' as 'car', and therefore give the wrong definition

Seeing cognitive processes in this way can be very helpful in helping us to understand the problems that are being experienced by people with neurological conditions. For example, if someone has experienced a stroke which has affected their left hemisphere then they may well experience several, significant language difficulties.

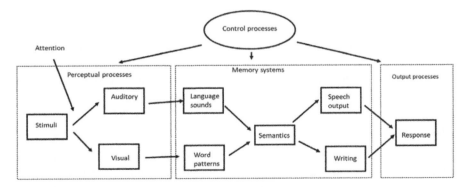

Figure 8.1 The human cognitive architecture

It is clear then that a thorough understanding of cognitive psychology is essential to working psychologically with neurological client groups. It will enable the effective counselling psychologist to understand the problems they observe in their clients, to formulate the cognitive difficulties and to come up with sufficiently justified intervention strategies.

We will now consider the different cognitive processes in a little more detail.

Perception

Perception involves the early processes in detecting stimuli in the outside world and forming an adequate internal representation. This is the first fundamental stage of processing which will be important in all cognitive tasks. Thus, any client who is struggling to perform a range of tasks could have difficulties at the perceptual level. It could be that they cannot see visual stimuli being presented adequately, or that the internal representation they are able to create is significantly distorted. This may often be the case where the occipital lobes of the brain have been damaged as this is the part of the brain that deals with early visual processing. Similarly, clients may have problems with sound perception. If this is significant it may present a challenge to performing any cognitive task, since most tasks will require some kind of verbal explanation. This could preclude the administration of many standardised cognitive tasks.

Attention

Even if a client appears to have intact perception, they still need to be able to direct their attention appropriately towards relevant stimuli. Attention processes are usually broken down into several components. For example, people need to be able to direct their attention, to shift their attention when necessary and to sustain their concentration overtime. The Test of Everyday Attention (Robertson et al., 1994[1]) is a battery of tests which assesses each of these different skills, using a variety of different formats which resemble real world tasks. There are a number of test batteries which use realistic tasks and thus claim to have 'ecological validity'. It has been suggested that this can enhance their generalisability (i.e. to predict the extent to which the person will experience difficulties in their everyday lives).

Memory

The examples referred to in relation to Figure 8.1 illustrate how knowledge in semantic memory can be very important in the performance of many cognitive tasks. Vocabulary tasks are one common example. These types of tasks are interesting for another reason. Vocabulary is generally thought to be quite resistant to different types of brain damage. Therefore, such tests are often used to estimate the persons premorbid ability. Obviously if the person has significant language difficulties then some other way of doing this would be needed, such as looking at their occupation or educational level.

Besides semantic memory there are many other important types of information held in our representational system. We have an ongoing sense of what has happened to us and what experiences we have had. This is often referred to as episodic memory. If we add to this our complex sense of time and detailed knowledge about ourselves and our interests, then this makes up auto-biographical memory. These are the aspects of memory which are often most affected in degenerative conditions such as Alzheimer's disease. This loss of past memories is referred to as retrograde amnesia. Clients with traumatic head injury will typically have a period of retrograde amnesia extending backwards from their injury. The extent of this amnesia is often used as a marker of severity.

Another way in which memory is often disrupted is where the person is unable to access their recent episodic memories. The technical term for this is anterograde amnesia. It can be a profound and extremely debilitating condition, in which the person becomes increasingly locked in their past and unable to update their sense of self with recent experiences and events.

There are many test batteries which have been developed to assess memory functions. From the ecological perspective there is the Rivermead Behavioural Memory Test (RBMT– Wall, Wilson & Baddeley, 1994). A more traditional battery which has now been revised a number of times is the Wechsler Memory Scales (Wechsler 2008).

Language

Language is a complex set of skills which includes being able to listen to and understand other people and reply verbally to them. Linked to this is the skill acquired at school in terms of being able to read the patterns of letters on paper to decipher particular words and, if necessary, to read these out.

Where counselling psychologists work in a multidisciplinary team, they will often have the advantage of being able to work with colleagues from speech and language therapy. Such colleagues can be invaluable in helping us to think about how best to communicate with our clients. They also tend to be specialised and experienced in the art of helping our clients to relearn the skills of speech and writing. As with other areas of functioning, there are specialist tests for the assessment of language – for example, the Boston Aphasia Tests (Goodglass, Kaplan & Weintraub, 2001).

Planning and problem solving

Novel problem solving is a higher-order skill underpinned by processes located in the frontal part of the brain (Stuss & Knight, 2013). This is a vital skill for clients to be able to navigate their everyday lives. Without being able to do this, clients will struggle to organise themselves and deal with new issues and problems as they arise. A widely used battery within the ecological tradition is the Behavioural Assessment of the Dysexecutive Syndrome (Wilson et al,. 1998).

Assessment of cognitive functions

In the above outline of the various areas of cognitive function, several examples of test batteries were cited. Besides these specialist tests, there are also comprehensive batteries which are designed to assess the full range of cognitive functions. One of the most widely used is that originally devised by David Wechsler in the 1930s, the Wechsler Adult Intelligence Scale (WAIS – Wechsler, Coalson & Raiford, 2008). This includes a range of different tests which tap into the full set of cognitive abilities. The WAIS does not measure long-term memory in any depth, and it is therefore often used alongside the Wechsler Memory Scales. These tests are seen as comprehensive and definitive, and therefore likely to form the backbone of assessment for practitioners working within a medico legal context. In addition, counselling psychologists looking to make a move into working with neurological clients would do well to become familiar with these tests, as they are widely known and used (and experience of using them is likely to be queried at interviews!).

Given the length of time taken to administer the full suite of Wechsler tests, assessment in rehabilitation settings will typically use shorter batteries. The Repeatable Battery for the Assessment of Neuropsychological Status (RBANS – Randolph et al., 1998) is widely used. It takes about forty minutes to complete.

Working with cognitive difficulties

Carrying out a full assessment of a client's cognitive function will take a considerable amount of time and effort. The activity therefore needs to be well justified. There are a number of sound arguments as to why this is a worthwhile use of valuable professional resources.

First of all, it allows us as psychologists to understand the underlying cognitive issues being presented by the client. This then enables us to formulate the client's difficulties (Caramazza & Coltheart, 2006). If we can identify the strengths and weaknesses that the client now possesses, this can be quite useful in formulating future strategies. For example, if the client now has quite impaired verbal memory but their visual memory is largely intact, then they may be encouraged to try to process the things they need to remember prospectively using a visual strategy.

A second reason is that clients often find it very difficult to comprehend and understand the difficulties they now face. Having someone explain their difficulties to them in easy-to-understand terms can be enormously helpful.

Finally, an understanding of the client's difficulties will enable us to devise remediation strategies (Sohlberg & Mateer, 2001). This could involve the client practising the cognitive skills to see if these can be reacquired. Traditionally there has been some debate about the extent to which practising abstract tasks can lead to generalisation and improvement in day-to-day activities (Wilson & Evans, 2003). Unfortunately, many of our clients will struggle to regain their previous cognitive skills. In this case we may need to look to alternative coping strategies. For example, in the past diaries were commonly used as a way of helping clients with memory difficulties.

Psychological and emotional

Clients living with neurological conditions will typically have to contend with a wide range of psychological reactions and issues. Depending upon the severity of their condition, the person may have to deal with a degree of loss in terms of the person they were before. This could be profound, in that the person may now not be able to perform a range of cognitive or physical tasks which they were previously capable of (Miller, 1993). This may cause loss in other aspects of their lives. They may now be unable to return to their previous occupation and family relationships and dynamics maybe completely altered. All of this will require a considerable degree of adjustment.

In some cases, the process of adjustment may be complicated by the fact that the client has an impaired degree of insight. They may have quite unrealistic expectations about how their future will unfold. This can have a serious impact on personal relationships (Burridge et al., 2007).

Where clients do have good insight and are undergoing a challenging period of adjustment, then this will possibly produce a variety of emotional reactions. The person may become very depressed about their situation, and they might be very anxious about the future and what it holds. There may often be a degree of trauma, particularly where the brain damage was caused through some dramatic means such as a severe accident or an assault (Bennet & Raymond, 1997).

Neurological conditions do not just affect the person with the brain damage. There is also an impact on the rest of their family (Florian, Katz & Lahav, 1989). The nature of this will vary depending on their age and family situation. If the client is eventually going to return home after a stay in hospital or rehabilitation, then the whole family may need to go through a process of adjustment and change.

All of this means that there is considerable scope for psychological input. Counselling psychologists, with well-developed therapeutic skills, should be very well placed for working with these psychological and emotional impacts of neurological conditions. Unfortunately, this type of therapeutic working has sometimes been neglected in neurological settings. This may partly be due to the lack of psychologists working in the area. The likely future increase in the number of counselling psychologists working in the field may be a positive step forward.

In terms of specific guidance as to how to work therapeutically with neurological client groups, there are now several texts available which give some guidance (e.g., Klonoff, 2010). There are also a number of useful journal articles. For example, Judd and Wilson (2005) give a very useful account of the ways in which therapy may need to be varied when working with neurological client groups. Ward and Hogan (2015) present a case study illustrating the potential issues which can arise in this setting.

Counselling psychologists working in relevant contexts

There have been a small number of counselling psychologists working within neurological contexts for many years – for example, in services aimed at older adults. It is less common to find counselling psychologists working with brain damage in rehabilitation settings, but it is not unheard of.

Similarly, counselling psychologists have been able, for many years, to access and use cognitive tests aimed at understanding neurological conditions. The Division of Counselling Psychology has provided advanced specialist training in the use of such tests, including the Wechsler Adult Intelligence Scale.

However, it has not been possible up to now for such applied psychologists to enter specialist neuropsychological training with a view to being entered on the British Psychological Society's specialist register of clinical neuropsychologists. After years of lobbying this is now changing.

At the time of writing (January 2021), the regulations within the British Psychological Society around specialist neuropsychology training are being altered. It is now possible for applied psychologists with a background in counselling psychology to apply for specialist training in neuropsychology. This is very welcome news. Having said that, this is not a pathway to be trodden lightly. It will require several years of theoretical and practical training. At the end, successful candidates will be able to register on what will likely become the register of practitioner neuropsychologists.

It is worth noting that even if people do not choose to go down this full training route, they can, if they have worked within a relevant setting for at least two years, join the neuropsychology division as a full member. It would be useful if more counselling psychologists were to pursue this and make their voices heard within the division. Historically, many clinical psychologists worked in the neurological field without pursuing the full training. Some people have adopted titles such as 'clinical psychologist in neuropsychology'. Such a strategy would be open to counselling psychologists.

Concluding comments

This chapter has sought to give an overview of working with neurological populations. It is hoped that this will be of interest to colleagues and inspire some to seek to work in this challenging but interesting area. It would be wonderful to see counselling psychologists choosing to access the specialist training in neuropsychology and taking their place in the years ahead as consultants in this field. At the same time, others might be encouraged to work in the field even if they choose not to undertake the full training. As with any area of psychology, the key to safe and ethical practice is to ensure that you are fully trained and supervised for the role that you are undertaking.

Note

1 In the interests of transparency, note the current chapter author is a co-author of this battery.

References

Bennett, T. L., & Raymond, M. J. (1997). Emotional consequences and psychotherapy for individuals with mild brain injury. *Applied Neuropsychology*, 4(1), 55–61.

Burridge, A. C., Huw Williams, W., Yates, P. J., Harris, A., & Ward, C. (2007). Spousal relationship satisfaction following acquired brain injury: The role of insight and socio-emotional skill. *Neuropsychological rehabilitation*, 17(1), 95–105.

Caramazza, A., & Coltheart, M. (2006). Cognitive neuropsychology twenty years on. *Cognitive Neuropsychology*, 23(1), 3–12.

Coetzer, R. (2007). Psychotherapy following traumatic brain injury: Integrating theory and practice. *The Journal of head trauma rehabilitation*, 22(1), 39–47.

Crum, R. M., Anthony, J. C., Bassett, S. S., & Folstein, M. F. (1993). Population-based norms for the Mini-Mental State Examination by age and educational level. *Jama*, 269(18), 2386–2391.

Drozdick, L. W., Wahlstrom, D., Zhu, J., & Weiss, L. G. (2012). The Wechsler Adult Intelligence Scale—Fourth Edition and the Wechsler Memory Scale—Fourth Edition. In D. P. Flanagan & P. L. Harrison (eds), *Contemporary Intellectual Assessment: Theories, Tests, and Issues* (pp. 197–223). The Guilford Press.

Ellis, A. W., & Young, A. W. (2013). *Human Cognitive Neuropsychology: A Textbook with Readings*. Psychology Press.

Eysenck, M. W., & Keane, M. T. (2020). *Cognitive Psychology: A Student's Handbook* (8th edition). Taylor & Francis.

Florian, V., Katz, S., & Lahav, V. (1989). Impact of traumatic brain damage on family dynamics and functioning: a review. *Brain Injury*, 3(3), 219–233.

Formisano, R., Azicnuda, E., Sefid, M. K., Zampolini, M., Scarponi, F., & Avesani, R. (2017). Early rehabilitation: benefits in patients with severe acquired brain injury. *Neurological Sciences*, 38(1), 181–184.

Goodglass, H., Kaplan, E., & Weintraub, S. (2001). *BDAE: The Boston Diagnostic Aphasia Examination*. Lippincott Williams & Wilkins.

Heilman, M. K. M., & Valenstein, E. (2010). *Clinical Neuropsychology*. Oxford University Press.

Judd, D., & Wilson, S. L. (2005). Psychotherapy with brain injury survivors: An investigation of the challenges encountered by clinicians and their modifications to therapeutic practice. *Brain Injury*, 19(6), 437–449.

Klonoff, P. S. (2010). *Psychotherapy after Brain Injury: Principles and Techniques.* Guilford Press.

Miller, L. (1993). *Psychotherapy of the Brain-injured Patient: Reclaiming the Shattered Self.* W. W. Norton & Co.

Morgan, J. E., & Ricker, J. H. (eds). (2016). *Textbook of Clinical Neuropsychology.* Taylor & Francis.

Nestor, P. J., Scheltens, P., & Hodges, J. R. (2004). Advances in the early detection of Alzheimer's disease. *Nature Medicine*, 10(7), S34–S41.

NHS England (2020). Neurological conditions. www.england.nhs.uk/ourwork/clinical-p olicy/ltc/our-work-on-long-term conditions/neurological/ [Accessed 30 October 2020].

Randolph, C., Tierney, M. C., Mohr, E., & Chase, T. N. (1998). The Repeatable Battery for the Assessment of Neuropsychological Status (RBANS): Preliminary clinical validity. *Journal of Clinical and Experimental Neuropsychology*, 20(3), 310–319.

Robertson, I. H., Ward, T., Ridgeway, V., Nimmo-Smith, I., & Thames Valley Test Company (1994). The Test of Everyday Attention. Pearson Assessment.

Salmon, D. P., & Bondi, M. W. (2009). Neuropsychological assessment of dementia. *Annual Review of Psychology*, 60, 257.

Sepulcre, J., Vanotti, S., Hernández, R., Sandoval, G., Cáceres, F., Garcea, O., & Villoslada, P. (2006). Cognitive impairment in patients with multiple sclerosis using the Brief Repeatable Battery-Neuropsychology test. *Multiple Sclerosis Journal*, 12(2), 187–195.

Sohlberg, M. M., & Mateer, C. A. (eds). (2001). *Cognitive Rehabilitation: An Integrative Neuropsychological Approach.* Guilford Press.

Strub, R. L. (1989). Frontal lobe syndrome in a patient with bilateral globus pallidus lesions. *Archives of Neurology*, 46(9), 1024–1027.

Stuss, D. T., & Knight, R. T. (eds). (2013). *Principles of Frontal Lobe Function.* Oxford University Press.

Wall, C. D., Wilson, B. A., & Baddeley, A. D. (1994). The Extended Rivermead Behavioural Memory Test: A measure of everyday memory performance in normal adults. *Memory*, 2(2), 149–166.

Ward, T., & Hogan, K. (2015). Using client-centered psychotherapy embedded within a pluralistic integrative approach to help a client with executive dysfunction: The case of 'Judith'. *Pragmatic Case Studies in Psychotherapy*, 11(1), 1–20.

Ward, T., & Plagnol, A. (2019). *Cognitive Psychodynamics as an Integrative Framework in Counselling Psychology and Psychotherapy.* Palgrave MacMillan.

Wechsler, D. (2008). *Wechsler Adult Intelligence Scale–Fourth Edition.* NCS Pearson.

Wechsler, D., Coalson, D. L., & Raiford, S. E. (2008). *WAIS-IV: Technical and Interpretative Manual.* NCS Pearson.

Wilson, B. A., & Evans, J. (2003). Does cognitive rehabilitation work? Clinical and economic considerations and outcomes. *Clinical Neuropsychology and Cost Outcome Research: A Beginning*, 16, 329–345.

Wilson, B. A., Evans, J. J., Emslie, H., Alderman, N., & Burgess, P. (1998). The development of an ecologically valid test for assessing patients with a dysexecutive syndrome. *Neuropsychological Rehabilitation*, 8(3), 213–228.

Worthington, A. D., Matthews, S., Melia, Y., & Oddy, M. (2006). Cost-benefits associated with social outcome from neurobehavioural rehabilitation. *Brain Injury*, 20 (9), 947–957.

Chapter 9

Working with people who have unusual experiences

Pam Jameson

Introduction

This chapter will focus on understanding the concept of psychosis, explaining the roles and skills required of a psychologist working into a psychosis team and considering the challenges and rewards of the role.

For the purposes of this chapter, the term 'unusual experiences' refers to:

1   Perceiving a phenomenon that others do not experience. For example, hearing voices or feeling insects crawling on your skin. The medical term for this is hallucination.
2   Experiencing beliefs that have little evidence or likelihood in reality. For example, the belief that you are being monitored as part of a conspiracy, or that you have supernatural abilities. The medical term for this is delusion.

Understanding unusual experiences

'The term "psychosis" covers a set of related conditions, of which the commonest is schizophrenia' (National Collaborating Centre for Mental Health, 2014, p. 14). To be diagnosed with schizophrenia, an individual must have experienced one month of symptoms, to include at least one of the following: 1) thought echo, insertion/withdrawal, or broadcasting; 2) delusions of control, influence or passivity; 3) hallucinatory voices; 4) persisted delusions that are culturally inappropriate or completely impossible; or at least two of the following, i) persistent hallucinations, ii) neologisms, breaks in train of through resulting in incoherent speech, iii) catatonic behaviour, iv) negative symptoms such as marked apathy or bluntness in emotional response (World Health Organisation, 1994).

Clearly, unusual experiences have not always been defined or understood in this way; however, it is beyond the scope of this chapter to do justice to the history of psychosis. The reader is directed to Bentall (2003) and Whitaker (2002, 2010) for further reading. As one would expect, our knowledge of

DOI: 10.4324/9781003159339-10

history is limited by subjective records, and, as remains the case today, the way that people make sense of unusual experiences is heavily embedded in culture. The concept of psychosis has been debated, revised and renamed repeatedly over hundreds of years, beginning with the original classification system by Kraepelin (1883, cited in Bentall, 2003), and culminating in the now widely accepted classification systems published by the American Psychiatric Association and the International Classification of Diseases by the World Health Organisation (Bentall, 2003). Despite abundant evidence against the reliability and validity of psychiatric diagnosis (see Bentall, 2003 for a well-documented discussion), this system continues to be widely used.

As criticism of the schizophrenia diagnosis has grown (Bentall et al., 1988; Romme, 2009; Johnstone, 2011; Dillon, 2011), research has moved away from a purely biological model. In the 1970s, Zubin introduced the vulnerability-stress hypotheses, suggesting that people become unwell through an interaction of pre-existing vulnerabilities and current environmental stressors (Boyle, 2011). However, there remains an inherent implication that the experience of abuse is not in itself enough to justify distress (Johnstone, 2011). Psychosis in particular may be susceptible to being understood in biological terms as it is often difficult to see a direct link between a person's presentation, unusual experiences and the traumas experienced. As Herman (1992) explains, 'people who have survived atrocities often tell their stories in a highly emotional, contradictory, and fragmented manner which undermines their credibility and thereby serves the twin imperatives of truth-telling and secrecy' (Herman, 1992, p. 1). Additionally, persistent focus on a biological basis for psychosis can be very profitable for some – for example, drug companies (Whitaker, 2002; Whitaker, 2010).

There now exists an irrefutable amount of evidence linking adverse childhood experiences to psychosis (Gerhardt, 2014; Herman, 1992; Read & Bentall, 2012), and in addition, less direct cultural and social factors appear influential. For example, recovery appears better in developing countries (Jablensky et al., 1992), and inequality appears to be a strong predictor of poor mental health (Wilkinson & Pickett, 2010).

Although there are biochemical and structural abnormalities in the brain of those diagnosed with psychosis, the same differences are present in people who have experienced trauma (Read & Bentall, 2012). In a remarkable shift over the past fifty years, researchers are now questioning whether the aetiology of psychosis is not biological, but may in fact be traumatic experiences. We are still some way from a fully satisfactory explanation of why people develop unusual experiences; however, there is now strong evidence that psychosis and unusual experiences are heavily influenced by the distressing events that people endure (Boyle, 2011).

Instead of asking 'what is wrong with you?' we should be asking 'what has happened to you?' (Dillon, 2011). Jacqui Dillon is the chair for the Hearing Voices Network UK. The Hearing Voices Network advocates that hearing voices is a normal human experience and that voices are meaningful in the context of someone's life. 'Hearing voices' is used as an umbrella term and includes seeing visions and having other similar experiences (including touch, taste and smell). The relationship a person has with his/her voices is vital, but 'getting rid of the voices is neither necessary, nor that important' (Romme, 2009, p. 7). In fact, two thirds of those who hear voices do not access mental health services (Romme, 2009). The difference between those who seek help and those who don't appears to be related to the meaning people make of their voices and the resulting level of distress.

Commonly, mental health services focus on symptoms; however, symptoms are often a normal response to abnormal stressful experiences. In implying that voices are part of an illness, the person may be disempowered, requiring 'experts' to make them better. The suggestion that voice hearing and delusional beliefs are pathological can invalidate the life experiences of that person. Additionally, there is an argument that pathologising the voice hearer colludes in preventing abusers from being held accountable (Dillon, 2011).

Although questions have been raised about psychology as a profession (Newnes, 2011; Moloney, 2013,) as well as psychiatry, in the treatment of those with mental health diagnoses, a counselling psychologist may be in a good position to relate to those with unusual experiences. Rather than an expert who *does to*, counselling psychologists, with emphasis on the therapeutic relationship, are well placed to *do with*, and from a position of curious learner, collaboratively work towards understanding. In order to work in this area, one has to be prepared to not know. One has to sit with uncertainty, and work towards reformulating a person's experiences and life journey, following the person rather than leading. 'When you understand your own "symptoms" as meaningful and essential survival strategies, a more respectful and loving acceptance of yourself begins to emerge' (Dillon, 2011, p. 115).

Setting

People diagnosed with psychosis are primarily seen within secondary care services in the NHS. Secondary care community teams[1], or CMHTs (community mental health teams), are "the main vehicle for co-ordinating and delivering specialist community mental health care in England" (Chew-Graham et al., 2007, p. 1). Due to the complex needs of service users, CMHTs consist of a multi-disciplinary workforce, primarily made up of community psychiatric nurses (CPNs), occupational therapists (OTs) and social workers, but can also include additional skilled roles such as support workers, associate practitioners, and assistant psychologists. CMHTs generally have at least one psychiatrist, non-medical prescribers and at least one psychologist or psychological therapist (Chew-Graham et al., 2007).

There is much debate in the literature regarding the purpose and functioning of a CMHT, however, the NICE guidelines recommend a recovery-orientated rehabilitation service. Recovery does not always mean that the person will stop having unusual experiences, but rather that they are able to manage these differently so that distress is minimised, there is a return to a state of wellness, and quality of life is improved (National Institute for Mental Health in England, 2005).

At the time of writing, there exists a diagnostic split in the CMHTs within the writer's employing Trust, so that service users are seen within either a psychosis CMHT or an affective disorders CMHT.

Role of the counselling psychologist in a psychosis CMHT

A psychologist working within a CMHT will typically be expected to have specific skills, and cover a range of roles within his/her job description. Below is a summary of the day-to-day role:

- Assessment and treatment planning. Psychological assessments should inform formulation and intervention planning.
- Psychometric and neuropsychological testing to inform formulation and intervention planning.
- Individual psychological therapy and intervention. National Institute for Health and Care Excellence (NICE, 2015) guidelines currently recommend CBT and family therapy. However, there is a growing evidence base for other ways of working such as CAT (Kerr, 2001), CFT (Gumley et al., 2010; Braehler et al., 2012), mindfulness (Chadwick et al., 2005; Chadwick, 2014) and EMDR (Adams et al., 2020), depending on service user choice, skill of the therapist and formulation.
- Clinical supervision of staff within the CMHT and trainee psychologists, assistant psychologists, and qualified psychologists.
- Group work, such as Hearing Voices groups[2], and compassion-focused therapy groups. Groups will depend on service user choice and demand, as well as on the skills of the psychologist within the team.
- Leadership role, teaching and training. It is recognised that psychological knowledge and understanding can have a much wider influence when psychologists have a role in leadership and team working (The British Psychological Society, 2007). Psychologists lead, and input into, multi-disciplinary team meetings (MDTs), and provide training to increase the skill base of the team in order to ensure psychological interventions can be offered on a wide scale. Psychologists may also teach within local recovery colleges with 'experts by experience', and within counselling and clinical psychology doctorate programmes.
- Psychologists are also involved in research and publication.

Challenges and rewards of the role

The case studies below are anonymised and brief to give a flavour of working psychologically with those with unusual experiences. In both cases the initial formulations were vital in considering what may be most helpful, and in what order.

Jack

Jack is a 60-year-old gentleman who has been in services from early adulthood, with several hospital admissions following suicide attempts. Despite this he had a successful professional career, and is married with adult children. He reported hearing critical voices, seeing things that no one else could see, and feeling a strong mistrust of others. He reported that he had been told that he had a faulty brain. When seen for psychological assessment, it was clear that he made no links between his traumatic childhood and his current difficulties. Jack's childhood was extremely traumatic. He suffered relentless physical and sexual abuses, as well as severe emotional abuse and neglect. Those who were supposed to protect and love him, subjected him to terror, leading him believing that somehow he must be evil in order to deserve this.

A highly intelligent man, he attended a brief psychoeducation group on trauma, and quickly understood the implications of his childhood experiences. From this understanding he was then willing to attend a Hearing Voices group, which was pivotal in Jack's recovery. He began to understand that he was not alone in having unusual experiences, and he started to trust the people in the group. He understood that there was nothing wrong with his brain, but that his unusual experiences and beliefs were an adaptive response to his childhood. He then went on to a 24-session cognitive analytic therapy (CAT), which helped him to understand the relational patterns that permeated his life. Intellectual understanding began to move into feeling, and he attended a compassion focused therapy (CFT) group to help him begin to change his relationship with himself and his voices. Rather than trying to ignore his voices, or being distressed by what they say, Jack now listens, and tries to understand what message the voices are trying to convey.

Eva

Eva is a 37-year-old single mother. Her childhood experiences were of emotional misattunement and invalidation. In her teenage years she was victim of a sexual assault, which was sadly misjudged by a group of friends, leaving her feeling invalidated, misunderstood and alone in her traumatic experience. She tried to manage her feelings using drugs, and was admitted to hospital, where unfortunately she experienced further invalidation and lack of understanding.

Eva reports hearing critical voices telling her that she is being monitored and that people intend to kill her. She struggles to trust others, and has strong negative feelings about her own self-worth. She was given a diagnosis of emotionally unstable personality disorder at 22 years of age, but also attended a Hearing Voices group.

She had some difficulties with her CPN, whom she experienced as dismissing and invalidating. Staff were polarised in diagnostic opinion, and eventually she was transferred to the psychosis team.

Eva worked with the psychologist for several periods of therapy over approximately two years. Initially dissociating within session, she became more comfortable and was able to remain present. The psychologist was able to help Eva be better understood within the team, explaining her formulation and beliefs to four members of staff so that Eva could always access someone who understood her. A more effective crisis plan was negotiated with the crisis team, explaining what she needed when she telephoned. Both of these interventions helped Eva to be better understood, and therefore validated, increasing her trust in others. Self-harming decreased as she became more aware of and able to understand her emotions.

After a rare admission to hospital, it was decided that psychosis was not the primary diagnosis and therefore she should be moved to the affective disorders team. In an unfortunate breakdown in the system, decisions were made by those who did not know Eva well, and the opinions of the psychologist and the CPN went unheard. This was a difficult time for Eva who felt she had lost the support of those who understood her, repeating her childhood experiences of feeling misunderstood and alone. Thankfully, Eva has moved on in her recovery since this time, and is now employed in a carer's role supporting vulnerable people.

Progress in recovery is often slow, and changes to the traditional therapeutic frame, such as flexibility in number of sessions, timing or location, are often useful in engaging with those who have experienced significant trauma. Emphasis on building a therapeutic and trusting relationship is vital, and psychologists should also consider the effects of antipsychotics on the ability to engage therapeutically. Long-term work in individual psychological therapy is possible, but not practical. Psychologists are often a minority in a team and have to make choices between offering few service users a lot, or a lot of service users a little. This is an ethical conflict that is difficult to balance and may often mean that service users receive shorter episodes of psychological intervention. There are very few 'light bulb moments' in therapy and a psychologist choosing to work in this area may need to redefine the term 'rewarding'. Working with less complex and entrenched difficulties, psychologists will likely have the satisfaction of witnessing much greater change than they are likely to see in the field of psychosis. I was fortunate to observe Jack and Eva throughout their journeys, via the Hearing Voices Group, and after several years both reported hearing a positive voice for the first time, and both changed the way they viewed themselves.

The philosophy of a Hearing Voices group is that all members are equal, and professional boundaries can be tricky to manage. To be present in such a group, you give more of yourself than you may in a one-to-one therapy. You may often find yourself in difficult situations whereby the philosophy of the group does not fit comfortably with the role of being an NHS employee. Management of risk, maintaining confidentiality and not offering an 'intervention' are prime examples of a disparity between the Hearing Voices Network and the NHS. Despite this, being involved with a Hearing Voices group was the most rewarding and enjoyable part of my job. I was lucky enough to facilitate the group for over six years, and saw phenomenal progress in the group members. It was a real honour to be accepted and trusted by the people in the group, and well worth the tricky dilemmas that inevitably ensue from such disparate philosophies. Both Jack and Eva benefitted from and contributed to the group.

CMHTs are fast-paced, reactive environments. Situations requiring urgent action are routine. Having psychologists within the leadership team can be containing for staff, and although decisiveness is required, counselling psychologists can also bring a better-honed ability to create space to think rather than react. This is useful for the team, but the offset is that some other aspects of the role can be squeezed in order to accommodate the urgent matters. This may often result in little time to think or to prepare for psychological therapy sessions, and it can be challenging to prioritise different aspects of the role.

The beauty of a CMHT is the collection of different professionals and expertise. However, strong personalities and different professional backgrounds can make dynamics within and between teams a challenge. Despite improvements, we remain in a system dominated by a medical discourse, and psychologists feel they have to comply with this in order to survive within the system (Newnes, 2011). Perhaps the most challenging aspect of the role is to witness a service user's unhealthy relational patterns being inadvertently repeated by services, as it can be hard to make oneself heard in a system that remains medically oriented. An example of this is given in Eva's story above. We must build good relationships and alliances, but also maintain professional identity and integrity. Certainly, we have to be resilient, confident and autonomous in order to manage the demands of a CMHT, the isolation and frustration of being a lone profession, and the vicarious trauma that inevitably comes with working with those who have been traumatised.

Research into vicarious trauma (Rothschild, 2006) suggests that listening to stories of abuse and neglect undoubtedly take a toll on the listener, and can lead to burnout. This combined with being in a high-pressure environment increases the need for good self-care. Psychologists will find their own way here, but examples include mindfulness, nature, exercise and being with loved ones. Clinical supervision is vital in offering support and space to think, as well as helping counselling psychologists to understand and manage team dynamics which impact upon the service user. Regular supervision is invaluable in remaining grounded and aligned with professional values and practices.

Further training can be helpful in formulating within the team and the wider system. CAT in particular is fundamentally grounding in understanding the dynamics that exist in teams, individual Trusts, the NHS and our culture, and how these affect staff and service users.

By far the most valuable part of the job is direct work with service users. From sitting with and listening to those who have unusual experiences, I have developed huge respect for the strength, resilience and creativity of the human spirit. Despite all the difficulties and challenges of this role, it is one I am honoured to have had. This chapter is written by a counselling psychologist for psychologists who are interested in working in the field of psychosis. By its design and nature, it is biased toward the views of psychologists. Those diagnosed with psychosis often go unheard by society, so for this reason I'd like to give the final words to Jack and Eva, and also thank them for reading, critiquing and contributing to this chapter.

Jack

'I have suffered with poor mental health all my life and been in and out of mental health services with negative experiences until I started working with the psychologist. I have always been told my brain is wired up differently and believed I had a faulty brain. Over recent years working with the psychologist has given my life new purpose. She started by asking not what is wrong with me but what has happened to me and it has become clear that my childhood has played the major role in my mental ill health, the effect on me was profound.

I have been on a number of courses with the psychologist and all have been amazing in my road to recovery. She has fought with me, and for me, over a long period of time and helped me to see past my mental health and explore my childhood and the reasons behind my problems. I had always felt lost and alone before but by working with her and introducing me to a "hearing voices" group, I realise that I am not alone and once a week when we meet I feel I don't have to be on my own, and feel more normal.

Without the help I doubt I would be here now. I know my mental health will not be totally cured, but at least by working with her I now have purpose in my life. I now see mental health services as a very positive experience and I will never be able to repay the support that has been given to me.'

Eva

'Working with a psychologist was very scary. However, over time I was able to "stay" in the conversation rather than disassociate. I was treated as an individual rather than "another case". I wanted not to be "fixed" but to gain the knowledge enabling me to validate my own feelings and emotions. I was beginning to not only name the emotion, but also to sit with it.

Going into a hearing voices group was very scary and ironically provoked the voices. I felt less frightened the more I went and, to my surprise, some members had experiences similar to mine! The group, our group, became a 'safe place' to talk about feelings, emotions and distress. Nobody mocked or laughed. I gained acknowledgement, support and confidence from the other members.

Walking became my release. Initially I just tried to reach the next lamppost or bench. Gradually I became fitter, and no longer needed my inhalers. My mind was becoming calmer and the little light began to glow. Where I once kept my head down, I started to smile at people and count how many smiles were returned.

I tried for years to block out the voices. But once I decided to listen (on my terms!), I felt empowered. The first step for me was to say *my* voices, not *the* voices. My voices seemed to be trying to protect me. They were on my side, not trying to hurt me or scare me. My relationship with the voices began to change.'

Notes

1 Early Intervention Psychosis Teams (EIP) are also community based, but work with people who are experiencing a first episode of psychosis, offering time-limited, intensive interventions. The scope of this chapter covers a Psychosis CMHT, where service users typically have longer, more enduring experiences of psychosis.
2 It should be noted that Hearing Voices groups are intended to be facilitated by those who have unusual experiences. However, depending on the attitude and behaviours of the staff, they can be positively facilitated by NHS workers, although remain difficult to navigate ethically within an NHS context. The complexity of facilitating a Hearing Voices group in the NHS will be discussed later in the chapter.

References

Adams, R., Ohlsen, S., & Wood, E. (2020). Eye Movement Desensitization and Reprocessing (EMDR) for the treatment of psychosis: A systematic review. *European Journal of Psychotraumatology*, 11(1), 2–13.

Bentall, R. P., Jackson, H. F., & Pilgrim, D. (1988). Abandoning the concept of 'schizophrenia': Some implications of validity arguments for psychological research into psychotic phenomena. *British Journal of Clinical Psychology*, 27(4), 303–324.

Bentall, R. P. (2003). *Madness Explained: Psychosis and Human Nature*. Penguin.

Boyle, M. (2011). Making the world go away, and how psychology and psychiatry benefit. In M. Rapley, J. Moncrieff & J. Dillon (eds), *De-medicalizing Misery Psychiatry, Psychology and the Human Condition* (pp. 27–43). Palgrave Macmillan.

Braehler, C., Gumley, A., Harper, J., Wallace, S., Norrie, J., & Gilbert, P. (2012). Exploring change processes in compassion focused therapy in psychosis: Results of a feasibility randomized controlled trial. *Clinical Psychology*, 52(2), 199–214.

Chadwick, P., Newman Taylor, C., & Abba, N. (2005). Mindfulness groups for people with psychosis. *Behavioural and cognitive psychotherapy*, 33(3), 351–359.

Chadwick, P. (2014). Mindfulness for psychosis. *British Journal of Psychiatry*, 204, 333–334.

Chew-Graham, C., Slade, M., Montana, C., Stewart, M., & Gask, L. (2007). A qualitative study of referral to community mental health teams in the UK: Exploring the rhetoric and the reality. *BMC Health Services Research*, 7, 117–125.

Dillon, J. (2011). The personal *is* the political. In M. Rapley, J. Moncrieff & J. Dillon (eds), *De-medicalizing Misery: Psychiatry, Psychology and the Human Condition* (pp. 141–157). Palgrave Macmillan.

Gerhardt, S. (2014). *Why Love Matters: How Affection Shapes a Baby's Brain* (2nd ed.). Routledge.

Gumley, A., Braehler, C., Laithwaite, H., MacBeth, A., & Gilbert, P. (2010). A compassion focused model of recovery after psychosis. *International Journal of Cognitive Therapy*, 3(2), 186–201.

Herman, J. L. (1992). *Trauma and Recovery: From Domestic Abuse to Political Terror*. Pandora.

Jablensky, A., Sartorius, N., Ernbery, G., Anker, M., Korten, A., Cooper, J. E., Day R., & Bertelsen, A. (1992). Schizophrenia: Manifestations, incidence and course in different cultures. A World Health Organization Ten-Country Study. *Psychological Medicine: Monograph Supplement* 20. Cambridge University Press.

Johnstone, L. (2011). Can traumatic events traumatize people? Trauma, madness and 'psychosis'. In M. Rapley, J. Moncrieff & J. Dillon (eds), *De-medicalizing Misery: Psychiatry, Psychology and the Human Condition* (pp. 99–109). Palgrave Macmillan.

Kerr, I. B. (2001). Brief cognitive analytic therapy for post-acute manic psychosis on a psychiatric intensive care unit. *Clinical Psychology & Psychotherapy*, 8(2), 117–129.

Moloney, P. (2013). *The Therapy Industry: The Irresistible Rise of the Talking Cure, and Why It Doesn't Work*. Pluto Press.

National Collaborating Centre for Mental Health (2014). Psychosis and schizophrenia in adults: Treatment and management. National Institute for Health and Care Excellence, London. www.nice.org.uk/guidance/cg178/evidence/full-guideline-490503565.

NICE (National Institute for Health and Care Excellence) (2015). Psychosis and schizophrenia in adult *s*. www.nice.org.uk/guidance/qs80.

National Institute for Mental Health in England (2005). NIMHE guiding statement on recovery. http://studymore.org.uk/nimherec.pdf.

Newnes, C. (2011). Toxic psychology. In M. Rapley, J. Moncrieff & J. Dillon (eds), *De-medicalizing Misery: Psychiatry, Psychology and the Human Condition* (pp. 211–225). Palgrave Macmillan.

Rapley, M., Moncrieff, J., & Dillon, J. (2011). Carving nature at its joints? DSM and the medicalization of everyday life. In M. Rapley, J. Moncrieff & J. Dillon (eds), *De-medicalizing Misery: Psychiatry, Psychology and the Human Condition* (pp. 1–9). Palgrave Macmillan.

Read, J., & Bentall, R. P. (2012). Negative childhood experiences and mental health: Theoretical, clinical and primary prevention implications. *British Journal of Psychiatry*, 200, 89–91.

Romme, M. (2009). Important steps to recovery with voices. In M. Romme, S. Escher, J. Dillon, D. Corstens & M. Morris (eds), *Living with Voices: 50 Stories of Recovery* (pp. 7–22). PCCS Books.

Romme, M. (2009). The disease concept of hearing voices and its harmful aspects. In M. Romme, S. Escher, J. Dillon, D. Corstens & M. Morris (eds), *Living with Voices: 50 Stories of Recovery* (pp. 23–38). PCCS Books.

Rothschild, B. (2006). *Help for the helper: The psychophysiology of compassion fatigue and vicarious trauma*. Norton.

The British Psychological Society (2007). New ways of working for applied psychologists in health and social care: Working psychologically in teams. chrome-extension://efaidnbmnnnibpcajpcglclefindmkaj/viewer.html?pdfurl=https%3A%2F%2Fwww.wiltshirepsychology.co.uk%2FWorking%2520Psychologically%2520in%2520Teams.pdf&clen=366461&chunk=true.

Wilkinson. R., & Pickett, K. (2010). *The Spirit Level: Why Equality is Better for Everyone*. Penguin.

Whitaker, R. (2002). *Mad in America: Bad Science, Bad Medicine, and the Enduring Mistreatment of the Mentally Ill*. Basic Books.

Whitaker, R. (2010). *Anatomy of an Epidemic: Magic Bullets, Psychiatric Drugs, and the Astonishing Rise of Mental Illness in America*. Broadway.

World Health Organisation (1994). *Pocket Guide to the ICD-10 Classification of Mental and Behavioural Disorders*. Churchill Livingstone.

Chapter 10

Working in an adult mental health affective disorders service

Jessica McCarrick

The Affective Disorders service provides assessment and treatment for adults presenting with significant mental health problems associated with disorders of mood, emotion, behaviour and personality. There are services in other parts of the country that have similar delivery aims and are organised between psychosis and non-psychosis pathways; however, the current service structure is not commonplace in other mental health trusts, with a tendency towards more general community mental health teams. The multidisciplinary service allows for a rich amalgamation of skills and understandings brought together to develop detailed collaborative care plans. The role of a counselling psychologist within an affective disorders service can be as diverse and interesting as the population it works with.

This chapter has been approached by thinking about what you, the reader, may wish to learn about the role of a counselling psychologist in this service. The aim is to deliver an honest reflection to capture the blessings and challenges of the role. The author has opted to refer to the 'affective service', which feels congruent with counselling psychology humanistic values and perspective of human distress. The term 'disorders' is underpinned by the medical model and may lead to a reductionist view when not integrated with an understanding of psychological distress and social contexts (Gillon, 2007).

Throughout the chapter 'Siobhan's' story will bring to life the descriptions and reflections. 'Siobhan' is not based on an individual client, but her story is reflective of some of the difficulties clients and those working with them may experience.

The Affective service

The Affective service is an NHS secondary care, community mental health team which provides assessment, formulation and treatment for adults aged from 18 years old. Clients present with severe and enduring mental health difficulties which are typically, but not exclusively, underpinned by complex trauma histories and early attachment problems, although there are other factors which can contribute, such as neurodevelopmental or cognitive issues.

DOI: 10.4324/9781003159339-11

Clients may present with significant risk, such as suicidal ideation and attempts, risk to others and/or safeguarding concerns. The Affective service also holds the waiting list for people referred for an autism spectrum or attention deficit hyperactivity disorder assessment and monitors those who are receiving lithium treatment.

The service consists of a multidisciplinary team (MDT), usually including a team manager, advanced practitioner, consultant psychiatrist, nurse consultant, community psychiatric nurses, applied psychologist, psychological therapists, occupational therapist and support workers. An MDT diverse in professional backgrounds and training is essential to meet the multiplicity of needs and ensures clients receive tailored, individualised care. The service is supported by the administrative team who keep things running smoothly. It is imperative that the system communicates well in order to ensure good care is delivered and daily team meetings are held to discuss concerns about clients. Communication is supported by a central electronic record keeping system which pulls everyone's work together into a unified record of care.

Mental health difficulties cannot be understood without appreciating the social and economic environment within which clients live. The service is situated in an area with high levels of socioeconomic deprivation. Those receiving care within secondary mental health services are typically more likely to be unemployed than the general population (Public Health England, 2019). These factors all contribute to increased psychological distress, with research highlighting how low socioeconomic status can precipitate mental health difficulties, and equally, mental health difficulties can lead to low socioeconomic status by limiting people's ability to function at work (Elliott, 2016; Perkins & Repper, 2014).

Referrals come from a range of sources, including the access team, crisis team, liaison psychiatry, liaison and diversion and inpatient mental health services, amongst others. The Affective service works closely alongside the access team who screen referrals from a range of sources. They lead on the initial assessment process and the counselling psychologist may attend regular meetings with access to support with decision making on some referrals. At times access clinicians request the team psychologist or psychological therapist to complete a psychological assessment for clients if they are uncertain whether somebody needs to be referred to the Affective service.

Clients in the Affective service are placed on either the 'standard' or 'care programme approach' (CPA) pathway. The standard pathway is for those who have a single aim of involvement, such as receiving psychological therapy, medication management or awaiting an autism/ADHD assessment in the absence of other mental health difficulties. The CPA pathway is for clients who require more intensive support and care coordination, such as clients open to safeguarding and at a high risk to themselves and/or others. There are currently national changes being planned to the configuration of the CPA and Affective service. These changes are planned to be rolled out over the next two to three years as a result of the community transformation work from the NHS and is set to integrate primary and secondary care and replace the CPA for community mental health services (NHS England/NHS Improvement and the National Collaborating Central for Mental Health, 2019).

The skills required for the role

The Affective service employs applied psychologists within a dual role, with 80% of their time dedicated to direct and indirect clinical work and 20% of their time dedicated to leadership duties. By the time a person reaches the Affective Disorder Service it is likely that they will have had input from various services, including crisis, liaison psychiatry, inpatient mental health services and primary care. There may be pre-existing information on the record keeping system which supports with the psychological assessment process. However, despite this helpful information, it is imperative to enter every initial meeting with a client having the mind-set of a beginner, rather than an expert. Although professionals have some knowledge and expertise on mental health, it is the client who is the expert on themselves and the joining together of these two minds is where true collaborative goal setting can begin.

Being a recovery focused service there is an emphasis upon working with clients towards mutually agreed goals in a time frame that is agreed upon from the beginning. Care coordinators generally start this journey with clients by completing a comprehensive and collaborative assessment which informs the formulation. A person-centred approach encourages clients to walk side by side with their care coordinator and other professionals and set mutually agreed aims of their involvement with the service. It is important to communicate hope from the outset that recovery is possible by setting goals which are manageable, achievable and timely. The counselling psychologist leads on MDT formulation meetings and through the collaborative assessment process the MDT can make suggestions, such as inviting the client to have a psychological assessment, which the care coordinator can then discuss with their client.

There are a range of psychological therapies available, including cognitive behaviour therapy, eye movement desensitisation and reprocessing (EMDR) therapy, dialectical behaviour therapy (DT), cognitive analytic therapy (CAT) and integrative therapy. These therapies are delivered by the counselling psychologist, psychological therapists and some care coordinators who are trained in and supervised to deliver psychological therapies. Having a range of different therapy options helps ensure clients access the most suitable treatment for their difficulties.

Clients can often experience and communicate high levels of distress. The service operates a working hour's duty system whereby clinicians are on hand to respond to clients who contact the service for support. In a service where all staff are busy with high caseloads and risk management, additional pressures can lead to high levels of stress. In their leadership role, counselling psychologists can notice what is going on for colleagues and provide proactive support. When thinking of a well-functioning Affective service, the concept of healthy reciprocal roles (Bradley, 2012) from CAT can be useful. The term reciprocal role refers to patterns of relating to the self and others, with healthy reciprocal roles referring to functioning patterns such as being attuned, available and receptive to feeling listened to and understood (Bradley, 2012). The concept of healthy reciprocal roles can provide a helpful way of basing relationships between colleagues and with management so that a psychologically safe environment is developed where staff are not penalised for making mistakes and are empowered and supported (Edmondson, 1999). If team members feel respected, listened to, understood and cared for, this fosters a psychologically healthy environment within which staff can then provide attuned, respectful care to clients. Healthy reciprocal roles within teams offer a safe, secure working environment mirroring a healthy, secure attachment base, which is imperative when working in challenging settings.

There is a fine balance between maintaining the boundaries of the role and being flexible enough to understand when to step into a more supportive role. For example, working with care coordinators to support highly distressed clients who attend for unplanned duty calls may not fit the usual protocol of psychological assessment, formulation and therapy, but is nevertheless psychologically informed care which supports both team and client. Observing the stress levels in the team and being mindful of the pressures by listening and offering time to chat about it over a cup of tea, or offering to help out in a practical sense, helps improve psychological safety. Although supporting the team is a central part of the skillset in this service, it is important to balance this, so that the psychological team have dedicated time to deliver therapies.

Building good relationships, not only with the team and clients but also with external agencies, is vital. Having knowledge of these services and how they operate helps ensure clients are receiving the right care in the right place. For example, there may be clients who are assessed in access and need to be 'stepped up' from primary to secondary care due to a decline in mental health, or alternatively, there may be clients in the Affective service who are ready to be closed to secondary care and could be 'stepped down' to primary care. Given the aforementioned planned national changes to service provision, it's likely that these boundaries between primary and secondary care will change and thus service delivery may differ. Despite these changes, good working relationships are nevertheless imperative. Multi-agency working helps reduce risk and improves safety by communicating clearly and working in collaboration with each other and the client.

Challenges of the role and personal reflections

The role is often challenging and stretches professional and clinical thinking and skills outside one's comfort zone. Referral rates are high and have increased significantly since the COVID-19 pandemic, possibly due to increasing psychological distress in society and the 'lockdowns' perpetuating avoidance behaviours which reinforce anxiety. High referral rates increase caseloads across the team and increase stress levels significantly. Hence, it can be easy to go into automatic pilot and in an effort to try and keep afloat see as many clients as possible for assessment, formulation and therapy. This mode can impact on reflective practice and decision making; it can also run the risk of compassion fatigue and burnout – and counselling psychologists are no exception. This mode cannot be sustained and may lead to ineffective care, which is why it is vital that there are safety measures in place of diary management, clinical and professional supervision, continuous professional development and the ability to pause and reflect. The emphasis on reflective practice in counselling psychology and the mandatory personal therapy during training is therefore beneficial to the role.

One of the most rewarding aspects is the opportunity to develop therapeutic relationships with clients who are facing great challenges in their lives. Meeting these people and being trusted to walk part of their journey with them is a true privilege. The opportunity to observe the progress that people can make from being at their 'rock bottom' place to living a life that holds meaning and value is undeniably rewarding. The service does not limit to a set number of sessions, which affords flexibility and autonomy for true collaborative working in therapy towards agreed aims.

It is important to be open-minded regarding how individuals view the concept of psychiatric diagnosis, as although some clients can find it stigmatising, others can equally find diagnosis provides them with a way of understanding their difficulties which validates their lived experiences. Working within the MDT offers a wraparound approach to care that can be crucial for clients who are struggling with their mental health. Diagnosis and medication, although not the whole answer, can provide understanding and support with stabilising people's mental health so that they can engage in psychological work.

The humanistic underpinnings of counselling psychology welcome clients bringing their whole self to the work, rather than being treated symptomatically, and this allows one to see just how resilient people are. For some clients it may be one of very few times they have trusted in someone. Not only is there the opportunity to build these meaningful therapeutic relationships, but due to the intensity of the work, relationships with colleagues can be very strong too. The team room can be a real safe space where the unique challenges of the job can be shared in order to give and receive the emotional containment and validation which is often needed. This safe space can be a place of shared laughter and comfort with colleagues who are bonded together in a way that those outside of the workplace may not fully understand.

Despite the challenges, another benefit of working within an MDT is that the counselling psychologist experiences the demands, pressures and stressors within the service, which generates a more accurate understanding and empathy for the team. There are times when the team are understandably pushed to their limits, exhausted and deflated, and at these times there can be a loss of psychological thinking and reflection. Once there is adequate support in place and the soothing system (Gilbert, 2010) has been adequately increased, then the counselling psychologist can be there to hear the stressors of the team and move towards encouraging psychological thinking and reflection.

Issues relating to leadership and diversity

Being present and approachable is imperative, and leadership activities include providing professional and clinical supervision and proactively leading on decision making. There are regular leadership meetings at which service issues are discussed and plans to address issues developed. The counselling psychologist and other members of the leadership team regularly reflect on staff wellbeing and needs, drawing upon common themes from staff supervision and everyday conversations. It was through the forum of the leadership meeting that a monthly team day was developed, whereby staff have time away from their regular duties and in place receive training, staff reflection and simply time to catch up. Given the high caseloads and pressure, this can feel like a welcome relief and provide vital space and time to get on top of their workload.

There is ample opportunity with the dual clinical and leadership role for setting the direction for the service and influencing psychological thinking. Monthly reflective supervision groups for staff are led by the psychology team. This group uses relational thinking and encourages self-reflection when thinking about a particular client that the team may be struggling to develop an effective therapeutic relationship with. There can be strong countertransference responses to clients and the concept of mentalisation (Bateman & Fonagy, 2016), which refers to the ability to understand behaviours of others and the self in terms of thoughts, feelings, needs and wishes, provides a good underpinning to these reflective spaces. In the often hectic day-to-day role of care coordinators it can be difficult to find sufficient head space to mentalise the thoughts, feelings, needs and wishes of the self and client. Reflective groups thereby offer a space to reflect on the professional's thoughts, feelings, needs and wishes and how these may be affecting responses to the client. This reflective space may be used at times when clients are having frequent contacts with services at times of heightened distress, such as with Siobhan.

Case study

Siobhan is a 22-year-old woman with a history of abuse in early childhood. Siobhan was removed from the care of her mother and moved between foster placements from the age of five and experienced further abuse in places which were supposed to offer care and safety. She survived by learning to suppress her feelings because to be perceived as vulnerable was too risky. The only emotion she allowed herself to express was anger.

Siobhan struggles to regulate her emotions and her relationships often have high levels of conflict. Recently, Siobhan has been involved in a domestic violence relationship and following child protection proceedings she has an interim care order in place for her two young children due to parental neglect and witnessing domestic violence. When Siobhan's children were removed, she took a large overdose of prescribed medication. Siobhan rang for emergency help and had treatment in hospital before having a brief admission to the mental health hospital. She was then transferred to the Affective service for further assessment and intervention.

Siobhan frequently expresses frustration with her care coordinator, who she feels is uncaring towards her, and can be verbally aggressive with professionals involved in her care. Siobhan will ring the service several times a day, and frequently expresses thoughts about ending her life, stating she has no reason to live. Recently this has escalated further and Siobhan has rung the service while at a local bridge, stating that nobody was helping her and she was going to jump off. Clinicians responding to these calls understandably feel concerned about Siobhan and emergency services are contacted immediately. The professionals involved feel that they do everything they can, actively listening to and validating Siobhan's emotions; however, they are feeling increasingly frustrated and helpless.

Siobhan's story mirrors the complexities that clients may present and the challenges that care coordinators and duty workers can face. When caught in the middle of these crises, it is difficult to respond in a reflective way, as often there is an urgent need to meet such as an emergency. Sometimes this can stir up difficult feelings in those who are supporting these clients. and the aforementioned reflective groups can be a helpful space for support.

An area of development is increasing access to the service for people from the Black, Asian, Minority Ethnic (BAME) population. Despite having a local population which is rich in ethnic diversity, this is not representative within the client base. Within this Affective service, the MDT is predominantly, but not exclusively, white British with a high female to male ratio. Increasing diversity across the team through staff recruitment may help reduce barriers to accessing the service for people from ethnically diverse backgrounds. Issues in staffing demographics have been recognised more broadly and innovations at a Trust-wide level have begun, including a scheme to support people from local BAME communities learn about mental health issues and at the same time, begin their NHS career. The barriers to accessing mental health services across the BAME community have been recognised by senior executives and a collective promise has been made to better support these people. A new process of 'reverse mentoring' has been initiated, whereby senior professionals are mentored by someone from a different background and less senior position. This improves understanding among senior professionals of the lived experience of people from diverse backgrounds. It is a promising start to increasing access to people from diverse populations to work within and/or access mental health services.

Ethical and legal considerations

Positive risk taking includes reviewing individual's strengths and thinking about what they can do, rather than what they can't. Applied psychologists support decision making in addressing harm, which involves differentiating between chronic and acute risk patterns. It is important to use a broad, all-encompassing definition of harm, which includes the range of contributory factors to a person being at higher risk, either to themselves or to or from others. Harms can arise from various sources, including but not limited to, prejudice and discrimination, social isolation, poverty and explicit or implicit power imbalances in caring relationships. Risk assessments cannot be done in isolation and need to be understood in the context of the client's psychological formulation, drawing upon the client's views, their carer's or family's views and the views of the MDT.

Despite efforts to ensure safety and utilising positive risk taking in a way that emphasises client's strengths and promotes them to live a life that holds meaning and purpose for them, sadly the system does not always get it right. Working in an Affective service means being exposed to high levels of risk and sometimes, very tragically, clients can take their own life. From clinical experience this is the most challenging aspect of the role and can lead to questioning one's professional abilities and decisions. Fundamentally, it contradicts the helping and healing nature of those attracted to caring professions. Research refers to the adverse effects of patient's deaths on individual clinicians, as well as the functioning of the whole team (Linke, Wojciak & Day, 2002). Personally it can stir up feelings including shock, grief and guilt, and professionally it can lead to burnout, compassion fatigue and increase defensive practice with risk, such as trying to prolong hospital stays (Grad, 2014). When the team experiences the loss of a client there are supportive processes in place, including team supervision, which is typically led by the personality and relational specialist service clinicians. Significant clinical and service reports – such as the findings from serious incident investigations and examples of good practice – are shared between the team and senior management, Self-care, reflective practice, support within the team and within supervision are all essential buffers to this hugely stressful aspect of the job.

Following assessment and the formulation meeting, a plan was agreed with Siobhan to arrange a medical review to discuss diagnosis and a psychological assessment to discuss therapy options. Throughout these initial months Siobhan developed trust in her care coordinator and communicated feeling hopeful and motivated to improve her mental health for herself and her children.

Siobhan attended her medical review and a diagnosis of emotionally unstable personality disorder was explored. Siobhan felt this diagnosis accurately described her difficulties. She found it comforting to know that she isn't the only person to experience intense emotional ups and downs.

During her psychological assessment it was agreed together that at this point in her recovery journey exploring trauma may be unsettling and possibly destabilising. Siobhan and the psychologist agreed that she is likely to benefit from developing skills around improving her emotional regulation, particularly when triggered by relationship conflicts. A treatment plan of the one-year DBT programme was discussed and Siobhan was keen to try this.

Over the past 18 months Siobhan has attended DBT and practises the skills regularly. Her children's social worker and care coordinator have noticed that she is more open to hearing constructive feedback during meetings about her children. There have been a couple of episodes of self-harm during this time, triggered by arguments with her friend; however, she did not require medical attention for this, sought emotional support and talked it through with her care team.

Siobhan completed DBT and started having increased contact with her children. After a further three months of stability with fortnightly 'check-ins' with her care coordinator, they started to discuss working towards discharge from service.

As discharge drew closer, Siobhan disclosed feeling scared of what she might do if she didn't have support. Assurance was offered that she will have support from crisis, while empathising and validating her anxiety; however, her distress escalated further. Several attempts were made to try to encourage Siobhan to develop a shared understanding of her anxieties; however, Siobhan would not respond to contact. Over the coming weeks Siobhan started to self-harm with increasing frequency and severity, resulting in a further overdose requiring hospital treatment.

At times, the very care provided to clients can itself become harmful. Sometimes, such as in Siobhan's story, these fears are so intense that they may communicate this by harming themselves. Counselling psychologists can support those involved in the client's care to develop a shared understanding of this communication and think about how to engage the client through the therapeutic relationship. It is helpful for all involved to think about this together, so that discharge plans are supported by those working with the client in different services. Teams can integrate and connect information in ways that an individual cannot do in isolation, which can improve complex decision making (BPS, 2007).

Sometimes, despite best efforts to work towards collaborative and supportive endings, it is not always possible. Discharge may trigger feelings of rejection and abandonment and clients may hold opposing views on the helpfulness of discharge from service for their recovery. This can conflict with humanistic values of counselling psychology, due to the explicit communication from the client of needing to remain in service. It is imperative to be mindful of the implicit power dynamic between care provider and receiver and ensure that clients' needs are considered centrally. The decision-making process involved when clients express that they do not want to be discharged is further complicated when faced with high risk. Counselling psychologists can lead on ensuring all professionals involved, carefully consider the short and long-term gains and risks of discharge to ensure MDT decisions are fully balanced. The views communicated by clients under high levels of distress may not align with the recovery aims communicated when in more of a reflective space. Drawing upon previous conversations with the person and understanding their unique strengths, values and wishes from life can help to balance the conflict felt if the professionals do not 'agree' with the client's expressed need to remain in service. Understanding the longer-term gains for a person, such as building a life outside of the identity of having a mental health diagnosis, can help to illuminate the broader picture. If services are risk averse and hold clients on an open-ended basis then this too can increase harm by communicating that professionals do not believe the client can cope without them, which could foster feelings of helplessness, rather than promoting client's unique strengths and resilience.

Summary

The role of a counselling psychologist in an Affective service is rich in variety, from the clients that one works with to the various clinical and leadership roles involved. The role is suitable for those who appreciate the benefits of MDT working, and it provides ample opportunities to develop professionally, clinically and personally. Although the role is rich with challenges, counselling psychology training, with its emphasis on reflective practice and personal therapy, is an excellent basis for the resilience needed to work in a busy Affective service.

References

Bateman, A. & Fonagy, P. (2016). *Mentalization-Based Treatment for Personality Disorders: A Practical Guide.* Oxford University Press.
Bradley, J. (2012). A hopeful sequential diagrammatic reformulation. *Reformulation,* Summer, 13–15.
BPS (British Psychological Society) (2007). New ways of working for applied psychologists in health and social care: Working psychologically in teams. chrome-extension://efaidnbmnnnibpcajpcglclefindmkaj/viewer.html?pdfurl=https%3A%2F%2Fwww.wiltshirepsychology.co.uk%2FWorking%2520Psychologically%2520in%2520Teams.pdf&clen=366461&chunk=true.

Edmondson, A. (1999). Psychological safety and learning behaviour in work teams. *Administrative Science Quarterly*, 44(2), 350–383.

Elliott, I. (2016). Poverty and mental health: A review to inform the Joseph Rowntree Foundation's Anti-Poverty Strategy. June. Mental Health Foundation.

Gilbert, P. (2010). *Compassion Focused Therapy*. Routledge.

Gillon, E. (2007). *Person-Centred Counselling Psychology: An Introduction*. Sage.

Grad, O (2014). Guidelines to assist clinical staff after the suicide of a patient. International Association for Suicide Prevention. www.iasp.info.

Linke, S., Wojciak, J. & Day, S (2002). The impact of suicide on community mental health teams: Findings and recommendations. *Psychiatric Bulletin* 26, 50–52.

NHS England and NHS Improvement and the National Collaborating Central for Mental Health (2019). The Community Mental Health Framework for Adults and Older Adults. September. www.england.nhs.uk/wp-content/uploads/2019/09/community-mental-health-framework-for-adults-and-older-adults.pdf.

Perkins, R. & Repper, J. (2014). Challenging discrimination within mental health services: The importance of using lived experience in the work place [Editorial]. *Mental Health and Social Inclusion*, 18(3).

Public Health England (2019). State of the North East 2018: Public mental health and wellbeing. February. https://assets.publishing.service.gov.uk/government/uploads/system/uploads/attachment_data/file/779473/state_of_the_north_east_2018_public_mental_health_and_wellbeing.pdf.

Chapter 11

Severe and enduring anorexia nervosa

Gabriel Wynn

This chapter focuses specifically on issues of concern to counselling psychologists who work with adults with 'severe and enduring anorexia nervosa' (SE-AN). It explores why some people don't recover from anorexia nervosa (AN), summarises criteria for using the SE-AN label, and briefly reviews evidence-based SE-AN treatments. A rationale for counselling psychologists to develop socially informed formulations for SE-AN is discussed, along with alternatives to standard weight restoration treatment including reducing habituated behaviour and social isolation within a harm-minimisation framework.

What is anorexia nervosa?

'Anorexia' means loss of appetite. Involuntary disturbances in eating patterns are common reactions to acute stress, but these generally self-resolve over time with no lasting emotional or physiological consequences. On the other hand, anorexia nervosa (AN) is a debilitating psycho-physiological syndrome brought on and maintained by calculated and sustained dietary restriction and deliberate weight suppression to generally below body mass index (BMI) 17 for adults (American Psychiatric Association, 2013) or below 85% median BMI for age, height and gender in children (Royal College of Psychiatrists, 2012). Other characteristics of AN include cognitive inflexibility; perseveration and ritualised behaviour, especially around food; misjudgement of the ill effects of dietary restriction; perceptual distortions particularly around body image; fear of weight regain; and in some cases binge eating and/or damaging compensatory behaviour such as self-induced vomiting, over-exercise or misuse of laxatives or purgative medication. Women generally lose their period (amenorrhea). All these conditions are direct sequelae of being underweight (Fairburn, 2008). While people with AN diagnosis tend to deny feeling hungry, anxious perseveration about food belies their famished condition. Compounding psychiatric comorbidity is common in AN. It has the highest mortality rate of all psychiatric disorders due to malnutrition, medical issues or suicide (National Institute for Health and Care Excellence, 2017). A 2008 study by Bulik et al. found that about 16.9% of their AN cohort had

DOI: 10.4324/9781003159339-12

attempted suicide, with risk heightened by depression, drug or alcohol misuse, or post-traumatic stress. Attempt-to-mortality ratio is high in AN, with lethality of method and intent to die implicated (Guillaume et al., 2011).

What causes and maintains anorexia nervosa?

AN affects 8–10 times more females than males in Western and industrialised societies (Steinhausen & Mohr, 2015). This may be partly due to social value ascribed to female thinness. But while weight concern may be a cultural phenomenon, Keel & Klump (2003) (following Banks, 1992; Brumberg, 2000) report that ego-syntonic emaciation syndromes have been recorded in adolescent females across widely different cultures and historical periods. Religious asceticism, demonic possession, family commercial gain and other factors were hypothesised drivers in these cases rather than idealisation of thinness. Keel & Klump (2003) conclude that female susceptibility to long-term, potentially fatal food refusal transcends culture-bound weight concern. The common denominator is female social and economic power inequality. 'Dissatisfaction with appearance often serves as a stand-in for topics that are still invisible' (Thompson, 1994, p. 11 referenced in Gremillion, 2005). For example, class and racial oppression; cross-cultural migration and acculturation stress; hetero- and cis-sexism in the aetiology of eating disorders are worthy of further qualitative research (Altabe, 1998). A study evaluating the reliability and construct validity of popular eating disorder measures found significant limitations in their assessment of risk factors and cultural pressures for women of colour (Kelly et al., 2012). To date, the dominant body of Euro-American AN research largely comprises quantitative treatment comparisons and investigations of psychopathology in white females.

The primary precipitating and perpetuating factors for AN are dietary restriction and its metabolic consequences. While there is emerging evidence of genome-wide significant loci for AN, 'identifying strong hypotheses about their connections to specific genes is not straightforward' (Watson et al., 2019, p. 1207). Research has highlighted a range of predisposing psychosocial factors, where the greater the exposure, the greater the risk of developing AN (Fairburn et al., 1999). These can be roughly grouped as personal psychological vulnerabilities; family behavioural and relational factors; and adverse experiences related to sociocultural inequalities for girls and women (for a more detailed breakdown of predisposing factors, see Brewerton & Dennis, 2016).

Personal psychological vulnerabilities include negative emotions, poor self-concept and perfectionism (Fairburn et al., 1999) along with anxiety, depression and guilt (Bulik et al., 2006).

Family behavioural factors may include parental dieting or alcohol/drug overuse. Family relational issues may include interpersonal conflict; high parental demands; or physical punishment (Nagata et al., 1999). Relational loss or disconnection from family or friends can also pose risk (Pike et al., 2007). Family psychological factors include perinatal epigenetic processes associated with maternal anxiety, undernutrition and pre-term birth that can render the amygdala and hypothalamic-pituitary-adrenal axis stress responses in young people more susceptible to developing AN following childhood maltreatment (Favaro, Tenconi & Santonastaso, 2010).

Adverse experiences related to sociocultural inequalities include physical and sexual abuse (Pike et al., 2007) and consequential sexual shame and disgust (Schmidt et al., 1997). Studies have found that possibly 25%–50% of AN inpatients have experienced childhood sexual abuse (CSA) prior to the onset of ED (Calugi et al., 2018). CSA is correlated in AN patients with more binge eating and purging symptoms and worse anxiety, depression, low self-esteem and obsessive-compulsive traits than non-CSA patients. However, CSA and non-CSA patients show similar improvements in BMI outcomes following treatment focussed on weight restoration and normalisation of eating (Carter et al., 2006). Sexual abuse in childhood and adulthood is associated with the development of post-traumatic stress disorder (PTSD). Dubosc et al. (2012) found PTSD symptoms fully mediated the effect of sexual assault on disordered eating in young adults.

Starvation as a dissociative mechanism

Dissociation is a symptom of PTSD. It is conceptualised broadly here as avoidance and disconnection from one's body, sense of reality, or the external world, as protection from stress (MIND, 2019). There is strong evidence for ED comorbidity with dissociative disorders (Brewerton & Dennis, 2016). Starvation induces dissociated consciousness. For example, participants in a study by Thompson (1992) described the effects of starvation and binge eating as numbing; sedation; protection against sexual predation; comfort in social isolation; distraction from shame, fear, depression and racial humiliation; and an expression of disruption in body-consciousness. Schott's (2017) critical race and feminist analysis of pro-ED social media environments describes a state of emotional and physiological 'homelessness' as the tragic destination of extreme dieting as a rite of passage to womanhood. Similar psychological and physiological destitution can be interpreted in Oldershaw, Startup and Lavender's (2019) phenomenological metaphor of the 'lost emotional self' which points to the alexithymic detachment from subjective experience seen in some people with AN. Reluctance to give up starvation in SE-AN could for some people be understood as maintaining a dissociative buffer against reality. Habitual dissociation may in turn form a maintaining factor in SE-AN.

Recovery from anorexia nervosa

Early intervention is key to recovery (NICE, 2017). Following treatment, relapse back to restrictive eating patterns and weight loss is common for those who have been eating disordered more than a year or two. Studies report up to half of those receiving treatment may relapse, particularly in the first year following treatment (Khalsa et al., 2017). Ben-Tovim et al. (2001) conducted a five-year follow-up study of people seen for AN assessment. While 56% of the AN participants had recovered, there was no difference in outcome for those who did and those who did not receive treatment. Although the no-treatment group comprised only 6% of the participants, this finding might suggest that treatment helps those with more severe EDs catch up to recovery, or, alternatively that treatment makes no difference in the long run. At least 50%–75% of people receiving treatment eventually recover over approximately eight years. Unfortunately, the remaining 20%-25% don't recover, and go on to develop long-term, persistent AN, and concomitant physical, social and occupational disabilities (Steinhausen, 2002).

Why do some people not recover?

Questions around why some people do not get better from AN has long vexed researchers and clinicians. Research points to synergistic effects of childhood maltreatment and the long-term consequences of metabolic energy conservation on neurocognitive function. In periods of adversity one's capacity to predict negative outcomes of impulsive self-protective behaviours such as strict dieting can become impaired, leading to these behaviours becoming routine (Schwabe & Wolf, 2009). In terms of brain function, initial periods of goal-directed dieting are rewarded by production of endogenous opioids (associated with ventral striatum and amygdala activity). Over time, dietary restriction becomes habitual and entrenched (associated with dorsal lateral striatum activity). Dietary restriction becomes further ingrained by compulsivity and anxiety associated with starvation (Godier & Park, 2014; Pallister & Waller, 2008). Essentially, the brain adapts to restricted energy intake with increasing dependence on habits and rituals as survival shortcuts, with severely curtailed capacity for reflection, imagination, learning and exploratory lifestyle changes required for recovery (Steinglass & Foerde, 2016).

What is 'severe and enduring anorexia nervosa'?

Debates around labelling and classifying non-remitting AN focus on determining markers of duration and severity. Severity can be gauged by several previously failed courses of evidence-based ED treatment; and substantial medical, psychiatric, social or occupational functional impairment. Expert opinion on duration varies from three to ten years with no significant period of remission (Hay & Touyz, 2018). In line with counselling psychology's anti-pathologising ethos, direct use of the SE-AN label with service users is ill-advised. The SE-AN label should not be applied to children and adolescents (Broomfield et al., 2017). Terms such as 'treatment resistance' or 'recalcitrance' are blaming and should be avoided. The term 'chronic,' although accurately pointing to AN's persistence, has fallen out of favour because it connotes defeat. Counselling psychologists are advised to maintain hope that with the right support people with SE-AN can make modest but meaningful improvements in their quality of life.

Counselling psychologists and eating disorders care

Care in multidisciplinary specialist outpatient community ED services (CEDS) is recommended for SE-AN (Wonderlich et al., 2020). Counselling psychologists working in community and hospital ED settings are likely to spend a proportion of their time delivering psychological therapy. Those working in multidisciplinary teams may be expected to facilitate whole-group formulation discussions (Johnstone, 2016) and to make substantial contributions to care plan approach (CPA) processes. They may also provide supervision to other clinicians or trainee psychologists; or engage in research and training. The field of eating disorders treatment is constantly evolving. Providing lectures or attending CPD events helps keep counselling psychologist practice up to date, and also supports professional networking. Management roles in eating disorders settings may require further training to support best practice.

Medical, nursing and pharmacological care for SE-AN is discussed by Robinson and Nicholls (2015). Neuropsychiatric transcranial stimulation therapies are discussed by Treasure et al. (2015). Dietetic care for SE-AN is discussed by Heruc et al. (2020). Hospital treatment for SE-AN people should be sought in line with local protocols for medical or psychiatric instability, and before risk becomes life-threatening. Involuntary detention to hospital for people with SE-AN is controversial and legally complex. England and Wales Court of Protection (2016) has observed in relation to SE-AN:

> There is a strong but not absolute presumption that it is in a person's best interests to receive treatment that helps her to stay alive. There may be circumstances in which treatment is not in the person's best interests, perhaps because it is futile or unduly burdensome.

Patients can experience involuntary treatment as disempowering. It should be avoided wherever possible (Clausen, 2020).

Reflection: The 'good enough' community care team

Supporting people with SE-AN can at times be stressful for the counselling psychologist. Service users adamantly reject what seems to the psychologist to be obviously helpful measures to improve nutrition and psychosocial functioning. Others may agree to carefully designed formulations and treatment plans in order to please the therapist, but then not follow through, all the while pushing themselves ever further toward the dangerous boundary between life and death. Sometimes the therapist sitting with a severely emaciated fellow human being can experience visceral shock, fear and helplessness around such extreme self-inflicted suffering. People with SE-AN have generally experienced multiple treatment failures across the lifespan, and find attending therapy a pointless obligation they resist through stasis. It is important for all these reasons that the psychologist not take more than one or two SE-AN people in their caseload at any given time, to avoid burnout. Maintaining self-care routines and robust emotional boundaries are critical (Selva, 2021). Qualities of 'good enough' care teams working with SE-AN, include an organisational culture of enduring patience and compassion, not only towards service users, but towards each other. Leaders prioritise the stability of a knowledgeable therapeutic workforce, with cohesive morale and low staff turnover. Experienced clinical governance and excellent cross-disciplinary communication are essential, as are team and individual supervision.

Evidence-based psychotherapy treatments for SE-AN

Recovery-oriented AN therapies aim for weight restoration and relinquishment of weight suppression as a basis for self-evaluation. However, these goals are generally unacceptable to people with SE-AN. Experts instead advocate harm-minimisation approaches focusing on improving quality of life, cognitive flexibility, mood and social adjustment with application of minimum weight thresholds rather than pressure to gain weight (Hay, McIntosh & Bulik, 2016).

This section briefly reviews three well-established forms of evidence-based therapy for SE-AN: Cognitive behaviour therapy (CBT), specialist supportive clinical management (SSCM) and Maudsley AN treatment for adults (MANTRA).

A number of related forms of CBT address AN, including cognitive behaviour therapy for AN (CBT-AN) (Pike, Carter & Olmsted et al., 2010); enhanced cognitive behaviour therapy (CBT-E) (Fairburn 2008); and cognitive behaviour therapy for SE-AN (CBT-SE-AN) (Pike & Olmsted, 2016). Six to eight-month manualised approaches aim to support any therapeutic harm-reduction goals the individual can agree to, while also addressing cognitive and behavioural maintaining features of AN, promoting motivation and overcoming obstacles to change. Touyz and colleagues (2013) conducted a randomised controlled study comparing outpatient CBT-SE-AN with SSCM. Both cohorts achieved moderate to good outcomes that were maintained at 12-month follow-up. Long-term (5+ years) follow-up shows no difference in outcome between CBT and SSCM for AN (Carter et al., 2011), with at least half the participants deemed to have a good outcome. Calugi et al. (2018) found CBT-E was equally effective at 12-month follow-up with AN inpatients who did and did not report a history of CSA. This suggests starvation-related dissociative features don't necessarily interfere with therapy, and may resolve with weight restoration.

SSCM (Hay, McIntosh & Bulik, 2016) is a 12-month protocol based on assessment and active monitoring of key ED behaviours and health indices; psychoeducation and nutritional counselling; and supportive patient-led (rather than manualised) psychotherapy that respects the person's defences while promoting regular eating, extinguishing compensatory behaviours and restoring weight. SSCM avoids formulation, motivation enhancement, cognitive interventions and homework. A randomised controlled trial comparing outpatient SSCM with MANTRA found equivalent significant improvements in BMI, weight, ED symptoms, affective symptoms and psychosocial impairments (Schmidt et al., 2015). MANTRA received more positive participant feedback and tended to produce better weight outcomes for more severely unwell participants.

MANTRA (Schmidt, Wade & Treasure, 2014) (also known as cognitive interpersonal therapy, Schmidt, Startup & Treasure, 2019) is a 4–6-month motivation enhancement and formulation-based approach that emphasises experiential writing. Nutritional rehabilitation is followed by remediation work on neuro-cognitive inflexibility, pro-anorexia beliefs and avoidance of emotion. It also promotes expansion of domains of self-evaluation beyond eating disordered concerns. On the interpersonal front it addresses social avoidance, passivity and anxious over-perception of social threat; and unhelpful family responses to anorexia such as accommodating ED rituals, and emotional reactions such as over-protectiveness, frustration, anger or abandonment.

None of these therapies expressly deals with trauma. Of the three therapies highlighted here MANTRA is the only one that expressly addresses unhelpful family involvement.

Therapies found to be effective for bulimia nervosa (BN) or binge eating disorder (BED) are not necessarily effective for AN or SE-AN. For example, third-wave CBT including dialectical behaviour therapy (DBT), schema therapy, acceptance and commitment therapy (ACT), mindfulness-based interventions (MBI) and compassion-focused therapy (CFT) have an emerging evidence base for other EDs, but not AN (Linardon et al., 2017).

Socially informed formulation

The counselling psychologist's work involves making a compelling case through formulation and socially rehabilitative treatment for the person with SE-AN to safely psychologically 're-home' themselves where possible within generative relationships. Supporting this idea is a narrative inquiry into recovery from long-term AN by Dawson, Rhodes and Touyz, (2014). Participants described how improvements in current relationships and the establishment of new relationships helped them reach, and move beyond, a 'tipping point of change'. While these findings only draw an association between social milieu and recovery, it might be theorised that both social support and others' expectations for normative eating are helpful.

In considering formulation for SE-AN, the counselling psychologist is first cautioned not to assume that standard cognitive-emotional-behavioural-physiological formulation is always useful. SSCM therapy (described above) is effective without formulation. Furthermore, the delivery of what a psychologist may deem a good formulation could be a bad experience for the recipient. For example, Gladwin & Evangeli (2012) found in a study of the impact of CAT-influenced case formulations for AN, that participants given letters assessed to be 'higher quality' actually lost weight over the course of therapy. The authors surmise that participant negative reaction to content, timing or method of delivery may have influenced this outcome. Overly-complex, therapist-led formulations that focus only on individual problem-maintaining factors may damage client hope.

Bearing these warnings in mind, the psychologist might co-create socially informed formulations with people they work with, by emphasising narrative themes connected to predisposing cultural, ethnic, racial and interpersonal dynamics and traumas (Allen et al., 2016; Ellickson-Larew et al., 2020). The traumatic pain and loss inherent to living with SE-AN should not be overlooked. Good formulation also locates and extends accounts of personal resilience and creativity. Formulations may be further enhanced by drawing attention to social trauma (e.g. Plumb, 2004); social inequality (e.g. McClelland, 2016); or socio-cultural practices around embodiment (Musolino et al., 2020) for those who might benefit from these perspectives.

In conclusion, counselling psychology work with people with SE-AN balances compassionate emphasis on improving self-care, with respect for individual rights not to change, and vigilance about the ever-present risks of premature death from complications related to long-term malnutrition or suicide.

References

Allen, K.L., O'Hara, C.B., Bartholdy, S. ... & Schmidt, U. (2016). Written case formulations in the treatment of anorexia nervosa: Evidence for therapeutic benefits. *International Journal of Eating Disorders*, 49(9), 874–882. doi:10.1002/eat.22561.

Altabe, M. (1998). Ethnicity and body image: Quantitative and qualitative analysis. *International Journal of Eating Disorders*, 23(2), 153–159. doi:10.1002/(SICI)1098-108X(199803)23:2-153:AID-EAT5-3.0.CO;2-J.

American Psychiatric Association (2013). *Diagnostic and Statistical Manual of Mental Disorders (DSM-5)*. American Psychiatric Publishing.

Banks, C.G. (1992). 'Culture' in culture-bound syndromes: the case of anorexia nervosa. *Social Science and Medicine*, 34(8), 867–884. doi:10.1016/0277-9536(92)90256-P.

Ben-Tovim, D.I., Walker, K., Gilchrist, P., Freeman, R., Kalucy, R. & Esterman, A. (2001). Outcomes in patients with eating disorders: A 5-year study. *Lancet*, 357 (9264), 1254–1257. doi:10.1016/S0140-6736(00)04406-8.

Brewerton, T.D. & Dennis, A.B. (2016). Perpetuating factors in severe and enduring anorexia nervosa. In S. Touyz, D. Le Grange, Lacey, J.H. & Hay, P. (eds), *Managing Severe and Enduring Anorexia Nervosa* (pp. 28–63). Routledge.

Broomfield, C., Stedal, K., Touyz, S. & Rhodes P. (2017). Labeling and defining severe and enduring anorexia nervosa: A systematic review and critical analysis. *International Journal of Eating Disorders*, 50, 611–623. doi:10.1002/eat.22715.

Brumberg, J.J. (2000). *Fasting Girls: The History of Anorexia Nervosa*. Vintage.

Bulik, C.M., Sullivan, P.F., Tozzi, F., Furberg, H., Lichtenstein, P. & Pedersen, N.L. (2006). Prevalence, heritability, and prospective risk factors for anorexia nervosa. *Archives of General Psychiatry*, 63(3), 305–312. doi:10.1001/archpsyc.63.3.305.

Bulik, C.M., Thornton, L., Pinheiro, A.P., Plotnicov, K., Klump, K.L., Brandt, H., Crawford, S., Fichter, M.M., Halmi, K.A., Johnson, C., Kaplan, A.S., Mitchell, J., Nutzinger, D., Strober, M., Treasure, J., Woodside, D.B., Berrettini, W.H. & Kaye, W.H. (2008). Suicide attempts in anorexia nervosa. *Psychosomatic Medicine*, 70(3), 378–383.

Calugi, S., Franchini, C., Pivari, S., Conti, M., El Ghoch, M. & Dalle Grave, R. (2018). Anorexia nervosa and childhood sexual abuse: Treatment outcomes of intensive enhanced cognitive behavioural therapy. *Psychiatry Research*, 262, 477–481. doi:10.1016/j.psychres.2017.09.027.

Carter, J.C., Bewell, C., Blackmore, E. & Woodside, D.B. (2006). The impact of childhood sexual abuse in anorexia nervosa. *Child Abuse and Neglect*, 30(3), 257–269. doi:10.1016/j.chiabu.2005.09.004.

Carter, F.A., Jordan, J., McIntosh, V.V., Luty, S.E., McKenzie, J.M., Frampton, C.M., Bulik, C.M. & Joyce, P.R. (2011). The long-term efficacy of three psychotherapies for anorexia nervosa: A randomized, controlled trial. *International Journal of Eating Disorders*, 44, 647–654. doi:10.1002/eat.20879.

Clausen, L. (2020) Perspectives on involuntary treatment of anorexia nervosa. *Frontiers in Psychiatry*, 21 October. doi:10.3389/fpsyt.2020.533288.

Dawson, L., Rhodes, P. & Touyz, S. (2014). 'Doing the impossible': The process of recovery from chronic anorexia nervosa. *Qualitative Health Research*, 24(4), 494–505. doi:10.1177/1049732314524029.

Dubosc, A., Capitaine, M., Franko, D.L., Bui, E., Brunet, A., Chabrol, H. & Rodgers, R.F. (2012). Early adult sexual assault and disordered eating: The mediating role of posttraumatic stress symptoms. *Journal of Traumatic Stress*, 25, 50–56. doi:10.1002/jts.21664.

Ellickson-Larew, S.A., Carney, J.R., Coady, A.T., Barnes, J.B., Gunthal, B. & Litz, B.T. (2020). Trauma and stressor-related disorders. In M.A. Antony & D.H. Barlow (eds), *Handbook of Assessment and Treatment Planning for Psychological Disorders* (3rd ed.) (pp. 295–334). Guilford.

England and Wales Court of Protection (2016). Judgment 13: W (Medical Treatment: Anorexia). Available from www.casemine.com/judgement/uk/5a8ff75c60d03e7f57eabbc5/amp.

Fairburn, C.G. (2008). *Cognitive Behaviour Therapy and Eating Disorders*. Guilford.

Fairburn, C.G., Cooper, Z., Doll, H.A. & Welch, S.L. (1999). Risk factors for anorexia: Three integrated case control comparisons. *Archives of General Psychiatry*, 56 (5), 468–476. doi:10.1001/archpsyc.56.5.468.

Favaro, A., Tenconi, E., Santonastaso, P. (2010). The interaction between perinatal factors and childhood abuse in the risk of developing anorexia nervosa. *Psychological Medicine*, 40, 657–665. doi:10.1017/S0033291709990973.

Gladwin, A.M. & Evangeli, M. (2012). Shared written case formulations and weight change in outpatient therapy for anorexia nervosa: A naturalistic single case series. *Clinical Psychology and Psychotherapy*, 20, 267–275. doi:10.1002/cpp.1764.

Godier, L.R. & Park, R.J. (2014). Compulsivity in anorexia nervosa: A transdiagnostic concept. *Frontiers in Psychology*, 5(778). doi:10.3389/fpsyg.2014.00778.

Gremillion, H. (2005). The cultural politics of body size. *Annual Review of Anthropology*, 34, 13–32. doi:10.1146/annurev.anthro.33.070203.143814.

Guillaume S., Jaussent I., Olié E., Genty, C., Bringer, J., Courtet, P. & Schmidt, U. (2011). Characteristics of suicide attempts in anorexia and bulimia nervosa: A case-control study. *PLoS One*, 6(8), e23578. doi:10.1371/journal.pone.0023578.

Hay, P., McIntosh, V. & Bulik, C. (2016). Specialist Supportive Clinical Management for severe and enduring anorexia nervosa: A clinician's manual. In S. Touyz, D. Le Grange, Lacey, J.H. & Hay, P. (eds), *Managing Severe and Enduring Anorexia Nervosa* (pp. 112–127). Routledge.

Hay, P. & Touyz, S. (2018). Classification challenges in the field of eating disorders: Can severe and enduring anorexia nervosa be better defined? *Journal of Eating Disorders*, 6 (41). doi:10.1186/s40337-018-0229-8.

Heruc, G., Hart, S., Stiles, G., Fleming, K., Casey, A., Sutherland, F., Jeffrey, S., Roberton, M. & Hurst, K. (2020). ANZAED practice and training standards for dietitians providing eating disorder treatment. *Journal of Eating Disorders*, 8(77). doi:10.1186/s40337-020-00334-z.

Johnstone, L. (2016). Using formulation in teams. In L. Johnstone & R. Dallos (eds), *Formulation in Psychology and Psychotherapy* (2nd ed.) (pp. 216–242). Routledge.

Keel, P. & Klump, K. (2003). Are eating disorders culture-bound syndromes? Implications for conceptualizing their etiology. *Psychological Bulletin*, 129(5), 747–769. doi:10.1037/0033-2909.129.5.747.

Kelly, N.R., Mitchell, K.S., Gow, R.W., Trace, S.E., Lydecker, J.A., Bair, C.E. & Mazzeo, S. (2012). An evaluation of the reliability and construct validity of eating disorder measures in white and black women. *Psychological Assessment*, 24(3), 608–617. doi:10.1037/a0026457.

Khalsa, S.S., Portnoff, L.C., McCurdy-McKinnon, D. & Feusner, J.D. (2017). What happens after treatment? A systematic review of relapse, remission, and recovery in anorexia nervosa. *Journal of Eating Disorders*, 5(20). doi:10.1186/s40337-017-0145-3.

Linardon, J., Fairburn, C.G., Fitzsimmons-Craft, E.E., Wilfley, D.E. & Brennan, L. (2017). The empirical status of the third-wave behaviour therapies for the treatment of eating disorders: A systematic review. *Clinical Psychology Review*, 58, 125–140. doi:10.1016/j.cpr.2017.10.005.

McClelland, L. (2016). Reformulating the impact of social inequalities: Power and social justice. In L. Johnstone and R. Dallos (eds), *Formulation in Psychology and Psychotherapy* (2nd ed.) (pp. 121–144). Routledge.

MIND (2019). About dissociation. Available from www.mind.org.uk/media-a/2936/dissociation-and-dissociative-disorders-2019.pdf.

Musolino, C.M., Warin, M. & Gilchrist, P. (2020). Embodiment as a paradigm for understanding and treating SE-AN: Locating the self in culture. *Frontiers in Psychiatry*, 11(534). doi:10.3389/fpsyt.2020.00534.

Nagata, T., Kiriike, N., Iketani, T., Kawarada, Y. & Tanaka, H. (1999), Hisotry and child sexual or physical abuse in Japanese patients with eating disorders: Relationship with dissociation and impulsive behaviours. *Psychological Medicine*, 29(4), 935–942. doi:10.1017/S0033291799008557.

NICE (National Institute of Health and Care Excellence) (2017). Eating disorders: Recognition and treatment. NICE.

Oldershaw, A., Startup, H. & Lavender, 2019. Anorexia nervosa and a lost emotional self: A psychological formulation for the development, maintenance, and treatment of anorexia nervosa. *Frontiers in Psychology*, 10(219). doi:10.3389/fpsyg.2019.00219.

Pallister, E. & Waller, G. (2008). Anxiety in the eating disorders: understanding the overlap. *Clinical Psychology Review*, 28(3), 366–386. doi:10.1016/j.cpr.2007.07.001.

Pike, K.M., Carter, J.C. & Olmsted, M.P. (2010). Cognitive-behavioral therapy for anorexia nervosa. In C. M. Grilo & J. E. Mitchell (eds), *The Treatment of Eating Disorders: A Clinical Handbook* (pp. 83–107). Guilford.

Pike, K.M., Hilbert, A., Wilfley, D.E., Fairburn, C.G., Dohm, F.A., Walsh, B.T. & Striegel-Moore, R.H. (2007). Toward an understanding of risk factors for anorexia nervosa: A case-control study. *Psychological Medicine*, 38(10), 1–11. doi:10.1017/S0033291707002310.

Pike, K.M. & Olmsted, M.P. (2016). Cognitive behavioural therapy for severe and enduring anorexia nervosa. In S. Touyz, D. Le Grange, J.H. Lacey & P. Hay (eds), *Managing Severe and Enduring Anorexia Nervosa* (pp. 128–145). Routledge.

Plumb, S. (2004). The social/trauma model: Mapping the mental health consequences of childhood sexual abuse and similar experiences. In J. Tew (ed.), *Social Perspectives in Mental Health: Developing Social Models to Understand and Work with Mental Distress* (pp. 112–128). Jessica Kingsley.

Robinson, P.H. & Nicholls, D. (2015). *Critical Care for Anorexia Nervosa: The MARSIPAN Guidelines in Practice*. Springer.

Royal College of Psychiatrists (2012). Junior MARSIPAN: Management of really sick patients under 18 with anorexia nervosa. College Report CR168. www.rcpsych.ac.uk/docs/default-source/improving-care/better-mh-policy/college-reports/college-report-cr168.pdf?sfvrsn=e38d0c3b_2.

Schmidt, U., Tiller, J., Blanchard, M., Andrews, B. & Treasure, J. (1997). Is there a specific trauma precipitating anorexia nervosa? *Psychological Medicine*, 27(3), 523–530. doi:10.1017/S0033291796004369.

Schmidt, U., Wade, T.D. & Treasure, J. (2014). The Maudsley model of anorexia nervosa treatment for adults (MANTRA): Development, key features, and preliminary evidence. *Journal of Cognitive Psychotherapy*, 28(1), 48–71. doi:10.1891/0889-8391.28.1.48.

Schmidt, U., Magill, N., Renwick, B., Keyes, A., Kenyon, M., Dejong, H., Lose, A., Broadbent, H., Loomes, R., Yasin, H., Watson, C., Ghelani, S., Bonin, E-M., Serpell, L., Richards, L., Johnson-Sabine, E., Boughton, N., Whitehead, L., Beecham, J., Treasure, J., Landau, S. & Nezu, A.M. (2015). The Maudsley outpatient study of treatments for anorexia nervosa and related conditions (MOSAIC): Comparison of the Maudsley model of anorexia nervosa treatment for adults (MANTRA) with specialist supportive clinical management (SSCM) in outpatients with broadly defined anorexia nervosa: A randomized controlled trial. *Journal of Consulting and Clinical Psychology*, 83(4), 796–807. doi:10.1037/ccp0000019.

Schmidt, U., Startup, H. & Treasure, J. (2019). *A Cognitive Interpersonal Therapy Workbook for Treating Anorexia Nervosa*. Routledge.

Schott, N.D. (2017). Race, online space and the feminine: Unmapping 'Black Girl Thinspiration'. *Critical Sociology*, 43(7–8), 1029–1043. doi:10.1177/0896920516652456.

Schwabe, L. & Wolf, O.T. (2009). Stress prompts habit behavior in humans. *Journal of Neuroscience*, 29(22), 7191–7198; doi:10.1523/JNEUROSCI.0979-09.2009.

Selva, J. (2021). How to set healthy boundaries. *Positive Psychology.com*. https://positivepsychology.com/great-self-care-setting-healthy-boundaries/.

Steinglass, J.E. & Foerde, K. (2016). How does anorexia nervosa become resistant to change? In S. Touyz, D. Le Grange, H. Lacey & P. Hay (eds), *Managing Severe and Enduring Anorexia Nervosa* (pp. 64–75). Routledge.

Steinhausen, H.-C. (2002). The outcome of anorexia nervosa in the 20th century. *American Journal of Psychiatry*, 159(8), 1284–1293. doi:10.1176/appi.ajp.159.8.1284.

Steinhausen, H.C. & Mohr, C.J. (2015). Time trends in lifetime incidence rates of first-time diagnosed anorexia nervosa and bulimia nervosa across 16 years in a Danish nationwide psychiatric registry study. *International Journal of Eating Disorders*, 48 (7), 845–850. doi:10.1002/eat.22402.

Thompson, B.W. (1992). 'A way outa no way': Eating problems among African-American, Latina and white women. *Gender and Society*, 6(4), 546–561. doi:10.1177/089124392006004002.

Thompson, B.W. (1994). *A Hunger So Wide and So Deep: American Women Speak Out on Eating Problems*. University of Minneapolis Press.

Touyz, S., le Grange, D., Lacey, H., Hay, P., Smith, R., Maguire, S. et al. (2013). Treating severe and enduring anorexia nervosa: A randomized controlled trial. *Psychological Medicine*, 43, 2501–2511. doi:10.1017/S0033291713000949.

Treasure, J., Cardi, V., Leppanen, J. & Turton, R. (2015). New treatment approaches for severe and enduring eating disorders. *Physiology & Behavior*, 152, 456–465. doi:10.1016/j.physbeh.2015.06.007.

Watson, H.J., Tilmaz, Z., Thornton, L.M. … & Bulik, C.M. (2019). Genome-wide association study identifies eight risk loci and implicates metabo-psychiatric origins for anorexia nervosa. *Nature Genetics*, 51(8), 1207–1214. doi:10.1038/s41588-019-0439-2.

Williams, J. (2004). Women's mental health: Taking inequality into account. In J. Tew (ed.). *Social Perspectives in Mental Health: Developing Social Models to Understand and Work with Mental Distress* (pp. 151–167). Jessica Kingsley.

Wonderlich, S.A., Bulik, C.M., Schmidt, U., Steiger, H. & Hoek, H.W. (2020). Severe and enduring anorexia nervosa: Update and observations about the current clinical reality. *International Journal of Eating Disorders*, 53, 1303–1312. doi:10.1002/eat.23283.

Chapter 12

Working as a counselling psychologist in an NHS Occupational Health setting

Julia Ann Harrison

Introduction

The following chapter aims to introduce an NHS staff psychology service (SPS) which sits within Occupational Health. Various functions of the service will be presented and the unique role of the counselling psychologist in this field will be explored. While some examples are drawn from my own experience, I have also considered the wider NHS context of this role. The aim is to provide an overview of what you might expect to experience as a counselling psychologist within this setting.

An SPS can comprise counsellors, CBT therapists and both clinical and counselling psychologists. A service can offer staff proactive programmes for dealing with work stress-related issues in line with Health and Safety Executive (HSE) guidelines (2005a, 2005b), including individual and team interventions to improve the mental health, wellbeing and effectiveness of staff. Additionally, it will also respond to traumatic incidents or other events likely to cause psychological distress to individuals or within teams. Opportunity to engage in development of initiatives which contribute to staff wellbeing is likely to exist within this setting – for example, an organisational mental health strategy, a psychological wellbeing policy, a mediation service or conflict coaching.

Supporting National Health Service Staff in the Workplace

Employers have a duty of care to reduce the risk of stress-related problems in staff (HSE, 1974; HSE, 1992). The Boorman review (2009) highlighted the importance of prioritising staff health and wellbeing within the National Health Service (NHS) and made recommendations on how to achieve this. Boorman's rationale is that staff who are supported and healthier will be less likely to take sick absence, be happier at work and produce better patient outcomes. There exists a growing evidence base for links between staff wellbeing and patient outcomes (Royal College of Physicians of London, 2015; West et al., 2011) with the understanding that a good level of staff wellbeing

DOI: 10.4324/9781003159339-13

is a precursor to positive patient experience (Maben et al., 2012). It makes sense that a healthy and satisfied workforce can improve staff morale, potentially increase the effectiveness of individuals, teams and the wider organisation, and may see a reduction in sick absence, ultimately improving patient experience.

The Boorman report recommends NHS Trusts implement guidance from the National Institute for Health and Clinical Excellence (NICE) on promoting mental health and wellbeing at work, as well as guidance from the National Mental Health and Employment Strategy. Key recommendations from NICE (2019) include adopting a proactive approach to staff health and wellbeing, recognising the value of Occupational Health in supporting staff to remain at work.

Occupational Health

Within the NHS, Occupational Health includes nurses, doctors, administrative staff and managers and provides specialist advice to employees and management regarding health, safety and welfare in line with the rights of employees under the Human Rights Act (1998). The purpose of Occupational Health is to promote and maintain the health of employees and prevent accidents and ill health at work in accordance with the organisation's Equality, Diversity and Human Rights Policy. The aim is to treat all staff equally, fairly and without discrimination regardless of protected characteristics. Advising on reasonable adjustments, supporting staff with illness or disability to remain at work is also a responsibility of Occupational Health in accordance with disability discrimination legislation within the Equality Act (2010). An NHS Trust may employ several thousand members of staff across business units including Nursing and Midwifery, Surgery, Corporate and Estates. Occupational Health can provide a range of services to staff at individual, team and organisational levels including pre-employment checks, referrals to physiotherapy, sight/hearing tests, sick absence management and an SPS.

Service Provision and Delivery

Following referral, clients may receive a telephone triage call to screen in relation to risk and consider which interventions would be most appropriate. Interventions vary and may include individual therapy, guided self-help materials, short-term telephone support or signposting to another agency – for example, Improving Access to Psychological Therapies (IAPT), a community mental health team (CMHT), a bereavement service or a carer's organisation. An SPS can also provide training for staff and line managers, with some offering resilience training courses, mindfulness sessions and other bespoke training as required by the organisation such as mental health awareness or risk pathway training.

Referrals

Referrals to SPS are commonly from Occupational Health nurses and may also be self-referral. Work-related difficulties such as stress, conflict and change are common reasons for referral. Acute or vicarious trauma can be seen in staff who may have experienced a traumatic or critical event at work. The Health and Safety Executive (2004) identifies six key areas that can be causes of work-related stress: demands of the job/workload; sense of control; level of support from managers; relationships at work which include conflict or unacceptable behaviour; clear roles with less role conflict; change and how it is managed. It can be common within therapy sessions to hear some of these issues if the reason for the difficulty is work related. However, staff can face many personal issues and life events which impact on their ability to function well at work. Personal reasons for referral include relationship difficulties, bereavement and caring responsibilities; mental disorders such as anxiety and depression also frequently present. Trauma presentations can be found across both work-related and personal referrals.

Psychometrics

Within an SPS, Clinical Outcomes in Routine Evaluation (CORE) 10 can be used as a client self-report measure pre- and post-therapy (Evans et al., 2000). This is designed to measure client's subjective levels of distress, with a score above 33 generally considered to reflect clinically significant levels of distress, indicating the individual may benefit from therapeutic intervention. Standardised screening tools such as the Patient Health Questionnaire (PHQ-9) for depression developed by Spitzer, Kroenke and Williams (1999) and the seven-item general anxiety disorder scale (GAD-7) (Spitzer, Kroenke, Williams & Löwe, 2006) are commonly used, and can be helpful in gaining insight into client experience and also in providing an indication of whether to refer client onward to their GP. In line with Occupational Health department policy and Health and Safety legislation (1974), staff have a responsibility to ensure they do not place themselves or others at risk of harm. There is a requirement therefore for staff to be open and honest regarding their wellbeing and levels of distress when completing psychometrics. This also highlights the responsibility of the counselling psychologist to respond accordingly, addressing any concerns with the client such as safety or risk. As well as an effective way to highlight difficulties and inform treatment planning, psychometric data in the form of pre- and post-therapy scores can be used to produce reports in view to informing the effectiveness of the service.

Roles of the Counselling Psychologist within an SPS

The main purpose of a role within an SPS is the provision of effective psychological therapies to employees of the NHS Trust. In addition to individual therapy, there may be opportunity to facilitate resilience training courses for staff groups, training for managers, service development and research and supervision. As mentioned previously, support may be required for individuals or teams in the case of a traumatic event to support staff in managing the immediate emotional effects. There is also a requirement to adhere to NHS Trust policy including safeguarding in the event of any disclosure or concern regarding safety or risk and to support staff who are victims of domestic violence, which involves liaison with the Trust safeguarding team. Counselling psychologists are trained to work as part of diverse teams, within recognised therapeutic frameworks appropriate for evidence-based, time-limited and focused interventions. With a phenomenological and humanistic philosophy, they are well positioned to consider the rich diversity of an NHS workforce and their experiences.

Individual Therapy Clinics

Within individual therapy clinics, counselling psychologists provide specialist assessment and psychological treatment for staff experiencing emotional/stress-related problems at work, while recognising that staff may also be experiencing personal difficulties which impact on their mental health and ability to function well at work.

Central to the way in which a counselling psychologist works is *formulation*. This collaborative process between client and clinician offers a psychological explanation of origin and maintenance of the client's difficulties (Johnstone & Dallos, 2014), appreciating the client's unique experience and informing treatment choice. Therapeutic interventions delivered within the SPS will vary depending on client need, determined by the process of assessment and formulation. Interventions are based on a range of evidence-based models of including psychodynamic, humanistic and cognitive behaviour therapy (CBT) approaches. Acceptance and commitment therapy (ACT) (Hayes, Strosahl & Wilson, 1999) incorporates mindfulness and values-based living skills with the aim of increasing psychological flexibility and has seen very good outcomes in healthcare staff, with improvements in mental health evident (Flaxman & Bond, 2010; Waters et al., 2018).

Resilience Training

The implementation of targeted prevention strategies to improve the mental wellbeing of staff is in line with NICE guidelines (2019) and also the government's Foresight report (2008), which calls for *preventative* as opposed to a more traditional *reactive* approach.

Training courses are often available to staff with the aim of building on resilience skills by developing psychological flexibility, reducing the likelihood of stress and burnout (Lloyd et al., 2017; Reeve et al., 2018) commonly reported among staff within the NHS at an estimated cost of up to £400 million a year (NHS Employers, 2019). Evidence shows improvements in the mental health of healthcare staff following group interventions using ACT (Flaxman et al., 2013; Frögéli et al., 2016; Waters et al., 2018; Gaupp et al., 2020). I found delivering these courses highly rewarding; it was my privilege to work with so many inspiring healthcare professionals who work in demanding roles and to observe positive shift towards psychological flexibility. Additionally, this represents an opportunity for counselling psychologists to develop professional skills and knowledge in relation to the ACT model as well as confidence working with groups.

Training for Managers

Managers play an important role in the prevention or alleviation of stress among their staff (Department of Health, 2012; Health and Safety Executive, 2014). NICE (2009; 2019) identifies the crucial role managers play in supporting staff; however, managers may not always feel they have the skills to do so. An SPS may develop specialist training for managers geared to helping them monitor and maintain staff wellbeing – for example, a stress risk assessment process or encouraging managers to talk to staff about their mental health and wellbeing. Within the role a counselling psychologist can expect to contribute to the provision of training to existing managers or be part of induction programmes for new managers, aligning with national guidance around a preventative approach to mental wellbeing in the workplace (Boorman, 2009; Foresight, 2008; NICE, 2019).

Service Development and Research

Development of quality improvement projects within the service can involve client satisfaction or other questionnaires, highlighting what is working well in the service and areas for improvement. Projects or research using patient data must be handled in line with The Data Protection Act (DPA) General Data Protection Regulation law (GDPR, 2018).

NICE (2019) recommendations regular monitoring of staff sickness absence and audit of referral trends which can be indicative of stress hotspot areas as well as revealing some of the potentially underrepresented, vulnerable or marginalised groups in the organisation. This information can be reported to the site or business unit concerned, prompting risk assessment. Monitoring data such as referral rates and waiting times can give an indication of how a service is doing against key performance targets with implications for the allocation of resources. Reports indicating average waiting times, triage outcomes and pre- and post-therapy outcome reports are examples of where service development skills are required.

The profession of counselling psychology aims to meet the need for clinically relevant evidence and has progressed towards a scientist-practitioner model, integrating an empirical evidence base with a reflective ethos and the aim of congruence between model of research and values (BPS, 2005). The role of the counselling psychologist as researcher is important in order to maintain a body of knowledge which is clinically applicable.

Supervision

Clinical supervision represents a way of monitoring practice; ensuring safety (BPS, 2005), compliance with professional standards and caseload management. Within an SPS, this would be provided by an experienced and senior member of clinical staff who may be either a counselling or a clinical psychologist.

Supervision can provide reassurance that correct procedures have been followed, additionally it can be an opportunity for psychological de-briefing and to consider what support you may need to manage your own emotional responses. While supporting NHS staff, risk of vicarious trauma exists, therefore it is important to have a supervisor sensitive to the effects of working with trauma, to recognise potential signs in order to respond with understanding and support. In my own experience of vicarious trauma, it was incredibly helpful that my supervisor expressed empathy, often encouraging me to focus on the strengths, resilience and post-traumatic growth of my client (Lonn & Haiyasoso, 2016).

Supervision of trainees is an important role within the organisation, representing an opportunity to ensure good-quality, safe and ethical practice in the counselling psychology profession. Responsibilities of the supervisor include assisting trainees in understanding their various roles and responsibilities and ensuring specified core professional competencies are demonstrated in the context of both their training institution and specific policy and procedures within Occupational Health. Trainee supervision may take various forms including one-to-one, peer, observation, role-play or audio and video recordings of client sessions. There are many benefits to providing supervision to trainees, including contributing to their professional development and linking with university counselling psychology doctoral programmes, which can be an effective way to maintain professional identity. As a trainee myself I benefitted from supportive supervisors providing endless guidance and encouragement, so to provide clinical supervision to a trainee is a wonderful, meaningful way to give something back to the profession.

Ethical Considerations

One potential source of conflict when working as a counselling psychologist with staff employed in the same organisation is a 'them and us' culture; staff facing disciplinary or investigation processes, aware that you are employed within Occupational Health, may worry about confidentiality or feel afraid information could be used against them.

The risk of a dual relationship exists when conflicting roles arise – for example, your clinical supervisor in this setting is likely to be a senior manager in the organisation, perhaps your own line manager. This can add a layer of complexity to the supervisory relationship, potentially blurring boundaries and affecting mutual respect within clinical supervision.

Another consideration is that staff members enrolling on training programmes may be current or former clients, potentially giving rise to dual relationship issues. For example, delivery of training may require elements of self-disclosure on the part of the counselling psychologist which could impact on a therapeutic dynamic. There is also a reasonable chance that in mandatory training situations within the organisation, you may find yourself sharing a classroom with a client. This is not necessarily problematic; however, it raises boundary issues and requires some sensitivity in how it is managed for the client and yourself.

Other dilemmas can arise if referrals are received from various staff members involved in the same dispute; understandably, this could present an ethical dilemma, especially when relationships are not always apparent right away and come to light during therapy.

Ethical dilemmas will always exist given the complexity of our humanity as well as organisational and other dynamics. However, there are ways dilemmas can be addressed including team meetings, clinical and peer supervision, accessing relevant policy and procedure and professional guidelines.

Leadership and Diversity

Counselling psychology embraces inclusive practice, celebrating diversity within the workforce. As a counselling psychologist within Occupational Health, providing an active leadership role on the issue of diversity is an opportunity to make a positive difference, bringing social justice to life. However, perhaps the question posited by Bell and Tribe (2018), 'how to turn social justice values into social justice action?', is relevant, highlighting potential barriers such as a sense of powerlessness regarding making a difference, especially when systems may appear resistant to change.

What comes to mind for me as a counselling psychologist when I consider leadership and diversity is *social justice*. Social justice can be defined as the addressing of social inequality (Bell & Tribe, 2018), creating a more equal society. There are several ways in which counselling psychologists can consider social equality within their organisation; for example, within the therapeutic setting where individuals are prized, valued and appreciated for their uniqueness (BPS, 2018). This also extends to colleagues, with appreciation of diversity within the team and valuing a mix of experience and expertise across all staff within the NHS. Identification of under-represented groups such as black and minority ethnic (BME) or lesbian, gay, bisexual or transgender (LGBT), for example. The NHS Trust may employ equality, diversity and inclusion leads, responsible for recognising and eliminating barriers; therein lies potential to work together towards social equality of staff. Furthermore, which business units have higher rates of Occupational Health referrals? Which have lower, and why? It is important to consider ways to reach out and encourage marginalised cohorts of staff to engage, as some have only limited access to Trust emails or intranet that would inform them of the support available. Therefore, just placing accessible information in staff rooms and canteens may be helpful.

The NHS Trust may have various support network groups for staff – for example, staff with specific physical health, neurodevelopmental or mental health conditions. Network groups may include staff with autism, unpaid carers with a work-life balance, menopause awareness groups, etc. As a counselling psychologist within Occupational Health there exists an opportunity to participate, offering a psychological perspective within meetings and gaining insight around specific issues faced in the workplace by potentially marginalised or 'hard to reach' cohorts. This has the potential to inform both Trust policy and service delivery around developing and nurturing a culture of social equality in the workplace.

Personal Reflections

The philosophical underpinning of counselling psychology fits well within Occupational Health, where there is a fundamental drive to maintain the health and wellbeing of staff. Humanistic theory (Rogers, 1951; Maslow, 1954) understands people as unique, inherently good and holds the belief that given the necessary conditions (positive regard, empathy, congruence) people will shift towards wellbeing. The therapeutic relationship forms a part of those conditions, with the counselling psychologist aware of the healing effects of being 'fully present' with their clients (Rogers, 1980) and the profound reparative effect of the therapeutic relationship (Clarkson, 2003). The discipline of phenomenology is a field of philosophy developed in the 20th century (Heidegger, 1962; Husserl, 1963) that considers 'first person' subjective experience of the individual, based on theories from 19th and 20th-century philosophy (Sartre, 1956; Heidegger, 1962). Existentialism focuses upon a search for meaning in human existence, and in a therapeutic setting it considers personal meaning when facing challenging issues. I have heard it said many times by healthcare professionals that experiencing trauma inherent within their role changed their view of the world. It seems to me that counselling psychology philosophy sits comfortably within an NHS setting, where empathy, compassion, healing and meaning making following trauma seems so necessary.

In addition to the relevance of counselling psychology philosophy in this setting, I notice how the core values intrinsic to counselling psychology also align: working ethically and effectively to be reflective scientist-practitioners; creatively, compassionately and collaboratively working with clients. Within this context there is a real sense of shared purpose and values with our clients, the NHS workforce, as they work to provide the best possible patient care.

Challenges of the Role

Several challenges exist in a dynamic environment such as an NHS Occupational Health department. High workload, stress and burnout –the counselling psychologist is essentially susceptible to the same stressors as their clients, especially in challenging times such as winter pressure, staff shortage or pandemic. During these times, services often see a rise in referrals with increased pressure to meet deadlines.

Relevant to the NHS setting, emergency workers and other medical staff can experience trauma as a result of, for example, exposure to fatal injuries and handling the deceased. Healthcare workers such as paramedics, doctors, nurses, porters, etc., are vulnerable to becoming traumatised following these events and may present with symptoms including post-traumatic stress, somatoform responses, depression or anxiety (Briere & Scott, 2014). It is not uncommon to encounter clients with trauma presentations within this setting, and this can lead to the experiencing of vicarious trauma in ourselves as clinicians providing support.

Another challenge within this setting can be stigma with regard to accessing mental health support at work. Some who may benefit from the service may choose not to attend due to fear of being seen or judged by colleagues, and this may present a risk of some staff becoming marginalised. Raising awareness with line managers regarding signs and symptoms to look out for in their staff which may indicate stress, burnout, anxiety or depression can equip managers with the necessary skills to offer support and advice to staff who may be hesitant to present to Occupational Health.

Organisational factors and the context of the service must be considered; while the counselling psychologist is primarily concerned with the wellbeing of their client, there may be a sense of pressure to encourage the staff member back to work as soon as possible. Indeed, it is within the remit of Occupational Health to support staff who are absent in a return to work as soon as possible, with the belief that returning to work at the right time can assist recovery, as opposed to a prolonged absence which may exacerbate anxiety for the staff member as well as having practical implications for the organisation.

Summary

Owing to the coronavirus pandemic evident in the UK from early 2020, the NHS, with its army of healthcare workers, has never been more important or more valued. Despite increased focus on the mental health and wellbeing of NHS staff, the effects of stress, burnout, compassion fatigue, trauma and more continue to be seen. Remarkably, though, even in the face of challenging circumstances, the NHS workforce remains willing to stand on the front line and serve the nation. The humanistic, phenomenological and existential philosophy of counselling psychology sits congruently within such an environment, calling as it does for empathy, compassion and ongoing meaning making. To work as a counselling psychologist providing support to NHS staff is at times challenging, but for the most part one of the most meaningful roles I could ever imagine.

References

Bell, D., & Tribe, R. (2018). Social justice, diversity and leadership. *European Journal of Counselling Psychology*, 7(1), 111–125.

Boorman, S. (2009). NHS health and wellbeing: Final report. NHS Health and Wellbeing Review.

Briere, J. N., & Scott, C. (2014). *Principles of Trauma Therapy: A Guide to Symptoms, Evaluation, and Treatment* (2nd ed., DSM-5 update). Sage.

BPS (British Psychological Society) (2005). Division of Counselling Psychology: Professional practice guidelines. BPS.

BPS (British Psychological Society) (2018). Code of ethics and conduct. BPS.

Burr, V. (2003). *Social Constructionism* (2nd ed.). Abingdon, UK: Routledge.

Clarkson, P. (2003). *The Therapeutic Relationship*. London: John Wiley & Sons.

Department of Health (2012). Advice for employers on workplace adjustments for mental health conditions. www.nhshealthatwork.co.uk/images/library/files/Governm ent%20policy/Mental_Health_Adjustments_Guidance_May_2012.pdf.

Evans, C., Mellor-Clark, J., Margison, F., Barkham, M., Audin, K., Connell, J., & McGrath, G. (2000). CORE: Clinical outcomes in routine evaluation. *Journal of Mental Health*, 9(3), 247–255.

Flaxman, P. E., & Bond, F. W. (2006). Acceptance and commitment therapy in the workplace. In R. A. Baer (ed.), *Mindfulness-based Treatment Approaches*. San Diego, CA: Elsevier.

Flaxman, P. E., & Bond, F. W. (2010). A randomised worksite comparison of acceptance and commitment therapy and stress inoculation training. *Behaviour Research and Therapy*, 48(8), 816–820.

Flaxman, P. E., Bond, F. W., & Livheim, F. (2013). *The Mindful and Effective Employee: An Acceptance and Commitment Therapy Training Manual for Improving Well-being and Performance*. Oakland, CA: New Harbinger Publications.

Foresight Mental Capital and Wellbeing Project (2008). Final project report. Mental capital and wellbeing: Making the most of ourselves in the 21st century. The Government Office for Science, London. www.gov.uk/government/uploads/system/uploa ds/attachment_data/file/292453/mental-capital-wellbeing-summary.pdf.

Frögéli, E., Djordjevic, A., Rudman, A., Livheim, F., & Gustavsson, P. (2016). A randomized controlled pilot trial of acceptance and commitment training (ACT) for preventing stress-related ill health among future nurses. *Anxiety, Stress, & Coping*, 29(2), 202–218.

Gaupp, R., Walter, M., Bader, K., Benoy, C., & Lang, U. E. (2020). A two-day acceptance and commitment therapy (ACT) workshop increases presence and work functioning in healthcare workers. *Frontiers in Psychiatry*, 11, 861.

GDPR (2018). Guide to the General Data Protection Regulation. *GOV.UK*. www.gov.uk/government/publications/guide-to-the-general-data-protection-regulation.

Hayes, S. C., Strosahl, K., & Wilson, K. G. (1999). *Acceptance and Commitment Therapy: An Experiential Approach to Behavior Change*. New York; London.

HSE (Health and Safety Executive) (1974). *Health and Safety at Work Act 1974*. HSE Books.

HSE (Health and Safety Executive) (1992). *Management of Health and Safety at Work Regulations 1992*. HSE Books.

HSE (Health and Safety Executive) (2004). Working together to reduce stress at work: A guide for employees. www.hse.gov.uk/pubns/indg424.pdf.

HSE (Health and Safety Executive) (2005a). The Management Standards for Work-related Stress. www.hse.gov.uk/stress/standards/standards.htm.

HSE (Health & Safety Executive) (2005b). Tackling work-related stress: A manager's guide to improving and maintaining employee health and well-being. www.hse.gov.uk.

HSE (Health and Safety Executive) (2014). Return to work questionnaire. www.hse.gov.uk/stress/assets/docs/returntowork.pdf.

Heidegger, M. (1962). *Being and Time*. Trans. by John Macquarrie and Edward Robinson. New York: Harper & Row.

Husserl, E. (1963 [1913]). *Ideas: General Introduction to Pure Phenomenology*. Trans. by W. R. Boyce Gibson. New York, London: Collier.

Johnstone, L., & Dallos, R. (2013). *Formulation in Psychology and Psychotherapy: Making Sense of People's Problems*. Routledge.

Lloyd, J., Bond, F. W., & Flaxman, P. E. (2017). Work-related self-efficacy as a moderator of the impact of a worksite stress management training intervention: Intrinsic work motivation as a higher order condition of effect. *Journal of Occupational Health Psychology*, 22(1), 115.

Lonn, M. R., & Haiyasoso, M. (2016). Helping counselors 'stay in their chair': Addressing vicarious trauma in supervision. *VISTAS 2016*, 1–12. www.counseling.org/docs/default-source/vistas/article_90_2016.pdf?sfvrsn=4.

Maben, J., Peccei, R., Robert, G., Adams, M., Richardson, A., & Murrells, T. (2012). Patients' experiences of care and the influence of staff motivation, affect and well-being. Final report. UK National Institute for Health Research Service Delivery and Organisation Programme

Maslow, A. (1954). *Motivation and Personality*. New York: Harper.

NHS Employers (2019). Stress and its impact on the workplace. www.nhsemployers.org/retention-and-staff-experience/health-and-wellbeing/taking-a-targeted-approach/taking-a-targeted-approach/stress-and-its-impact-on-the-workplace.

NHS (2019). NHS Workforce Race Equality Standard: 2018 data analysis report for NHS trusts. www.england.nhs.uk/wp-content/uploads/2018/12/wres-2018-report-v1.pdf.

NICE (National Institute for Health and Clinical Excellence) (2009). Promoting mental wellbeing at work. www.nice.org.uk/guidance/ph22/resources/mental-wellbeing-at-work-pdf-1996233648325.

NICE (National Institute for Health and Care Excellence) (2019). Workplace health: Long-term sickness absence and capability to work. NICE guideline NG146. www. nice.org.uk/.

Reeve, A., Tickle, A., & Moghaddam, N. (2018). Are acceptance and commitment therapy-based interventions effective for reducing burnout in direct-care staff? A systematic review and meta-analysis. *Mental Health Review Journal*, 23(3), 131–155. https://doi.org/10.1108/MHRJ-11-2017-0052.

Rogers, C. (1951). *Client-Centred Therapy*. Boston, MA: Houghton Mifflin.

Rogers, C. (1980). *A Way of Being*. Boston, New York: Houghton Mifflin.

Royal College of Physicians of London (2015). Work and wellbeing in the NHS: Why staff health matters to patient care. www.rcplondon.ac.uk/guidelines-policy/work-a ndwellbeing-nhs-why-staff-health-matters-patient-care.

Sartre, Jean-Paul (1956). *Being and Nothingness: An Essay on Phenomenological Ontology*. Trans. by Hazel E. Barnes. New York: Philosophical Library.

Spitzer, R. L., Kroenke, K., & Williams, J. B., with the Patient Health Questionnaire Primary Care Study Group. (1999). Validation and utility of a self-report version of PRIME-MD: the PHQ primary care study. *JAMA*, 282(18), 1737–1744.

Spitzer, R. L., Kroenke, K., Williams, J. B. W., & Löwe, B. (2006). A brief measure for assessing generalized anxiety disorder: the GAD-7. *Archives of Internal Medicine*, 166(10), 1092–1097.

The Equality Act (2010). The National Archives. Retrieved from www.legislation.gov. uk/ukpga/2010/15/contents.

The Data Protection Act (2018). The National Archives. Retrieved from www.gov.uk/ government/collections/data-protection-act-2018.

Waters, C. S., Frude, N., Flaxman, P. E., & Boyd, J. (2018). Acceptance and commit-ment therapy (ACT) for clinically distressed health care workers: Waitlist-controlled evaluation of an ACT workshop in a routine practice setting. *British Journal of Clinical Psychology*, 57(1), 82–98.

West, M. A., & Dawson, J. F. (2012). Employee engagement and NHS performance. Paper commissioned for The King's Fund review leadership and engagement for improvement in the NHS. www.kingsfund.org.uk/sites/default/files/employee-enga gement-nhs-performance-west-dawson-leadership-review2012-paper.pdf.

Willig, C. (2016). Constructivism and 'the real world': Can they co-exist? *Qualitative Methods in Psychology (QMiP) Bulletin*, 21, 33–38.

Chapter 13

Working relationally with trauma

Helen Nicholas

Setting the scene

This chapter will give you a taster of how a counselling psychologist works relationally with adult clients who have experienced traumatic events. Counselling psychologists undertake specialist placements during their doctoral training and this, together with their research, can help them decide which specialist area interests them. In my early career I noticed that many clients who presented with mental health issues in clinic would disclose past traumas. Their presenting issues and past traumas were key to the assessments and formulations I was completing. At times, clients would disclose these early on in therapy sessions and this would help me form a better picture of their presentation. Disclosing past traumas can be difficult for clients, and some took longer to build up trust in the therapeutic relationship before they would disclose in sessions. Although I may have suspected past traumas, it was important to let them go through their own process within therapy. I specialise in anxiety and trauma and have completed training in eye movement desensitisation and reprocessing (EMDR), gaining my accreditation as an EMDR therapist. In 2013, I contributed to a British Psychological Society (BPS) discussion document on 'working relationally with trauma' with colleagues from the BPS Division of Counselling Psychology (BPS, 2013). This document highlighted the importance of a relationally based approach when working with clients who have experienced traumas. Within my academic role, I taught workshops with colleagues on trauma-informed care to local counselling services and charitable organisations. This approach helped their staff think in a more trauma-sensitive way when working with clients and experts by experience in their organisations. One of my favourite books is Bessel Van der Kolk's *The Body Keeps the Score*, which highlights how emotions and therefore trauma is stored in our body. If you are interested in working with clients who have experienced trauma then I would highly recommend that you read this book. In 2018, I completed a 200-hour Ashtanga and Yin yoga teacher training and started to incorporate mind and body movement to help clients within therapy. There is so much still to learn

DOI: 10.4324/9781003159339-14

about the therapeutic benefits of yoga for clients and how trauma-sensitive yoga can help clients reconnect with their body awareness.

What is trauma?

At times, clients will talk about deep losses experienced in their life, but they may not have considered that these events are traumas. This highlights the misconception many have, that trauma relates more to military personnel and specifically combat trauma. Fundamentally, trauma is a feeling of threat and a perceived lack of safety. This means that although not everyone will meet the Diagnostic and Statistical Manual – 5 (DSM-5) (American Psychiatric Association, 2013) criteria for post-traumatic stress disorder (PTSD), they may have been impacted by and have symptoms of trauma. Shapiro (2001) wrote about the distinction between big 'T' trauma and small 't' trauma, where clients with big 'T' trauma would more likely meet the DSM criteria for PTSD. Examples might be crimes such as sexual assault; intimate partner violence; terrorist attacks; military combat; and natural disasters such as earthquakes and fires. People witnessing traumatic events are also vulnerable to trauma reactions and can become victims themselves. Traumas are highly distressing for clients and the big 'T', little 't' trauma distinction may not be useful for clients. If you are in clinical practice, you will know that clients do not tend to fit neatly into a model or formulation template. This is very much the case with clients who present with trauma. When completing your assessment and formulation, what might initially appear as a single incident traumatic event, for example a road traffic collision, might trigger complex past or childhood traumas, thus creating a more complex presentation. Clients who present with small 't' traumas are adversely affected by their experiences. The impact of the trauma is more important to consider than the cause; this will include how the trauma is stored and 'remembered' in their body (Van der Kolk, 2014).

Trauma is often bound up in relationships, whether this is directly through client's own lived experience or indirectly such as witnessing a crime or traumatic event. Clients who suffer trauma as an adult and who also had past traumatic experiences were found to be more affected 'by the later event than were victims of adult-onset trauma who did not have such a developmental history' (Bromberg, 2011, p. 58). Trauma has long-lasting effects on a client's mental health and can break the attachment bond, thus leaving the client feeling insecure and vulnerable. Adverse childhood events (ACEs) have been linked to a number of physical and psychological conditions, risk behaviours, development disruption and increased healthcare utilisations (Kalmakis & Chandler, 2015). In 1998, 13,494 adults completed a questionnaire on adverse childhood experiences. These included their experiences of psychological, physical or sexual abuse, violence against mother, or living with household members who were substance abusers, had mental health issues or were suicidal, or were imprisoned. The total amount of ACE categories was then compared to measures of adult risk behaviour, health status and disease. The result was a significant link between exposure to abuse or household dysfunction during childhood and a range of negative outcomes and risk factors (Felitti et al., 1998). The ACE study is a landmark study, and the original paper is well worth a read. You can also read the BPS (2019) briefing paper on ACEs, available on their website.

Trauma-informed assessment and treatment plan

The main question when working relationally with clients is 'what has happened to them?' There are a few standardised outcome measures and questionnaires counselling psychologists can use in their assessment of clients presenting with trauma. Clinicians will need to complete a holistic assessment, grounded in compassion and client-centred principles. One of the best ways for counselling psychologists to assess clients is through a semi-structured interview approach, taking the relationship into account. Clients need to feel that therapy is a safe environment in order to explore past traumas and therefore a relationally based approach is best. It may be beneficial to ask clients to also complete self-report measures to ascertain their levels of anxiety (e.g., GAD-7), depression (e.g., HADS, PHQ-9), and mental wellbeing (WEMWBS). Trauma specific questionnaires are available such as the Impact of Event Scale – Revised (IES-R); Posttraumatic Diagnostic Scale (PDS-5) and PTSD checklist for DSM-5 (PCL-5). If you suspect that the client is dissociating from the traumatic event, then the Dissociative Experiences Scale (DES) can be a useful tool to screen for any dissociative symptoms. These are also useful when writing expert witness reports in order to show whether the client meets the DSM-5 PTSD or adjustment disorder criteria. Psychometrics can help to provide meaningful information for an assessment report that is needed to ascertain the number of treatment sessions the client requires. Counselling psychologists are skilled in using a wide variety of psychometric and neuropsychometric tests.

The Power Threat Meaning (PTM) framework for trauma enables clinicians to engage with the client's narrative. For example, rather than using the DSM-5's manualised way of diagnosing clients, the PTM framework is more concerned with the story the client has about their experiences. This conceptual framework can be used with clients who are experiencing persistence of distress, unusual experiences and troubled or troubling behaviour. The PTM framework replaces 'what is wrong with you?' with four key questions (BPS, 2018, p. 190):

- What has happened to you? (How is *Power* operating in your life?)
- How did it affect you? (What kind of *Threats* does this pose?)
- What sense did you make of it? (What is the *Meaning* of these situations and experiences to you?)

- What did you have to do to survive? (What kinds of *Threat Response* are you using?)

We also think about their skills, resources and strengths.

- What are your strengths? (What access to *Power* resources do you have?)

• What is your story? (How does all this fit together?)

Case study

Jennifer, a 25-year-old woman, was referred through her insurance company for treatment following a road traffic collision (RTC). She was experiencing travel anxiety, negative intrusive thoughts and occasional flashbacks of the traumatic event. She was avoiding driving due to high levels of anxiety and would become nauseous when she needed to be a passenger in a vehicle. She would insist on only be driven by her mother whom she trusted, and would only be driven to and from work, which was five miles from her home. Jennifer was also struggling to concentrate at work and was finding it difficult to be around her colleagues. She noticed that she was becoming increasingly snappy with people around her and irritated in meetings at work. She had lost motivation to engage in activities that she used to enjoy, such as cycling, yoga and reading.

Some client referrals will include a brief assessment report or a basic triage assessment. When first presented with Jennifer's referral, it may seem like a single incident trauma. However, it is important to gain an understanding of the client's difficulties and to formulate a treatment plan based on a number of factors. For example, many clients find it difficult to disclose historical traumatic events and it may take them longer to trust you before disclosing. Outcome measures and psychometric tests can be useful tools when assessing the impact of the event on the client's daily life and can be used to track a client's progress through therapy. Referral and insurance company often ask for these to be completed at the assessment session, midway through therapy and then at discharge. However, psychometric measures may miss significant past events that could have been triggered. Some tend to focus on the most recent incident and mood over the past week or two. A comprehensive history taking and understanding of the client's past traumas can be taken in the form of a timeline of events and may include further clues as to what has happened to them. Incidences may include parental care issues (critical parent); losses throughout their life (death of nurturing figure); bullying (school, work); social interactions (friendships/relationships), and so forth.

As you can see, with the additional information Jennifer has provided, her single incident trauma is a more complex presentation with links between her past traumatic events and the RTC. Her present emotions are linked to many of her past traumas. Although one of the goals for therapy might be to address the travel anxiety, she will benefit from exploring her past traumas within a safe therapeutic setting. One of the strengths of counselling psychologists is that they work relationally with clients within a client-centred manner and at the client's pace. We are well suited to working relationally with clients who present with complex traumas.

Choosing a treatment approach will be based on the client's presentation, your formulation and your skills. You might be restricted to a set number of sessions – for example, by the NHS service or referral company agreement. At times, additional sessions can be requested, however, this can result in a break during treatment if there is a delay in authorisation. Clients might disclose more complex past traumas when therapy is coming to an end and additional sessions might not be possible. You may need to adjust your formulation and treatment plan accordingly. Working with Jennifer, we could choose trauma-focused CBT which will include psychoeducation around what trauma is, some grounding, relaxation and breathing techniques, cognitive restructuring skills and perhaps a few behavioural experiments to help engage Jennifer in driving again and to cope more effectively with her anxiety. We could choose to use EMDR to process Jennifer's distressing memories of her past experiences.

Reflection

Take a moment to think about a minor incident in your childhood, perhaps a time when you were embarrassed or humiliated.

Write down what you recall from the incident.

What image comes to mind?

What emotions do you fell?

What body sensations do you remember?

Many of us will be able to recall an event and possibly feel this in our bodies. We may connect with the experience of embarrassment and/or humiliation in the present. We can still experience these strong emotions even though the incident may have been many years ago. The Adaptive Information Processing (AIP) model, which guides EMDR as a therapeutic approach, suggests that the event that we recalled has been insufficiently processed and that the emotions and body sensations we are experiencing may be clouding our perceptions and actions in present situations. In Jennifer's case, the RTC has brought up the negative cognition and belief about herself now of 'I am in danger', which links to the same thought during the sexual assault. The aim of EMDR is to process these memories so that when Jennifer recalls them, she will not experience the distressing old emotions or body sensations. She will also be able to choose to recall the events rather than needing to 'push them away'. Francine Shapiro, who developed EMDR as a psychotherapeutic approach to trauma in 1987, has written extensively about this approach (Shapiro & Forrest, 1997). There is a growing database of research and literature on the effectiveness of EMDR and AIP on mental health. Many of these can be found on the EMDR International Association website in the Francine Shapiro Library, which is dedicated to scholarly articles on EMDR therapy and AIP.

With Jennifer, the appropriately qualified EMDR therapist will go through the eight phases of EMDR therapy using the standard protocol that attends to three prongs – past events that set the foundation for pathology, current situations that cause disturbance, and future templates for appropriate future action (Shapiro, 2001). It will be useful to have a timeline of the events so that processing can be done on all of them.

Beyond the therapy room

Trauma-informed and trauma-sensitive yoga

Yoga, as a mind-body practice, has been used as a therapeutic treatment approach to mental health and wellbeing (Cramer et al., 2018; Nguyen-Feng et al., 2019). Trauma-informed and trauma-sensitive yoga is yoga that has been appropriately adapted to the unique needs of individuals affect by and/or over-coming trauma. Yoga therapy includes specific postures (asanas); breathing (pranayama) exercises (Farhi, 1996); body awareness and movement; and relaxation and meditation practices. At times, I have incorporated specific yoga postures (asanas) within EMDR therapy sessions to help clients connect or reconnect with their bodies. Trauma-informed care is also about providing clients with a safe place to work through trauma and become more body aware. Van der Kolk wrote that 'self-regulation depends on having a friendly relationship with your body. Without it you have to rely on external regulation from medication, drugs like alcohol, constant reassurance or compulsive compliance with wishes of others' (Van der Kolk, 2014, p. 97). In trauma- sensitive yoga, the yoga teacher is more mindful of the environment, the physical practices and movements, the adjustments and hands-on assists given, and the language they use to guide students through the yoga class (Emerson, et al., 2009).

Body awareness

Body awareness is important because traumatised individuals often feel unsafe inside their bodies. Body psychotherapy, which works with the body as well as the mind, has body awareness at its core. Traumatised clients may be hyper-aroused and waiting for the next warning sign. They may also have learnt to ignore their bodies' reactions in order to numb their emotions and may find it difficult to fully relax and be present in their bodies. Body psychotherapists will engage the body through muscular, behavioural and sensory input without 'intruding on bodily integrity' (Rothschild, 2000, p. xiv). This is important in clients who have experienced trauma such as sexual or physical abuse, as respecting their boundaries and personal space is essential. Levine's (1997) Somatic Experiencing approach outlines how traumas can be played out soma-tically, in our bodies. He believes that the roots of trauma are in our bodies and are usually held as fear or helplessness, rather than through faulty thinking.

Counselling psychologists are uniquely placed to think beyond the therapy room. We focus on the client in a holistic way, taking into consideration their experiences from a broad range of approaches as well as using the therapeutic relationship in therapy. For example, in trauma-informed work, the client may bring their anxieties, sense of helplessness and hopelessness, guilt and shame to the therapy room. As counselling psychologists we can represent for the client stability, safety and someone to validate their emotions, and perhaps provide a space for them to reconnect with another person. Our doctoral training equips us to work with transference, countertransference, splitting and the complicated mix of relational factors that may come up in clients with complex trauma pre-sentations. This ability to tune in to the client's state of arousal might not have been something they have experienced before. Thinking beyond the therapy room allows the client to build trust and experience successful exchanges while trusting the process. Walking therapy, dance therapy, exercise therapy, ecother-apy and the benefits of being outdoors in nature have all been shown to have a positive effect on mental health (Hefferon, 2013). Incorporating outdoor activ-ities with different therapeutic approaches, such as EMDR, mindfulness and talking therapies, can help the client heal from traumatic events in their past.

Resourcing yourself as a trauma specialist

Work-related trauma

Work-related trauma can lead to psychological distress and have a cost on our own wellbeing. Secondary traumatisation, vicarious traumatisation, compassion fatigue and burnout are well recognised in the helping professions and amongst first responders (Rasmussen, 2005). It is important to focus on your experience of working with trauma; your own experience of trauma; your beliefs (for example, perfectionism), beliefs about the role of trauma treatment, and your trauma-informed approach(es) effectiveness. Rasmussen's research suggested an inter-subjective view of vicarious traumatisation, with affective attunement being a major component. He wrote that the therapist's capacity to be emotionally flexible and available to the client is weakened with vicarious trauma. The therapist is therefore unable to provide a holding environment, and unable to sustain affective attunement through empathic immersion in the client's subjective experience. Counselling psychologists can become disturbed by the client's narrative, entering into a painful and fragmented world of the client, judging whether the client is able to tolerate such feelings and, at times, needing to actively guide the client through the process. Secondary trauma stress may be experienced when witnessing the trauma narrative of clients as they relay their experiences to you in the therapy room. Sometimes we are exposed to visual reminders of their experiences, such as a photograph of their road traffic collision, a physical disfigurement or amputation.

Self-care and resilience

Joseph's (2012) book *What Doesn't Kill Us* explains post-traumatic growth and the adversity hypotheses whereby people require adversity, trauma and setbacks in order to grow, find fulfilment, develop as a person and find their inner strength. In 2015, the BPS and the New Savoy Partnership conducted a survey of therapists' mental health. The results showed that stress levels amongst psychologists were high, with some experiencing burnout, low morale and depression. Working with any client group can bring its own challenge, so being aware of when our resilience levels are fading is vital. Pemberton (2015, p. 13) suggests recognising three needs in clients, which are also useful for recognising in ourselves:

1 Building protection – through taking action
2 Building capacity – through developing resilience skills
3 Building renewal – through being helped to use the learning from difficulty to move forward.

As counselling psychologists, the importance of self-awareness is rooted in our philosophy, ethics and identity and is nurtured throughout our doctoral training. However, faced with a growing caseload of clients needing our support we can sometimes place our own needs on hold or focus less on our self-care than we should. At times we need to follow our own advice, possibly do more yoga, mindfulness or connect with nature. Recognising and engaging in the strategies that support you will help you be more connected and present for your trauma clients, as well as providing a secure base for them to explore their past. Resilience enables us to retain stability in our psychological functioning – and even though it may be reduced at times, it can be regained. A wide range of positive activities, such as movement-based exercises like yoga, will help you maintain sufficient levels of resilience.

Collegial support and supervision

It is recommended that you seek a trauma-informed supervisor or a supervisor who specialises in the approach you use such as TF-CBT or EMDR. Collegial support, peer support and employing a psychologist in a consultative or mentoring capacity can help to guide you (Bernard & Goodyear, 2019). There is great benefit in having a supervisory space for personal development, reflection and mentoring (Nicholas & Goodyear, 2020). Supervisors can bring expertise and specialist knowledge such as therapy and cognitive assessments that are relevant to the specific client groups you are working with. They can also offer an important platform for exploring your transference and countertransference, clinical caseload, and clinical work that may be triggering for you.

Counselling psychologists can take on a number of leadership roles such as supervising colleagues or other helping professionals, forming networking groups in their areas of specialism, training other professions in their areas of interest, and offering collegial support. It is important to keep up to date with practice guidelines, changes in policies, and the latest evidence-based research in order to practice competently. If you are registered with an accrediting body such as the EMDR Association UK, you will also need to renew your accreditation by evidencing your continued professional development. A good way of engaging in the profession is to present at conferences, write research articles or work with colleagues to produce blogs, social media posts and support events. You may want to join the BPS crisis, disaster and trauma psychology section, a trauma specific interest group, or an EMDR social media group in order to connect with colleagues who practice in the same area of specialism or use a specific therapeutic approach. Being well resourced can help us to expand our own window of tolerance and develop and maintain our levels of resilience and our boundary parameters.

Conclusion

This chapter has provided a taster of what it can be like as a counselling psychologist working relationally with trauma. As you can see, the work is varied and can be tailored around your own interests, specialist areas, therapeutic preferences and openness to thinking beyond the therapy room. As a therapist, your own self-awareness, body-awareness and self-care is vital. The next time you attend a yoga class, think about how a client who has experienced trauma might feel in the class, whether there any changes you would make to the words the yoga teacher uses, or whether some postures make you feel more vulnerable and might therefore trigger clients. Try to become more trauma sensitive and trauma informed.

A few useful resources

EMDR Association UK – https://emdrassociation.org.uk

The Francine Shapiro Library – https://emdr-europe.org/research/francine-shapiro-library/

U.S. Department of Veteran Affairs – www.ptsd.va.gov

References

American Psychiatric Association (2013). *Diagnostic and Statistical Manual of Mental Disorders* (5th ed.). American Psychiatric Association.

Bernard, J. M. & Goodyear, R. K. (2019). *Fundamentals of Clinical Supervision.* Pearson.

BPS (The British Psychological Society) (2013). Working relationally with trauma: A discussion. The British Psychological Society.

BPS (The British Psychological Society) (2018). The Power Threat Meaning framework: Towards the identification of patterns in emotional distress, unusual experiences and troubled or troubling behaviour, as an alternative to functional psychiatric diagnosis. www.bps.org.uk/sites/bps.org.uk/files/Policy%20-%20Files/PTM%20Main.pdf.

BPS (The British Psychological Society) (2019). Adverse childhood events (ACEs): Evidence briefing. www.bps.org.uk/sites/bps.org.uk/files/Policy/Policy%20-%20Files/Briefing%20Paper%20-%20Adverse%20Childhood%20Experiences.pdf.

Bromberg, P. M. (2011). *The Shadow of the Tsunami and the Growth of the Relational Mind.* Routledge Taylor & Francis Group.

Cramer, H., Anheyer, D., Saha, F. J. & Dobos, G. (2018). Yoga for posttraumatic stress disorder: A systematic review and meta-analysis. *BMC Psychiatry,* 18(72). https://doi.org/10.1186/s12888-018-1650-x.

Emerson, D., Sharma, R., Chaudhry, S. & Turner, J. (2009). Trauma-sensitive yoga: Principles, practice, and research. *International Journal of Yoga Therapy,* 19(1), 123–128. https://doi.org/10.17761/ijyt.19.1.h6476p8084l22160.

Farhi, D. 1996. *The Breathing Book: Good Health and Vitality through Essential Breath Work.* St Martin's Griffin.

Felitti, V. J., Anda, R. F., Nordenberg, D., Williamson, D. F., Spitz, A. M., Edwards, V., Koss, M. P. & Marks, J. S. (1998). Relationship of childhood abuse and household dysfunction to many of the leading causes of death in adults. The Adverse Childhood Experiences (ACE) Study. *American Journal of Preventive Medicine,* 14 (4), 245–258.

Joseph, S. (2011). *What Doesn't Kill Us: The New Psychology of Posttraumatic Growth.* Piatkus.

Kalmakis, K. A. & Chandler, G. E. (2015). Heath consequences of adverse childhood experiences: A systematic review. *Journal of the American Association of Nurse Practitioners,* 27(8), 457–465.

Hefferon, K. (2013). *Positive Psychology and the Body: The Somatopsychic Side to Flourishing*. Open University Press.

Levine, P. (1997). *Waking the Tiger: Healing Trauma*. North Atlantic Books.

Nicholas, H. & Goodyear, R. (2020). Supervision of a sample of clinical and counselling psychologists in the UK: A descriptive study of their practice, processes and perceived benefits. *European Journal of Counselling Psychology*, 9(1), 41–50.

Nguyen-Feng, V. N., Clark, C. J. & Butler, M. E. (2019). Yoga as an intervention for psychological symptoms following trauma: A systematic review and quantitative synthesis. *Psychological Services*, 16(3), 513–523. https://doi.org/10.1037/ser0000191.

Pemberton, C. (2015). *Resilience: A Practical Guide for Coaches*. Open University Press.

Rasmussen, B. (2005). An intersubjective perspective on vicarious trauma and its impact on the clinical process. *Journal of Social Work Practice*, 19(1), 19–30. doi:10.1080/02650530500071829.

Rothschild, B. (2000). *The Body Remembers: The Psychophysiology of Trauma and Trauma Treatment*. W.W. Norton & Co.

Shapiro, F. (2001). *Eye Movement Desensitization and Reprocessing: Basic Principles, Protocols and Procedures*. The Guildford Press.

Shapiro, F. & Forrest, M. S. (1997). *EMDR: The Breakthrough Therapy for Overcoming Anxiety, Stress and Trauma*. Basic Books.

Van der Kolk, B. (2014). *The Body Keeps the Score: Mind, Brain and Body in the Transformation of Trauma*. Penguin Books.

Chapter 14

Forensic settings

Janice Brydon

Setting the scene

Secure adolescent services are a part of the National Secure Forensic Mental Health Service for Young People (NSFMHSfYP) clinical management network. Each referral from youth justice settings is considered to determine the level of security required. The term 'secure' describes a setting which deprives a person of their liberty and detained against their will under the Mental Health Act (1983, as amended 2007) placing them in hospital. In 2015 over 1,450 young people were detained in secure settings at any one time; 300 were detained in secure mental health settings (NICE, 2011). Young people in secure setting are mainly detained either on remand or following sentence from a secure youth justice setting or alternatively detained under the Children's Act (2004) on welfare grounds.

Working within a Medium Secure Forensic Child Adolescent Mental Health Service (FCAMHS), a counselling psychologist would simultaneously focus on psychological and criminological psychology. That is, understanding not only assessment and treatment of mental health but also criminal behaviour, and combining both to alleviate distress, improve coping and ultimately reduce future recidivism and risk. Medium secure services operate within practices and policies which comply with standards and requirements produced by Quality Network for Inpatient CAMHS (QNIC), CQC and the Mental Health Act Code of Practice. The governance ensures that young people access safe, effective patient-centred services of high quality to address their problems safely and with dignity. Care is underpinned by legislation such as The Human Rights Act (1998), applied equally to young people in custody, eliminating discrimination and promoting equality.

A secure setting provides a safe environment to manage high risk and challenging behaviours appropriately. Care and treatment offered is a highly prescribed set of physical, relational and procedural security measures where young people are unable to leave enforced by physical measures. The Mental Health Act (2007) includes the law which governs the compulsory treatment of people who have a mental disorder. In practice, young people within the

DOI: 10.4324/9781003159339-15

Youth Justice System (YJS) are entitled to individualised, multi-disciplinary and evidence-based treatment. The government initiative, Future in Mind (Department of Health and NHS England, 2015, p. 15), promoted the need for 'improved care for children and young people in crisis, so they are treated in the right place, at the right time and as close to home as possible'. Most young people receive community-based care; however, some require intensive specialised inpatient care.

The skills required

The acquisition of a wide and varied range of generalised competencies are common to all psychologists and essential for practitioner psychologists. 'Competencies' are elements of competence that are observable, measurable, containable, practical, derived by experts, and flexible (Stratford, 1994). The core competencies, skills, and attitudes across different domains include carrying out assessment and formulation to inform diagnosis and treatment recommendations. The counselling psychologist would deliver psychological intervention and provide training and clinical supervision as a core competency (Falender et al., 2004).

Counselling psychologist's need to be scientifically minded, able to access and apply current scientific knowledge to facilitate evidence-based practice and interventions. The role of a counselling psychologist, according to BPS (2006, p. 14), is to apply core competencies to facilitate the following:

> Commitment to reducing psychological distress and enhancing and promoting psychological well-being through the systematic application of knowledge delivered from psychological theory and evidence.

Building on core competencies gained during doctoral training and placement is essential for all counselling psychologists involved with both mental health and criminal forensic arenas. Additional skills are gained through forensic placements, training or, as in my case, applying for a specialist role due to keen interest but without prior experience and through practice and application acquiring the necessary advanced knowledge and skills.

Developing a good understanding of judicial systems is essential for providing advice to mental health tribunals, crime analysis and when working within the boundaries of their competencies as an expert witness evidence for court.

A counselling psychologist would be expected to recognise that their personal moral beliefs and values may negatively influence professional relationships. The importance of being a competent self-reflective practitioner cannot be underestimated: reflective supervision helps to develop skills and competencies and cultivates an interpersonally sensitive style of engagement.

Counselling psychologists must work within the limits of their education, skills, training and professional experience, working in a manner that does not undermine the civil rights of the young person. Within this setting, working with young people in crisis and their families, the expectations and challenges of the role cannot be underestimated. However, every day is an opportunity to learn and grow both professional and personally, the work is intellectually stimulating, and it is extremely rewarding to witness the remarkable ability of humans to recover.

Assessments

Psychological assessment is an essential skill for most practitioner psychologists, providing the foundation for working with young people at risk to self or others and reoffending. Counselling psychologists regard the interview as an assessment technique that is central to their professional identity and a vital job function. A comprehensive assessment enables the clinician to understand the function, underlying process and impact of challenging behaviour.

The use of standardised tests provides projective assessments of personality and cognitive functioning; these can include semi-structured interviews, personality tests, psychometric assessments to test cognitive functioning and vocational interest, and brief scales to assess specific symptomology. Counselling psychologists within a psychiatric setting often use a standard battery of assessments to make up a uniform set of instruments with which psychology colleagues can develop proficiency and the multi-disciplinary team develop familiarity.

Gathering background information on young people helps to influence care, describe symptoms and level of current functioning, learn history related to the presenting problem, and refine the Diagnostic and Statistical Manual of Mental Disorders (DSM-5) diagnosis. Counselling psychologists working within a secure environment employ a 'needs and risks' approach rather than a purely diagnosis-led approach. They utilise assessment and procedures to obtain diagnostic information shared by the multi-disciplinary team (MDT) to facilitate individually tailored interventions and care plans. Counselling psychologists believe in the uniqueness of each individual; this philosophical rationale guides the use of assessment techniques to collect data on a range of cognitive and affective attributes – in practice, helping to gain an understanding of how each young person thinks, feels and acts.

Employing evidence-based measures helps to assess and gather information concerning a wide range of presenting issues, including: offending, violence, harm to self or others, assault, murder, sexual violence, stalking, crime, theft, drug dealing, arson, malignancy and lying. In addition, it helps to identify any challenges faced outside or within the secure setting and evaluate mental health and level of risk. The counselling psychologist requires an understanding of how the systems within the secure setting relating to procedural and relational security psychologically impact the young person. The assessment process is in itself therapeutic, enabling the young person to feel safe enough to begin to facilitate change. Ultimately the assessment process helps the young person gain insight into and knowledge about their own behaviour, enables accurate behaviour prediction and is an opportunity to strengthen the therapeutic relationship. The assessment helps the psychologist develop the insight into their client's world that enables them to guide and advise the MDT, family and young person.

The challenges of the role

The role of counselling psychologist within a forensic setting is complex, and not for the faint-hearted. The secure environment enables urgent treatment for complex young people presenting with the highest levels of risk of harm to self and others, including those who have committed significant crimes. The work involves managing and treating young people presenting with acute mental and behavioural disturbance, including neurodevelopmental disorders requiring a specific specialist inpatient service. General adolescent care settings are unable to meet the needs of high-risk young people requiring a secure setting to understand, address and meet their idiosyncratic needs. Young people who have a forensic history and mental health needs present a unique challenge to those who care for them, as they often have co-morbid disorders. Some of these are unrecognised for long periods due to difficulties in carrying out comprehensive assessments (Barlow & Turk, 2001).

A counselling psychologist requires specialist skills to work with this client group within the prescribed stringent levels of physical, relational and procedural security. They face challenging situations, including their young clients having their autonomy restricted – through physical restraint or seclusion to mitigate harm – or having to therapeutically engage a young person during the midst of a 'dirty protest'. Secure services deliver care which places primary importance on behavioural approaches, de-escalation and the psychopharmacological treatment of mental illness. Violent and aggressive behaviours are proactively managed to enable swift recovery from episodes of ill health or following injury, preventing young people dying prematurely. Services have facilities for the management of young people who require periods of care in seclusion, but separation from the main patient group can often create a barrier to engagement.

With all young people admitted to a secure setting, resisting engagement and disengagement is expected due to trust and attachment issues. The counselling psychologist may feel deskilled or overwhelmed at such times; however, maintaining the therapeutic relationship is essential for the provision of a time-limited intervention to support recovery. Care is guided by the care programme approach (CPA) process, providing multi-disciplinary evidence-based treatment. Counselling psychologists carry out the assessment of needs, formulation and risk, providing the basis for the care package. This will also involve collaborating with the young person and family/carers in decision-making that reflects the young person's wishes and aspirations. Supporting a young person's autonomy may conflict with restrictive approaches practised within a secure environment. It is essential to ensure as far as possible that the young person has a positive experience of care as enhancing their quality of life will have long-term benefits.

The range of roles within a forensic setting

Experts in human behaviour, counselling psychologists assume a diversity of roles within mental health secure services. It is expected that they undertake the full breadth of widely varied activities, including (but not limited to): providing psychological and psychosocial assessment and evidence-based interventions to young people, their families and groups; acting as advisor to the treatment team and providing training and support. Counselling psychology brings with it a variety of roles and responsibilities, and to maintain these roles and responsibilities, frequent self-reflection is required, facilitated within a supervisory relationship.

A crucial aspect of the counselling psychologist's role is 'interagency working' both internal and external to the secure setting – for example, working alongside the YJS to support the decision-making process regarding access to, accountability and discharge from the secure setting. The MDT integrates the expertise of a range of professional bodies, including psychiatry, psychology, child and adult services, occupational therapy, education, the local authority, the court system and advocates. Having awareness of the diverse range of clinical disciplines is central to meeting the young person's holistic needs; however, they may hold opposing views. Medical staff are rarely ready to identify or, of course, address psychological difficulties (Layard, 2005). Supporting collaborative working helps to address inequality, resolve conflict, improve communication and provide targeted interventions. The team is in place to assess, plan and manage care jointly, including supporting the family from the impact of their child's detention. Counselling psychologists are responsible for the behavioural and psychological aspects of treatment – providing assessment, formulation and treatment to understand and reduce psychological distress, as well as solutions to manage challenging behaviours, benefiting both the young person and staff.

Counselling psychologists are specially trained in consultation, acting as advisors or consultants to the treatment team of a young person's care; they provide information regarding the psychological well-being of the patients (BPS, Division of Counselling Psychology, 2007), but also offer specific recommendations that will assist medical staff. Counselling psychologists are highly skilled to engage the young person, MDT and the families; this may be both daunting and rewarding. The counselling psychologist ensures the family remains involved where appropriate in every aspect of the young person's care.

Integrating the young person's social support system into the care can be instrumental in a positive prognosis.

A counselling psychologist has the core skills sufficient to apply for jobs in forensic services – I was informed everything else could be learned. However, additional reading, training and, ideally, securing a trainee placement or volunteer post within adult or young people's service areas would equip you to work within this setting.

The therapeutic relationship

A central task of the counselling psychologist is the ability to establish a personal connection. The therapeutic relationship – that is, the shared agreement and emotional bond between therapist and client (Bordin, 1994) – is essential. Treatment interventions may be interpersonal in nature: 'it is incumbent on the therapist to facilitate the provision of an environment in which the child is permitted free expression' (Harper, 1994, p. 167).

Carl Rogers, founder of person-centred psychotherapy, described three necessary and sufficient core conditions for a successful therapeutic relationship to facilitate change: unconditional positive regard (UPR), empathy and congruence (or genuineness). UPR provided by caregivers during the early years of life can help contribute to feelings of self-worth as people grow older (Bozarth, 2013). Accepting that the young person is doing the best they can and born with the potential to develop in positive, loving ways (Rogers, 1961). Empathy and genuineness are crucial for the counselling psychologist to relate to another wholeheartedly and with understanding: 'if you are willing to enter his private world and see the way life appears to him, without any attempt to make evaluative judgments, you run the risk of being changed yourself' (Rogers, 1961, p. 283).

The elements of the therapeutic relationship considered effective have been investigated, and common therapeutic factors include empathy and collecting client feedback (Norcross, 2014). The counselling psychologist demonstrates a genuine interest in the young person as a unique individual, relating in ways that are sensitively tailored to their specific needs. This attunement is an effective way to form healthier, more secure attachments in order to make sense and feel the full pain of our story (Siegal, 2012). The focus is on the psychological health of the young person, rather than merely diagnosing and treating symptoms. Cultivating a responsive therapeutic relationship can be emotionally demanding; therefore, self-care and supervision are essential to mitigate against vicarious trauma. The counselling psychologist needs to enhance and build specific therapeutic skills to cater for a different range of needs, as the range of influences on young people's lives means that they are vulnerable to periods of disengagement from interventions (Cooper, Sutherland & Roberts, 2007).

A task force by the American Psychological Association's (APA) Society of Clinical Psychology set out to identify empirically supported treatments and found that the 'therapy relationship makes substantial and consistent contributions to psychotherapy outcome independent of the specific type of treatment' (Norcross, 2014). The therapeutic engagement may allow for 'a period of malleability during which there may be the opportunity to enable the development of positive identities' (McNeill, 2006, p. 133). It is through the quality of the relationship formed, that real progress can be made to reduce future offending.

Ethical and legal considerations

The majority of young people in secure environments are detained either on remand or following sentence from a secure youth justice setting or detained under the Children's Act (2004) on welfare grounds. Legislation such as The Human Rights Act (1998) is applied equally to young people in custody to eliminate discrimination and promote equality. Young people within the YJS are entitled to individually focused treatment. The legislation indicates the responsibilities of social, education, health and mental health services to care for young people who offend and holds these services accountable. The following significant factors concerning ethical and legal concerns have been considered.

Confidentiality

A counselling psychologist may encounter an array of ethical issues related to practice and protecting a young person's rights, which could be challenging, especially regarding confidentiality and the proper use of psychological information (Hudson-Allez, 2000). Confidential information is only shared with members of the MDT and the young person. Access to information is on a need-to-know basis, to disclose only that information which is necessary to achieve the purpose of the disclosure, and then only to people required to have that information (NHS England, 2016). The counselling psychologist has a duty to share any concerns related to risk of harm to self or others. Ethical considerations arise, especially concerning developing a therapeutic relationship where the young person can feel comfortable, safe, valued, respected and free to share their story. It is important to be very clear about confidentiality and its limits when commencing a new counselling relationship (Mitchell, Disque & Robertson, 2002).

Informed consent

The counselling psychologist should remain aware of the importance of informed consent, mindful that the young person is most likely to benefit from therapy when they enter the child-counsellor relationship voluntarily – that is, with their informed consent (Bond, 1992).

The counselling psychologist determines if the young person has the cognitive and emotional ability to understand the nature of, and decide about, the counselling relationship (Lawrence & Robinson Kurpius, 2000). It is important to provide young people with the opportunity to understand the counselling service being offered (BPS, 2009). Despite detention, they have the option of declining psychological services, after a discussion about its purposes, aims and restrictions. Young people deemed to be competent to make their own decisions, known as 'Gillick competent', can legitimately request that parents and family members are not involved in or informed of any aspect of their care.

Family members collaboration

The young person is understood within context and, as a result, ethical issues may arise. The counselling psychologist often needs to update the young person's family, as working in collaboration with family members is frequently critical for the treatment (Bennett, 2000).

Engaging with the wider team

Consulting with the young person to explain why consulting with or gathering information from the wider team such as schools, doctors, children's services and other professionals is important in order to maintain trust and safety.

Boundaries and power imbalance

The counselling psychologist has a responsibility to maintain appropriate and consistent boundaries that define the therapeutic relationship as a professional one. These include time, place, and the frame during the session, and appropriate touch (Gutheil & Gabbard, 1993). Ongoing self-reflection and supervision are essential for cultivating a safe and supportive environment for engagement and helping to identify and limit any power imbalance. To mitigate against dependency or becoming directive, the child-adult relationship should be young person led.

How the philosophy of counselling psychology is maintained

Established within the humanistic movement, counselling psychology holds a distinct philosophical position, acknowledging the strengths and resources of individuals at all levels of psychological functioning. The humanistic position represents dynamic ways of understanding human experience as well as creative ways of conceptualising and connecting the humanistic narrative and cognitive behavioural, existential and psychoanalytic theories. Counselling psychologists understand people from a non-judgmental viewpoint as 'relational beings'; it is this conception of the human which informs the way counselling psychologists practise – that is, they adopt a strongly relational stance (Cooper, 2008) in order to cultivate democratic, non-hierarchical client-therapist relationships and bring about meaningful change.

Counselling psychology as a discipline is understood to be a social science; however, the National Health Service in 2019 produced recent legislative changes resulting in a drive towards evidence-based interventions. Moving away from a more experiential approach in therapeutic decision-making towards the use of research may pose a challenge to the counselling psychologist's identity, activities and roles. Counselling psychology is concerned with engagement, subjectivity, inter-subjectivity and beliefs, with an explicit focus on a humanistic value base. For either the reflective or scientist practitioner, or both, this is often at odds with the empirical-positivistic approach.

Reflective practitioner

A reflective practitioner approach considers, and analyses, how the interaction within the therapeutic relationship impacts on the psychologist's and client's experience. The quality of the therapeutic relationship is central to the identity of the counselling psychologist as a collaborative helper reflecting upon their practice in supervision.

Scientist practitioner

A scientist practitioner approach considers competing ideologies which inform both research activity and clinical practice, conceptualising their practice in relation to research. It involves keeping up to date with research findings that have a 'research-orientation in their practice, and a practice relevance in their research' (Belar and Perry, 1992, p. 72). A counselling psychology philosophical orientation favours a holistic approach, prioritising the personal, subjective experience of the young person over and above notions of diagnosis from an expert. However, this can be challenging within settings where conceptualisations of 'sickness' and associated labels that align with the concept of mental illness prevail. The goal of therapeutic engagement is to help the young person arrive at a meaningful, cohesive life narrative rather than endeavour to fit their experiences into theoretical models. The task is for both scientific and reflective activities to be reconciled with the values underpinning the counselling psychologist's philosophy of practice associated with phenomenological and humanistic concerns (Rogers, 1961). This in addition to skills of empathic listening and reflecting essential to good practice – but in fact these skills define the practice of science within a psychotherapeutic context.

Personal reflections

A counselling psychologist's philosophical position as derived from a humanistic stance holds, as Carl Rogers states, that the conditions a young person requires for creating a growth-promoting climate where they can move towards their full potential are congruence, unconditional positive regard and empathy (Rogers, 1957). However, this approach can be challenging due to the focus on risk reduction, which often results in medical treatment interventions and detention against the young person's will. The counselling psychologist must understand the aetiology of offending behaviours that led to the young person's loss of liberty. On admission, young people are in crisis, making engagement difficult for the most competent counselling psychologist due to risk and challenging behaviours, attitude and mistrust.

Working with young people who mistrust can be challenging: the dilemma is whether to refer to a different clinician or continue knowing that any effort I make will be rebuffed. But providing the young person with a different experience in itself is therapeutic. It is understood that developmental trauma as a consequence of significant adversity during childhood can repair as a result of therapeutic engagement. The young person needs to be understood from an intrapersonal, interpersonal stance in order to facilitate developmental reparation towards long-term resolution.

Within a secure setting, the counselling psychologist spending time with the MDT is essential to promote positive collaborative working, mitigate against opposing views and support the unification of the team. The young person's worldview is shaped within the context of a family system, often driven by a need to survive or defend against harm by those positioned to protect. Some young people detained may be beyond self-preservation, perceiving no other option than suicide and therefore needing protection from themselves. Supervision and self-care are essential in mitigating against becoming overwhelmed, deskilled or burnt out.

A counselling psychologist needs to be both scientific and reflective practitioner to maintain a holistic position. The young person requires effective, evidence-based interventions; however, intervention to address developmental trauma requires an idiosyncratic approach facilitated by the therapeutic relationship. Although assessment is central to the professional identity of counselling psychologists, the incremental utility of assessment in counselling has not been established. Counselling psychology therefore needs to adopt scientific procedures for evaluating the efficacy of assessment techniques and practices. However, Goethe highlights the tendency to oversimplify the scientific practice, and science assumes we need a mediator, and views human subjective experience itself as the measure for change (Nisbet, 1972). This role can at times be challenging: patience, flexibility and trust in a gut instinct helped a young person who initially presented as relentlessly oppositional to finally yield. She informed me after weeks of non-engagement, 'Janice, the reason why I like you is that every time I tell you to fuck-off you keep coming back', and from then we worked closely and effectively.

The complex needs of the young people involved make it essential to merge the scientific and reflective practitioner approaches when working within a medium secure forensic setting. Despite the significant contribution of counselling psychology, few work in forensic medium secure settings. Working within a medical setting can be challenging, demanding and highly complex, and practitioners may feel under-resourced; however, specialist skills and knowledge can be quickly built upon to establish a very competent framework. Counselling psychologists will meet daily challenges; however, it is undoubtedly an environment for intellectual, personal and professional growth and development. Working with young people within secure settings, counselling psychologists have a lot to offer and a lot to gain.

References

Barlow, F. & Turk, J. (2001). Adolescents with learning disability and psychiatric illness: Two case reports. *Clinical Child Psychology and Psychiatry*, 6(1), 125–135. doi:10.1177/1359104501006001010.

Bordin, E. S. (1994). Theory and research on the therapeutic working alliance: New directions. In A. Horvath & L. Greenberg (eds), *The Working Alliance: Theory, Research, and Practice* (pp. 13–37). Wiley & Sons.

Bozarth, J. D. (2013). Unconditional positive regard. In M. Cooper, M. O'Hara & P. F. Schmid (eds), *The Handbook of Person-Centred Psychotherapy & Counselling* (pp. 180–192). Bloomsbury.

BPS (British Psychological Society) (2006). Discussion paper: Subject benchmarks for coaching psychology. www.bps.org.uk/sites/www.bps.org.uk/files/Accreditation/Clinical%20Accreditation%20Handbook%202019.pdf

BPS (British Psychological Society) (2009). Code of Ethics and Conduct. BPS.

BPS (British Psychological Society), Division of Counselling Psychology (2007). Professional practice guidelines. BPS.

Cooper, K., Sutherland, A. & Roberts, C. (2007). *Keeping Young People Engaged*. YJB.

Cooper, M. (2008). *Essential Research Findings in Counselling and Psychotherapy: The Facts are Friendly*. Sage.

Belar, C. D. & Perry, N. W. (1992). The national conference on scientist-practitioner education and training for the professional practice of psychology. *American Psychologist*, 47(1), 71–75.

Bennett, S. & Bennett, J. W. (2000). The process of evidence-based practice in occupational therapy: Informing clinical decisions. *Australian Occupational Therapy Journal*, 47, 171–180.

Bond, T. (1992). Ethical issues in counselling in education. *British Journal of guidance and Counselling*, 20(1), 51–63.

Gutheil, T. G. & Gabbard, G. O. (1993). The concept of boundaries in clinical practice: Theoretical and risk-management dimensions. *American Journal of Psychiatry*, 150(2), 188–196. https://doi.org/10.1176/ajp.150.2.188.

Department of Health and NHS England (2015). Future in mind: Promoting, protecting and improving our children and young people's mental health and wellbeing. chrome-extension://efaidnbmnnnibpcajpcglclefindmkaj/viewer.html?pdfurl=https%3A%2F%2Fassets.publishing.service.gov.uk%2Fgovernment%2Fuploads%2Fsystem

%2Fuploads%2Fattachment_data%2Ffile%2F414024%2FChildrens_Mental_Hea
lth.pdf&clen=1729426&chunk=true.

Falender, C. A., Cornish, J. A. E., Goodyear, R., Hatcher, R., Kaslow, N. J., Leventhal, G., ... & Grus, C. (2004). Defining competencies in psychology supervision: A consensus statement. *Journal of Clinical Psychology*, 60(7), 771–785.

Gillick v West Norfolk & Wisbech Area Health Authority (1985). UKHL 7 (17 October) from the British and Irish legal Information Institute (BAILII) website.

Harper, P. (1994). A spectrum of psychological therapies for children. In P. Clarkson and M. Pokorny (eds), *The Handbook of Psychotherapy* (pp. 158–171). Routledge.

Harper, R. & Hardy, S. (2000). An evaluation of motivational interviewing as a method of intervention with clients in a probation setting. *British Journal of Social Work*, 30, 393–400.

Hudson-Allez, Glyn (2000). What makes counsellors working in primary care distinct from counsellors working in other settings? *British Journal of Guidance and Counselling*, 28, 203–213.

Human Rights Act (1998). HMSO.

Lawrence, G. & Kurpius, S. E. R. (2000). Legal and ethical issues involved when counseling minors in nonschool settings. *Journal of Counseling & Development*, 78 (2), 130–136.

Layard, R. (2005). Mental health: Britain's biggest social problem?http://eprints.lse.ac.uk/id/eprint/47428.

NICE (National Institute for Health and Clinical Excellence) (2011). NHS evidence: Evidence in health and social care. www.nice.org.uk.

NHS England (2016). Confidentiality policy. www.england.nhs.uk/publication/confidentiality-policy/.

McNeill, F. (2006). A desistance paradigm for offender management. *Criminology and Criminal Justice*, 6(1), 39–62. doi:10.1177/1748895806060666.

Mitchell, C. W., Disque, G. J. & Robertson, P. (2002). When parents want to know: Responding to parental demands for confidential information. *Professional School Counseling*, 6, 156–161.

Nisbet, H. B. (1972). *Goethe and the Scientific Tradition*. Institute of German Studies.

Norcross, J. C. (ed.) (2011). *Psychotherapy Relationships That Work: Evidence-based Responsiveness* (2nd ed.). Oxford University Press.

Norcross, J. C. (2014). Conclusions and recommendations of the Interdivisional (APA Divisions 12 & 29) Task Force on Evidence-Based Therapy Relationships. June. https://societyforpsychotherapy.org/evidence-based-therapy-relationships/.

Rogers, C. R. (1957). The necessary and sufficient conditions of therapeutic personality change. *Journal of Consulting Psychology*, 21, 95–103.

Rogers, C. R. (1961). *On Becoming a Person*. Houghton Mifflin.

Siegel, D. J. (2012). *The Developing Mind: How Relationships and the Brain Interact to Shape Who We Are* (2nd ed.). The Guilford Press.

Stratford, R. (1994). A competency approach to educational psychology practice: The implications for quality. *Educational and Child Psychology*, 11, 21–28.

Section 3

Beyond healthcare

Chapter 15

Counselling psychologist as expert witness in family courts

Mark Bradley

Working as an expert witness in the courts is a challenging area of work. As a counselling psychologist, we can be called upon to give evidence in court as a professional or expert witness. The following chapter provides an overview of what this role entails, our responsibility to the court, the challenges and benefits of the role and the many opportunities for personal and professional growth. This chapter also aims to provide information with regard to the structure and formality of the court. More importantly, to reflect on what we as counselling psychologists have to offer the court in assisting with decision making regarding the lives of vulnerable people.

The chapter focuses primarily on working as an expert witness in family courts, which is where my experience mainly lies. However, broad themes discussed throughout the chapter are likely to be applicable to other courts, including criminal and civil. It is useful to provide a brief illustration of the court structure at this juncture.

Types of court

Courts in the UK have evolved over centuries and mostly comprise family courts, county courts, magistrates' courts and the High Court. There is also the Court of Appeal and the UK Supreme Court. Family cases can be heard in either a family court or, with more complex cases, the High Court. Trials for civil cases are mostly heard in a county court – for instance, cases involved in personal injury, clinical negligence and many other civil matters. The Crown Court is concerned with serious criminal offences which are indictable.

What is an expert and your legal responsibility?

Psychologists of all disciplines can be called upon to give an opinion and to disseminate psychological knowledge in a range of different settings, and the courtroom is one of them. However, there are a number of unique challenges within the court arena, which remains an adversarial environment. Psychologists have a range of skills and technical knowledge that can assist the court

DOI: 10.4324/9781003159339-16

make decisions about people's lives. However, the challenges inherent in the formality of the court process may deter psychologists from undertaking expert witness work.

As counselling psychologists we can be called upon to give evidence in court as a professional witness and expert witness. Professional witnesses are generally formal employees of one party and are responsible to the court in the same way as an independent expert witness is (BPS, 2016). However, as a professional witness there is always the possibility of bias due to the potentially conflicting nature of your responsibilities vis à vis the court and your client – particularly if you are providing treatment for the client. You can be asked by court to produce records or to give evidence in person.

There is a distinction between professional witness and expert witness. As an expert witness, your role ought to be much clearer and nonpartisan. The BPS (2016, p. 3) define an expert witness as follows:

> An expert is a person who, through special training, study or experience, is able to furnish the Court, tribunal or oral hearing with scientific or technical information which is likely to be outside the experience and knowledge of a Judge, magistrate, convenor or Jury.

Many types of expert provide evidence in court. However, an expert witness has a very specific role within the confines of their expertise. Professionals who put themselves forward as an expert do so on the basis of their knowledge within their field and area of specialism. It is not necessary to be an expert in the court process, and there has to be a first time for every psychologist when undertaking court work.

Counselling psychologists may be reluctant to undertake expert witness work due to the adversarial nature of court and feeling like an imposter within the process. However, it is important to remember that professionals in court are not qualified or experienced in your area of specialism, and you are there to give an opinion on the basis of your experience and clinical expertise. All expert assessments and opinions are underpinned by a declaration and statement of truth, which must be stated at the end of your report.

The specific content of this declaration may change in the future, but you will be notified of any changes within the letter of instruction received from the solicitor. Furthermore, if changes are to be made, these can be found in the Family Procedural Rules Part 25 and Practice Direction 25B (Gov.uk, 2021, May 17).

Prior to undertaking any court report, it is important that you familiarise yourself with the Family Procedure Rules Part 25 and Practice Direction 25B. Essentially, an expert's overriding duty is to the court, which takes precedence over any obligation to the person from whom the expert has received instructions or by whom the expert is paid. It is the primary duty of the psychologist to provide an independent opinion to the court through their objective, unbiased nonpartisan opinion about matters within their expertise. The key term here is 'independent', with no allegiance to any party.

The family court

The family justice system exists to help families avoid disputes as far as possible and to enable disputes between parents in the case of private law and between parents and local authorities in public law. Private cases are disputes that involve parents and concern their children – for example, in divorces or separations, who the children should live with, who they should see, where they should go to school or even if they can move to live abroad with one of their parents. The cases can also involve grandparents and other relatives. Public work is the term used for cases when local authorities take action to remove children from their parents' care because they are being hurt in some way. Such cases can lead to children being adopted, and this is also dealt with by a family judge.

Unlike criminal courts, family courts are slightly less adversarial, although challenges still exist. Your overriding duty is to assist the judge in these proceedings to make a decision in the best interest of the children. This latter point is key as it is all too easy to be swayed by the interests of parents given their own distress and specific needs. Ultimately, while you are instructed to provide a professional opinion on matters relevant to the court, the final decision-making rests with the judge, who is required to consider all of the evidence, including that of other professionals involved, and make a final judgement. The expert's job is to advise, the court's job is to decide, and your evidence forms part of the jigsaw which the judge puts together to form an overall opinion. Finally, it is important to remember that your role is to assist the court make a decision alongside other available evidence. While there may be instances when it is difficult to give an opinion, it is important that as far as possible you do not sit on the fence and that you give an opinion independent of the view of other professionals involved. The mandate of the court is to prioritise the child's welfare as the paramount consideration (Children Act 1989 s1 (1)).

Psychological assessments for family courts

The assessment is dependent upon what you have been specifically asked to consider by the court. More broadly, for family-based assessments, as with most standard psychological assessments, this may include documenting a person's understanding of the court process and reason for assessment, including usual assessment information and psychometric testing (where appropriate). Redar, Duncan and Lucey (2003) and Scaife (2013) provide an excellent overview of the assessment process and issues to consider during the course of the assessment. Essentially, we draw upon a range of evidence to formulate, provide opinion and make recommendations to the court.

Throughout the assessment, it is essential that we form our opinion on the evidence rather than seeking evidence to support our opinion. There is a clear difference between the two. In expert witness work, there is often a risk of confirmation biases within assessments – for instance, paying less attention to facts and evidence that do not support your whole proposition. The consequences of confirmation bias can be extremely serious, as demonstrated by the Cleveland Report, which was the response to a series of expert findings that led to 97 children being placed in care that were later discredited.

While questions that you may be required to answer when assessing families can be very specific, relating to matters that are of interest to the court, there are some broad similarities, which might include the following:

a   Please undertake a psychological assessment of the children/parents focusing upon their cognitive functioning, intellectual, educational, emotional, social and behavioural development and comment on any matters of concern.

b   Please comment upon the children's/parents understanding of their current situation.

c   Please comment upon any harm the children may have suffered in respect of her psychological, intellectual, educational, emotional, social and behavioural development and assess what the cause may be.

d   Please consider the children's relationships with their parents. Please can you consider what work could be completed to improve the difficulties in the relationship and whether such work could be beneficial?

e   What work or therapy may assist the children with any problems identified within your assessment? Please can you also identify timescales and how support may be accessed?

f   Does parent have, whether in their history or presentation, a disorder or emotional difficulty and if so, what is the diagnosis?

g   How does the above affect parent's functioning including their personal relationships?

h   What are the experiences/antecedents/aetiology which would explain their difficulties, if any (taking into account any available evidence base or clinical experience)?

i   If the need for treatment is indicated, what is the nature and likely duration?

j   What is the parent's capacity to engage in treatment/therapy?

k   Are you able to indicate the prognosis for, timescales for achieving and the likely durability of positive change?

l   If such treatment or therapy is suggested where might such treatment/therapy be provided or sourced from?

Obviously, these questions may differ somewhat depending on the issues at hand, but in my experience this is a fairly typical set.

The above questions are contained in what is referred to as a 'Letter of Instruction' (LOI). Amongst many things, the LOI stipulates who is to be assessed and when the report is to be completed and served to the court. The latter is known as the filing date, and the report is emailed to the lead solicitor for distribution. It is likely that upon submission of the report, the matter proceeds without the need for you to attend court. It is not unusual to receive additional questions in order to clarify in writing any matters that still need to be addressed, in an attempt to resolve any issues without the need for either a final hearing or giving evidence in person.

Counselling psychologist as expert

A counselling psychologist's role is to assist the court by undertaking comprehensive assessments that include developmental, psychological, social, relational and neuropsychological issues in complex situations through the application of psychological formulation (BPS, 2016). Comprehensive assessments require the interweaving of scientific principles with reflective practice and rely upon the application of a broad range of psychological theories and principles to specific contexts.

As stated by the BPS (2016, p. 4), 'the focus on dimensional rather than categorical approaches allow for the evaluation of strengths, weaknesses, capacity for change and potentially useful interventions'. For instance, the focus ought to be on formulation, taking a broad approach to understanding the needs of vulnerable people across time and the systemic factors that contribute to the issues being addressed. Diagnostic issues can be commented upon as may be expected by the court, but it is also important to help the court understand a person's journey beyond any given diagnosis.

Furthermore, while not exhaustive in relation to the role of counselling psychology in the court process, evidence may be required to evaluate specific or multiple issues such as mental health, behavioural and emotional functioning; mental capacity; neuropsychological functioning (e.g. memory, attention, executive functioning); personality functioning; the impact of substance misuse and/addiction; learning needs; psychological impact of disability; and psychological impact of trauma and/or abuse. Our role as expert may also include an understanding of interpersonal relationships, capacity for change, and personal developmental and therapeutic needs, on which we are well positioned.

There are personal and professional challenges in accepting and embracing this role as expert. First, the notion of expert challenges core humanistic principles and values that underpin our work as counselling psychologists. Expert witnesses broadly hold power in claiming knowledge and experience, for which they are paid. Counselling psychologists whose values are rooted in humanistic traditions may wish to hold on to a central position of equality within the relationship. Counselling psychologist as expert witness in court proceedings challenges our fundamental philosophy and the values that underpin our profession. While there is an inherent difference within the relational dynamic when compared to traditional therapeutic work, the aim is still to work in an anti-oppressive way and to tell the client's story as sensitively and respectfully as possible. For example, although our role is to assist the court in decision-making in the best interests of the child, it is also an opportunity to provide the court with an understanding of a parent's history and consider their individual therapeutic needs.

When undertaking expert witness work, you are provided with a court 'bundle', which is a file of court documents detailing all of the assessments that have been undertaken to date. This file includes a chronology of events, minutes of child protection conference minutes, medical records, social worker reports and any other information relevant to the case. It is rare that a parent's story is told in a therapeutic and sensitive way, which is understandable given the more immediate concerns regarding risk.

Undertaking assessments for court on parenting capacity opens up opportunities to share the parents' story of the challenges they have faced in their own lives and to consider what support may be helpful to them. While your opinion may well be for the children to be placed outside the family home, it is important that your assessment and formulation is balanced and reduces the shame already experienced by the parent. It is not uncommon for parents involved in care proceedings to have been exposed to trauma in their own lives – for instance, via domestic violence, substance misuse or mental health problems. Borrowing from the trauma-informed approach to emotional distress and following on from the basic tenet of the Power Threat Meaning Framework (BPS, 2018, p. 304), emotional distress and troubling behaviour are understandable when viewed in the context of adverse life experiences, interpersonal relationships, life events and social circumstances. As an expert witness, such a position inevitably situates you in a position of power, in which the client is to disclose their inner world while sitting with the fear of being judged by a professional they have never met before.

Counselling psychologists are particularly skilled at developing therapeutic and working alliances with clients. This is a challenge in court work given the potentially oppressive nature of the relationship, the speed at which assessments need to be undertaken and the need to remain nonpartisan throughout the process. It is essential that we work hard to be non-oppressive and to encourage parents and children to tell their story. This is obviously difficult given the potential consequences of open disclosure. In cases of alleged neglect and abuse, there are a range of factors that underpin defences mechanisms that are often deployed, leading to conflicting accounts provided at interview. The way in which you formulate and understand the position of the other is therefore challenged by these conflicting accounts, and it remains the case that we have to be consistently sensitive and mindful of the impact of their own adversities on their parenting capacity.

Ultimately, it is our role as counselling psychologists to undertake an assessment with the purpose of informing a decision regarding the safety and welfare of a child and whether or not children should be left in the care of their parent or parents. There are therefore inherent challenges with regard to the relationship with those being assessed – you are, after all, assessing their fitness to occupy a parenting role (Scaife, 2013). One way is to be constructive in your formulation and to focus on strengths from which parenting skills can build. The aim of building relationships within family-based assessments is to reduce shame and associated anxiety as much as possible, notwithstanding the inherent challenges.

From the therapy room to the court

Making the decision to carry out work for the court is often a difficult process and can trigger a great deal of apprehension and reflection. During our career, it is not uncommon to oscillate between self-confidence and self-doubt, ambition and anxiety, inner drive to procrastination. Stepping outside our comfort zone is a challenge.

So, what does the process look like and what would be helpful to know? First, becoming an expert witness means that you have some knowledge and understanding of psychological functioning within a specific field that is different to that of a layperson or professional from a different field. It doesn't mean that you are an expert in the formality of court proceedings and or that you have more expertise than any other psychologist working in a similar field. It simply means that you have the experience and knowledge to assist the court in gaining a better understanding of an individual's psychological functioning. With that in mind, let's go through the basic steps that might take you from therapy room to court.

The circumstances that may require you to give evidence in person

A party may challenge an expert's report by asking them to come to court and give evidence and answer questions on their report in person, which is known as a cross-examination. Questions asked of an expert in cross-examination might be aimed at showing:

- That the expert has not had or read all the relevant information and that this has undermined or affected their opinion or recommendations.
- The expert may have misunderstood some fact or explanation and that this has undermined or affected their opinion or recommendations.
- That they have misapplied or misused statistics or research, or that they have missed something important out of their report or analysis, and that this has undermined or affected their opinion or recommendations.

- That they have not carried out a test or done something they ought to have done before offering an opinion and that this has undermined or affected their opinion or recommendations.
- That they have not been fair or thorough in their work and that this has undermined or affected their opinion or recommendations.
- That they have not considered all options and that this has undermined or affected their opinion or recommendations, or that their recommendations generally can't be relied upon, perhaps for one of the reasons explored above (lack of independence, inaccurate representation of an interview, etc.).

Alternatively, they might be asked to reconsider or update their recommendation in light of some change of circumstances or new information. Or similarly, to further assist the judge in thinking through the case in person.

Going to court

It is the first image that comes into the mind of a psychologist when they contemplate offering their services to the court, and the last thing they think about the night before the court date arrives.

When accepting an instruction from a solicitor, you may be asked to set aside up to three days in order to attend a final hearing on a specific date, should this be required. However, you will be notified in advance if you are required to attend or not, and which day from the three days you set aside. You will not be required to attend for the full three days, at least not in my experience. Furthermore, while giving evidence may require you to commit to a full day, much of this will be spent sitting outside the court room. The length of time giving evidence can be anything from an hour upwards.

Before we get to that bit, let's walk through what happens beforehand. First, similar to airport security, you are searched upon arrival before being allowed to enjoy the experience of the court process. Courts vary in size and there is often a notice board in the foyer listing the cases being heard on that day and which court you are to attend. You are often asked to attend half an hour beforehand, whereupon you sit and wait outside the courtroom before being called to give evidence. Quite often the parents you have assessed will occupy the same space, which can be uncomfortable – particularly if your recommendations are for the children to be removed from their care.

Eventually, parents and counsel (solicitors) enter court and you are left with your own thoughts, waiting to be called in. After being called, you will be directed toward the witness box, whereupon you will see a file containing the same case papers that you were given to prepare your report. The judge is not in the court at this point but will have the various solicitors present. Typically, there is a solicitor for each parent, the local authority solicitor and the solicitor representing the children appointed by a guardian. Solicitors typically sit in the front row, with parents and social worker involved in the case behind. In family courts, solicitors, referred simply as 'counsel', and the judge do not wear wigs.

The case file will be open at your report and the court official will approach you beforehand to confirm whether you wish to take an oath or make an affirmation that your evidence is true. The oath is a religious commitment whereas an affirmation is non-religious.

At the point at which the judge enters the court, you and those in attendance must stand until permitted to sit. This is the time when you stand or sit, as is your preference, exuding effortless confidence, banishing all self-doubt – or at least that is the theory. You will first be asked by the lead solicitor representing the children to confirm your name, professional address and qualifications and that the signature on the report in front of you is your own. You will also be asked if the opinions stated in your report remain the same or have changed. As a side note, you may on occasion be served with additional documents or information upon your arrival for you to read prior to going into court that you may not have previously been made aware of. Upon reading this information, this particular question becomes more relevant.

The questioning from counsel then begins, which may initially start with the local authority or parent's counsel. Family proceedings are typically regarded as non-adversarial and therefore more inquisitorial, at least insofar as the court is concerned. However, for psychologists and experts more generally, it may still feel adversarial as the nature of cross examination is to test the expert's opinion on the basis of the evidence and to represent the view of their client.

A few basic points in relation to giving evidence should be made here. It is important that your opinion remains consistent unless your opinion has changed on the basis of new evidence presented to you. Furthermore, it is important that you are not tempted to talk about matters which fall outside your areas of expertise. It is also important that when answering questions, you direct your response to the judge or magistrate. A judge is to be referred to as 'Your Honour', whereas a magistrate is referred to as 'Sir' or 'Madam'. In the High Court and Appeal Court, judges are referred to as 'My Lord' or 'My Lady'.

It is also helpful if you do not engage in a two-way conversation with counsel and that you position your body in such a way that you are half turned towards the judge for ease. When asked a question, turn and face the lawyer, and when they have finished give your response to the judge. You will notice that the judge and other parties will be typing and making notes as you go along; it is therefore important that you talk slowly before turning back to receive the next question.

Giving evidence in court is not a natural thing to do and it can take years before you feel wholly confident and skilled. It is not uncommon for experts giving evidence to feel anxious, and the court understands that this is not your natural environment and makes allowances. It is important to be honest, clear and concise and not make use of psychological jargon in an effort to disguise your anxiety or compensate for feelings of insecurity. There is also no microphone in the hearing to amplify a witness's voice, so the witness needs to pitch their voice appropriately. You are usually positioned near the judge, so there should be no problem hearing your evidence.

The court always ask that you arrive between thirty minutes and an hour beforehand, and it is essential that you take this as an instruction rather than a polite request. You also need to be dressed smartly in formal attire. Turn off your mobile phone – this goes without saying, of course, but things do happen. Finally, in preparation, reread your report and the court bundle.

After hearing your evidence, you are then given permission to leave the court by the judge at which point, you thank the judge and before leaving the court, turn and bow. You should also bow when the judge enters or leaves the court at any point.

Summary

In summary, engaging in court work can be challenging, yet it is a rewarding area of practice for counselling psychologists. The challenge of this work helps further develop your analytical skills and your ability to be cross-examined. While this can feel daunting, you already have the skills to assess and formulate as these are integral to your existing role. Counselling psychologists are well positioned to help vulnerable individuals share their story and to disseminate psychological knowledge across a broad mix of professionals. While you may not be experienced in a court setting, you may well be very experienced as a psychologist, and your opinion may well be crucial in assisting the court make life-changing decisions in the best interests of children.

Finally, the court takes your opinion more seriously if you are balanced and reflective in your assessment, highlighting positives and strengths while remaining confident in your opinion, particularly if the opinion is one in which the children are to reside outside of the family home.

References

BPS (British Psychological Society) (2016). Guidance on the use of psychologists as expert witnesses in the Family Courts in England and Wales (standards, competencies and expectations). www.bps.org.uk/news-and-policy/psychologists-expert-witnesses-guidelines-and-procedures-england-wales-scotland.

BPS (British Psychological Society) (2018). The Power Threat Meaning framework: Towards the identification of patterns in emotional distress, unusual experiences and troubled or troubling behaviour, as an alternative to functional psychiatric diagnosis. www.bps.org.uk/sites/bps.org.uk/files/Policy%20-%20Files/PTM%20Main.pdf.

Great Britain & Masson, J. (1990). *Children Act 1989*. Sweet & Maxwell.

Family Procedure Rules Part 25 and Practice Direction 25B. www.justice.gov.uk.

Ministry of Health and successors (1987). Inquiry into Child Abuse in Cleveland: Report and papers. Her Majesty's Stationery Office, London.

Redar, P., Duncan, S. & Lucy, C. (2003). *Studies in the Assessment of Parenting*. Routledge.

Scaife, J. (2013). *Deciding Children's Futures: An Expert Guide to Assessments for Safeguarding and Promoting Children's Welfare in the Family Court*. Routledge.

Chapter 16

Working in independent private practice

Helen Nicholas and Daisy Best

Introduction

This chapter focuses on the potential career benefits of working in independent private practice (referred to throughout as 'private practice') as part of a portfolio career. It includes the development of a business idea and reflections on incorporating the 'businessperson' into our counselling psychology identity. Considerations around the therapeutic setting and the challenges have been included, in addition to legal and ethical considerations.

Based on our experience, we highlight the importance of building and maintaining networking connections with colleagues, marketing consistently and appropriately, and having proper regard for self-care and self-awareness.

A rationale for private practice

The British Psychological Society (BPS) Division of Counselling Psychology (DCoP) audited members across the UK in 2019 and found that approximately 56% of those surveyed were working in 'independent' practice. This includes those who are self-employed, directors of their own company or running a social enterprise where the counselling psychologist gains income from this as opposed to working for a private or public organisation.

Many counselling psychologists are attracted to 'portfolio careers' where you can work in a range of settings – for example, private practice *with* NHS employment or an academic role. A 2016 DCoP survey revealed that 53.7% of respondents work less than 0.5 whole-time equivalent in their primary roles and concluded that this may be explained by the preference for portfolio working. Private practice offers the flexibility to manage your own time and choose both the work that you undertake and, to some extent, the therapeutic approach(es) you work from, in addition to high earning potential. With privately paying clients, you may have the flexibility to work both short and long term and choose the diversity of the clients you work with, such as age range and presenting issues. This is likely to appeal to the humanistic philosophical position of counselling psychologists where client autonomy is a foundation

DOI: 10.4324/9781003159339-17

of their work. Choice about when to work and where to work from can enable your practice to fit around other commitments, which offers the potential for enhanced life satisfaction.

Conversely, the challenges of private practice include the risks, associated with any business, that are beyond our control – such as the number of referrals received, the reduced financial security associated with running a business and the lack of institutional support, which may leave you feeling isolated and exposed. Furthermore, marketing your business involves marketing yourself, as you are the 'service', and this requires time, commitment to maintain and refine your marketing strategy and confidence in what is provided and to whom.

For some, private practice can be viewed as providing an elite service for clients who can afford therapy, therefore, the implication is that counselling psychologists are gaining from richer members of society. This may appear to go against the ethical and moral values of being a psychologist. However, not all therapy is provided by those who are paying for it themselves as many will access treatment through health insurance or referral companies. Additionally, people who have the means to pay for therapy may have a preference for choosing who they access therapy from. The authors know countless examples of people who have been dissatisfied with lengthy NHS waiting lists or services that are not flexible enough to accommodate their preferred time for an appointment, therapeutic approach or required number of sessions. Furthermore, there remains a stigma for some about their medical records including reference to psychological therapy, and for this reason they prefer to access therapy privately.

Identity

Importantly, when first establishing a psychological therapy business, as a counselling psychologist you need to consider the focus of your business in terms of what you will offer. This is often in line with your own identity as a counselling psychologist and, dare we say, as a businessperson as well. You may have chosen to provide therapy; work as an expert witness; carry out clinical assessments; develop training courses; or provide a wider range of consultancy services. Whatever you decide to focus on, you will need to consider where your referrals will come from. Your training, experience, knowledge and skills may determine the type of therapeutic business you want to establish, taking into consideration your identity as a counselling psychologist. This can be a starting point in establishing the client group you would like to work with, the setting in which you would like to work, and the therapeutic approach(es) you choose. Working within your competencies and area of specialism ensures adherence to the requirements of the HCPC standards of proficiency (HCPC, 2015) and the BPS code of ethics (BPS, 2018).

Thinking of yourself as a businessperson may not come easily for you. Some counselling psychologists struggle with the financial aspects of running a business. Balancing the commercial interest and ethical responsibility, can be a challenge. Referrals can come from employee assistance programmes, health insurance companies and medico-legal services, as well as from private individuals. You will need to decide what your cancellation policy is or what to do when clients do not attend scheduled appointments. It is useful to reflect on your business boundaries and your views on the effect of charging/not charging on the therapeutic relationship. If the 'therapeutic relationship is considered to be the main vehicle through which psychological difficulties are understood and alleviated' (BPS, 2019, p. 6), then missed sessions or non-payment for session might have an impact on the relationship and you will need to consider how you will handle these situations.

Even if you struggle to consider yourself a businessperson, it is important to engage in a process of reflection about what this means so that you can consider and appreciate your transferable skills in networking, communication, independence and creativity. Ultimately, as identified by McMahon, Palmer and Wilding (2005, p. 48), 'Every business has a range of products or services … . Your business is no different.'

Building it

Aims of the business

As counselling psychologists, we may not want to consider the financial benefit of our work as a priority, yet when self-employed or a director of our own limited company, we may rely upon this as our main source of income. Financial gains need to be a vital aspect of business planning, including what you hope to gain in the way of financial renumeration.

It is important to consider what you hope to achieve in addition to financial gains. Consider what your reasons are for setting up in private practice, what it is that has created this motivation and what you want the end result to look like. One of the authors identified the wish to have more time at home, a more flexible working pattern, choice about her workload plus a specific, minimum income per year.

This is also the time to consider your target market. The target market may be related to age (children and adults), presentation (trauma, anxiety, mood disorders and chronic conditions) and source (self-referrals, healthcare companies, employers).

While considering your short (next three to six months), medium (next six to twelve months) and long-term (next twelve months to five years) plans, focus on 'Business Contingency Planning'. This might entail building your business while salaried, considering potential conflicts of interest and possible tax implications. During the COVID-19 pandemic from 2020, both authors had to move from providing in-person sessions to remote/online therapy sessions. This presented them with the need to adapt how they were working, and it also gave them the chance to consider new ways of working. Business contingency planning includes considering all the potential risks to the business and ways to mitigate against them. Risks may include another psychologist setting up a business in the same building, and ways to mitigate this might be, for example, working with them to identify strengths, areas of interest and skills/expertise and consider referring to each other.

Type of business

It is helpful to explore the pros and cons with a trusted accountant of being a company limited by guarantee or a sole trader. Sole traders carry all the financial risks associated with a private practice, however, it is easier to set up as a sole trader, and the legal, accounting and taxation requirements are less complicated (Weitz 2006). With a limited company, the business (rather than the person) owns the assets, and the company is registered as a limited company, which may inspire public confidence. Some organisations will only refer to you if you are a limited company.

Unique selling point

This is not about what counselling psychologists more broadly can offer but what you can offer based upon your skills, training, target audience, personal qualities and favourable payment terms. It can be a challenge to view ourselves as a commodity in this way, but at some point this offer will need to be communicated to others so now is the time to begin considering this. Imagine you are presenting yourself in thirty seconds, what would you say? What is your unique selling point?

Legal requirements

Consider here the business insurance that is required specifically if you are running the business from home as basic house insurance does not usually cover business use. Some residential buildings have restrictive covenants which means that the land is not allowed to be used for business activity. Professional indemnity insurance needs to be maintained, ensuring that you are covered for self-employment and considerations must be made to ensure compliance with General Data Protection Regulation (GDPR) and the Information Commissioners Office (ICO).

When you choose to accept referrals from rehabilitation services and insurance companies, they become your debtor. You will most likely be offered a contract to sign that outlines the terms and conditions of your business arrangement. This will include key factors such as payment terms. If they have not adhered to their terms of payment, you may have to pursue legal action and can claim your outstanding fee together with interest (see debt recovery and legal legislation in useful resources). Some insurance companies and legal sectors have payment terms 60–90 days after treatment or settlement of the case, which would affect your cash flow.

Logistics

Now that the focus of the business has been identified, it is time to begin putting all of those creative ideas into action. First, you need to consider a name for your business that reflects you or the location from which you practice. You can check the companies house register to ensure that your preferred name does not already exist. You can practice as a sole trader or in partnership or you may wish to register your company. Here are some of the potential set-up and running costs to consider.

Branding

Consider what your brand will be. Some counselling psychologists benefit from the input of a brand and/or website designer who can help with branding, website design and social media channels. You will need to think about what you want to convey in the imagery that you use alongside the name of your business. Ensure that your design(s) are not going to contravene copyright laws and consider the costs associated with your brand being designed by someone else. It is advisable to get a quote and to have a clear outline of what is included in the quote.

Website

It is advisable to set up a website that will help promote your business. Both authors have business websites where they provide information about their qualifications, the types of clients they work with, their approach to therapy, the cost of sessions and the location of their practice. It is worth considering becoming a member of local or national organisations that promote psychologists as this will help to increase the visibility of your services. Some organisations charge a fee for this.

Accounting

Unless you plan to submit your own tax return through the HMRC self-assessment tax return system, you may want to employ an accountant. For limited companies, your accountant will also need to submit your accounts to Companies House. You can reduce costs by keeping a monthly record of your invoices including all expenditure and income. Another option is to employ a bookkeeper or administrative person to organise your expenses and invoices for you. It will all depend on your own confidence levels, preferences and abilities. The same legal and financial rules apply regardless of the number of clients on your caseload, but if you are unsure, always consult a registered accountant. Ultimately, it is your responsibility to ensure that adequate and separate financial records are maintained.

The world of tax can be challenging. It is useful to know that all income is generally taxable apart for specific expenses that are allowable. Such expenses include office costs (stationery or phone bills), travel costs (parking, fuel, public transport fares), staff costs, bank and insurance charges, business rates, advertising and professional services (administrative staff, bookkeeper) and professional registration (BPS, HCPC). You will also need to contribute to national insurance and usually pay two types of national insurance (class 2 and class 4) as a self-employed individual, which is determined by your profit. The HMRC website (www.gov.uk/self-employed-national-insurance-rates) has a wide range of essential information that is useful for business owners. If you complete a self-assessment each year, the HMRC helpline staff are also available to talk you through the online form or any questions relating to your self-assessment.

Organisations

All counselling psychologists need to be registered with the HCPC in order to use the title 'counselling psychologist' and/or 'practitioner psychologist'. Many also choose to be members of the BPS as a chartered psychologist. If you are processing and/or storing personal data, you will need to register with the Information Commission's Office (ICO) and pay an annual fee. Personal data relating to others must be securely stored in accordance with the UK General Data Protection Regulation (GDPR).

Supervision

Factor in the cost of supervision in order to maintain your competencies. It is advisable to identify a supervisor with sufficient expertise in the nature of your work – for example, someone experienced with medico-legal assessments and reports if you are engaging in this work.

Therapy room

If you have decided not to rent a therapy room you will have additional set-up costs for office furniture such as a table, chairs and a desk. Ongoing costs for tissues, cleaning products, wear and tear of furniture need to be taken into consideration. Some counselling psychologists prefer to rent a room, where all the bills are included in the rental cost. If you are working out of a room in your home or in an owned therapy space, you will need to think about your expenses. Many of these are tax deductible and may include office equipment such as a computer, printer with a scanner function and stationery.

Both working from your own serviced office and renting a room by the hour have advantages and disadvantages. One author rents a serviced office in a building shared with other non-psychology businesses. The building has a reception area, disabled access (including a lift) and serviced toilets. The office is a rental so in the event the owners decide to sell the building or change its function, this office space could disappear. A legally overseen rental agreement ensures tenancy rights and a sufficient notice period for all parties, which can help in such circumstances. Renting a room that enables you to have flexible access (evenings and weekends) may also be important depending upon your chosen working pattern.

One author of this chapter has a purpose-built annexe on her property from which she offers private therapy. The advantages of this are that there are no rental costs, there is long-term security, she can access it at any time of day, and she doesn't need to commute to work. The challenges are that you need to ensure you find a way to keep your home life and work life separate, also that clients will know where you live which removes some of the privacy often associated with a therapeutic relationship. Bor and Stokes (2010, p. 31) consider how clients might experience us based upon our home environment as they 'will naturally project ideas, beliefs and feelings onto us about the kind of person we are based on the physical environment that they encounter'. This is perhaps something to be mindful of when considering what your clients will experience as they enter your property.

Importantly, wherever you practice from, you need to ensure that you have adequate space and privacy and that your clients have access to a toilet. You also need to ensure that your premises are accessible both for clients with disabilities and in terms of your location. Finally, your office needs to feel like a place that is suitable for therapy: comfortable and welcoming.

Working online

This chapter was written at a time when there was a worldwide lockdown due to COVID-19. Many counselling psychologists had to adapt their practice to either include remote working or – at least at times – be exclusively remote working. A wide variety of platforms became increasingly popular at that time – for instance, Zoom, Vsee, and Skype – with many focusing more on increasing their security and privacy policies. Some platforms charge a monthly fee for an upgraded system or to have more than one attendee on the call. For example, if you see couples for therapy (either co-habiting or in separate homes), provide group supervision or offer group peer networking, then this would apply to you.

Marketing

Once your business has been set up, you will need to establish yourself in the market, regardless of whether you are building your private practice over time, working in another setting or setting up straight after training. The influence of social media channels has grown exponentially and even though some counselling psychologists may feel uneasy about promoting themselves, it is essential in private practice. It is important to remember that you are running a business and may well choose to work with external companies such as psychological health referrers, insurance companies and, if you carry out expert witness reports, then solicitors: they all need to be able to locate you, and often very swiftly.

Target market

Think about who would access your services and where they might look. This may require some work in terms of learning what is already being offered and the gaps your service might fill. Consider who your competitors are and find out what services they offer. Follow them on LinkedIn, look at their websites, read their social media posts and consider what they offer that you don't and vice versa. It is worth networking with other private practitioner psychologists, who are more than likely willing to share ideas and experiences.

Where to market your practice

Social media networks can facilitate connection with your target market. Your marketing strategy may include publishing blogs or articles about subjects of interest. These can showcase your knowledge and experience to others as well as offering something of interest to your anticipated followers.

As a chartered member of the BPS, you can be listed in the Directory of Chartered Psychologists, and some clients may locate you via the HCPC register. You can also register with expert witness societies if providing this type of work and you can register with employee assistance programmes (EAPs), rehabilitation, private healthcare and personal injury companies. There are specific organisations that promote therapists and psychologists for a fee, and you can advertise your services through their website.

Networking with other businesses, as well as psychologists, can be a useful way to share with and learn from others. Most regions will have networking groups for small businesses, though some do charge a fee. When networking via social media or in person, consider that the importance of building relationships is the same in business interactions as it is with client work. Going in with a 'hard sell' is usually off-putting and tends to be viewed in a negative way. Getting to know people, listening to them and sharing ideas is a better way to build long-lasting relationships.

Marketing your practice

Ethical practice must always be at the foundation of how we work and marketing your private practice is no different. Be mindful of marketing yourself in an honest way and avoid making false promises, offering promotions or generating potential discontent in those who read your materials by headings such as 'Are you unable to cope with life at the moment?'. Be professional in all of your communication and promote what you offer in a genuine and honest way. Both authors are transparent in their communication of qualifications, experience, location and fees.

Self-care, resilience and staying connected

Work-life balance

One of the difficulties that private practitioners may face is their own barriers to self-care. For example, taking annual leave potentially means that no income will be received in that time period. Finding a work-life balance that suits you is essential, but this can be a struggle at times, especially as a businessperson working in a helping profession. You may experience pressure to take on additional clients or may find it difficult to say 'no' when your caseload is full. Some counselling psychologists feel guilty when declining work requests or taking time off for themselves. If this is you, then you may want to consider establishing a network of colleagues who you can refer clients to when your caseload is full, and they can do the same for you.

Carrying a case load that is manageable for you is important. You will need to decide whether you offer appointments during specific days, at certain times, in the evening and/or on weekends. This may mean working outside of 'office hours' or offering clients early morning sessions to fit in with their working day. Setting appropriate boundaries with your time can be challenging – for example, if you offer evening appointments, the demand for these may outweigh the availability. This can challenge the flexibility of your boundaries.

Staying connected

Part of your continuing professional development (CPD) as a counselling psychologist may be networking with other practitioners and being involved in peer consultation. There are a number of groups that can be found on social media, for example, the BPS special group for independent practitioners. Part of staying connected may be through supervising other counselling psychologists. Counselling psychologists take on a number of leadership roles such as mentoring, supervision, forming networking groups, training and collegial support. It is important to keep up to date with practice guidelines, changes in policies and the latest evidence-based research in order to practice competently. In private practice, counselling psychologists will often focus on an area of specialism or an area that is of personal interest to them. This may mean that you undertake additional training. You will need to pay for any conference attendance, workshops, courses and events yourself.

In private practice it is more difficult to carry out research unless you have links with a university or can collaborate with university colleagues. Some private practitioners secure associate lecturing contracts with local universities where they may teach on undergraduate and post graduate courses. Having this flexibility to engage in a wide range of areas benefits both your clinical work and your research. This links well to the philosophy of counselling psychology and the emphasis placed on practice-based and evidence-based knowledge.

Benefits and challenges of private practice

What we enjoy

Independence. With independence comes greater choice. Choice of client group, size of caseload, therapeutic approach with clients and range of work (for example, therapy, supervision, training, consultancy, expert witness).

Flexibility. There is greater freedom to work within the clinical hours set by you. This may mean that your clinic could work around other commitments, such as family, CPD and personal appointments. Therapy sessions are likely to be weekly; however, there is the opportunity to also offer fortnightly and monthly appointments.

Building the business you want. The freedom to create a business that best suits your skills and specialist area, working towards your strengths and areas of interest.

Freedom. No institutional procedures/limitations to work within and no manager monitoring your performance.

What can be challenging

Potential lack of collegial connection. Unless you join or belong to a networking group, being in private practice can be a solitary experience. This may not suit everyone.

Annual leave and sickness absence. If you don't work, you don't get paid. Although you can take out insurance to cover sickness.

Funding CPD events. Responsible for your own CPD, which means paying for workshops, courses and events. This is tax deductible as an expense to the business.

Tax. Tax planning and submitting self-assessment tax returns can be a challenge. You need to keep on top of daily invoices, payments, and business expenses.

Cash flow. Chasing outstanding invoices and the additional administration time this takes. Late payment affects your cash flow.

Reflections

Imagine you are going to set up your own practice.

- Where would it be?

- What would it be called and why?
- Where would you receive referrals from?
- Who would you work with – children, couples, families?
- What would be your areas of specialism?

Conclusion

This chapter has provided an introduction to counselling psychologists who are interested in establishing and maintaining an independent private practice. The work is varied and offers the option of more flexible working that being employed by others may not always provide. Creating links with a variety of routes to referral, having a sound marketing strategy and establishing a good support system helps make this a very financially viable, flexible, interesting and rewarding way of working.

Useful resources for practitioners:

BPS practice guidelines (English and Welsh versions) – www.bps.org.uk/news-and-policy/practice-guidelines.

BPS special group for independent practitioners – www.bps.org.uk/member-microsites/special-group-independent-practitioners/publications.

BPS (retrieved on 22 November 2020 with reference to 2016 survey) Careers in counselling psychology. chrome-extension://efaidnbmnnnibpcajpcglclefindmkaj/viewer.html?pdfurl=https%3A%2F%2Fwww.bps.org.uk%2Fsites%2Fwww.bps.org.uk%2Ffiles%2FMember%2520Networks%2FDivisions%2FDCoP%2FDr%2520Masrita%2520Ishaq%2527s%2520presentation%2520on%2520Careers%2520in%2520Psychology-Counselling%2520Psychology.pdf&clen=1365200&chunk=true.

BPS (2018) Employment support for counselling psychologists. ID2288 DCoP employment support v4.pdf.

BPS Research Digest – The 100+ most followed psychologists and neuroscientists on Twitter! https://digest.bps.org.uk/2015/11/06/the-100-most-followed-psychologists-and-neuroscientists-on-twitter/.

Debt recovery and legal legislation – www.gov.uk/late-commercial-payments-interest-debt-recovery.

Standards for the accreditation of doctoral programmes in counselling psychology – www.bps.org.uk/sites/www.bps.org.uk/files/Accreditation/Counselling%20Accreditation%20Handbook%202019.pdf.

References

Bor, R. and Stokes, A. (2010). *Setting Up in Independent Practice: A Handbook for Counsellors, Therapists and Psychologists*. Palgrave Macmillan.

BPS (British Psychological Society) (2018). Code of Ethics and Conduct. Retrieved from www.bps.org.uk/sites/www.bps.org.uk/files/Policy/Policy%20-%20Files/BPS%20Code%20of%20Ethics%20and%20Conduct%20%28Updated%20July%202018%29.pdf.

BPS (British Psychological Society) (2019). Standards for the accreditation of doctoral programmes in counselling psychology. Retrieved from www.bps.org.uk/sites/www.bps.org.uk/files/Accreditation/Counselling%20Accreditation%20Handbook%202019.pdf.

HCPC (Health and Care Professions Council) (2015). HCPC standards of proficiency for practitioner psychologists. Retrieved from www.hcpc-uk.org/standards/standards-of-proficiency/practitioner-psychologists/.

McMahon, G., Palmer, S. & Wilding, C. (2005). *The Essential Skills for Setting Up a Counselling & Psychotherapy Practice.* Routledge.

Weitz, P. (2006). *Setting Up & Maintaining an Effective Private Practice.* Karnac.

Chapter 17

Working as a counselling psychology lecturer in higher education

Motivating, evolving and challenging

Daisy Best

The following chapter will provide an overview of working as a lecturer within UK higher education (HE) institutions, with a specific focus on the teaching of the doctorate in counselling psychology. It is informed by my 12 years as a senior lecturer, including several years as the programme director of a doctorate in counselling psychology in England. The chapter will cover the context, relationships, leadership and personal reflections.

There are currently 13 Health and Care Professions Council (HCPC) approved programmes for the taught doctorate in counselling psychology across the United Kingdom. Programmes require HCPC approval in order for trainees to be eligible to apply for registration once qualified. Programmes can also obtain British Psychological Society (BPS) accreditation, and while this is considered to be good practice, it is not essential.

Professional standards and guidance

While programmes are individualised in terms of therapeutic approaches, the structure and delivery of doctorates and the BPS qualification in counselling psychology have to meet the same standards in order to achieve continued approval by the HCPC and accreditation from the BPS. The HCPC specify standards that all approved programmes must meet to provide eligibility for 'the learner to meet standards of proficiency for their profession' (2017, p. 1). Programmes are required to submit an annual monitoring declaration of how the HCPC standards are met. More specifically for practitioner psychologists and psychology protected titled professions are the HCPC (2015) Standards of Proficiency for Practitioner Psychologists that outline the requirements for trainees to achieve competencies as a psychologist.

The BPS (2019) provides an accreditation requirements and standards document that must be demonstrated by BPS accredited programmes. The standards include the design of the programme including content such as ethical and legal aspects while emphasising the role of the process of accreditation as a partnership.

DOI: 10.4324/9781003159339-18

The Quality Assurance Agency for UK Education (QAA, 2018a) has developed a quality code which provides 'fundamental principles' for all HE providers to ensure that expectations are clearly defined and quality is ensured in order to protect the public and students. More specifically, 'advice and guidance' has been written for research degrees that includes an outline of the research environment, support and communication for doctoral trainees (QAA, 2018b). To summarise, all documents detailed are important when designing and delivering a doctoral programme in counselling psychology within a UK HE institution.

The roles of a lecturer

Teaching

Despite the job title, the teaching aspect of lecturing is usually a smaller role within the overall workload of a lecturer. Teaching on the doctorate in counselling psychology usually begins at Level 6 (masters level) before moving to levels 7 and 8 (doctoral level), so the standard expected is high and preparation for lectures cannot be rushed. Lectures are not usually limited to theoretical concepts but include practical application with an ethical and legal underpinning, so this needs to be considered when designing taught sessions. Trainees need to grasp complex concepts while also developing a critical, applied understanding; hence, pedagogically informed lectures tend to be didactic and discursive.

Having worked alongside other counselling psychology lecturers, I have witnessed those who I believe to be more successful in the role and consider the following to be some of the vital elements. Thorough preparation for teaching is essential because trainees ask probing questions. Understandably, they want value for money so require evidence that the teaching has been carefully planned and is clearly aligned with the philosophy of the programme. Lecturers need to be prepared and sufficiently well acquainted with the subject matter to communicate information with confidence. We want to inspire trainees to learn more, beyond what we deliver, and a good foundation will enhance their engagement. Ultimately, the students will have their own definitions of what constitutes a good lecturer, so obtaining regular feedback is essential.

We need to be cognisant of the fact that we are role models for counselling psychology and, therefore, our values and ethics need to be visible to those we teach. Consistency, fairness, kindness, encouragement, congruence and clarity are helpful when responding to learners who may be unsure and anxious despite being also curious and determined. Trainees need to feel safe enough to ask questions or challenge ideas and concepts (Wood & Su, 2017). We cannot encourage critical thinking if we do not allow them to rehearse that with us. This also means that we must be open to feedback and make suitable changes where feasible within the scope of the standards and institutional protocols. We also need to be creative in how we deliver our taught sessions to ensure maximum engagement, with consideration for varied learning styles and potential learning difficulties such as dyslexia.

A sound ability and willingness to deliver material digitally is required. This may include teaching online, providing discussion groups for the sharing of information and ideas or digital methods of assessment. Digital learning has escalated because it provides a flexible, accessible mode which can be balanced with face-to-face relationships and the setting up of interactions where skills can be practised.

Finally, we want to aim to inspire our trainees to be as good as they can be and to further their passion and interest. Our own enthusiasm for the subjects we are teaching needs to be evident, and this will often come from our knowledge and the sharing of our clinical experience. Trainees always like to hear how knowledge can be synthesised into real life application, so pursuing opportunities to do this can only enhance their learning and motivation. Lecturers who are also experienced clinicians have a lot to offer.

The Office for Students (OfS, 2019) have developed the Teaching Excellence Framework (TEF) which rates universities on their teaching quality from Bronze to Gold based upon various metrics. Teaching excellence is based upon the quality of teaching, the environment in which students are taught and the outcomes for students, including employability. Engagement with the TEF is on a voluntary basis. When assessing what is meant by teaching excellence, indicators such as this can provide you with an idea of what external assessors are looking for.

Pastoral support

As adult learners, trainees may feel anxious about studying new concepts as they become more aware of what they don't know. This process of learning and not knowing has been described by Grand (2006) as 'painful' and 'unsettling':

> To be an adult is to know, to be authoritative. To have to learn is to be in a position of inferior strength. It is also a position of potential anxiety. Not knowing can feel and actually be problematic. But above all is the social anxiety of not knowing, of having to learn, of not being able to adopt the surety of authority and closure.
>
> (p. 169)

As most trainees have studied relentlessly to secure a place on the doctorate, they are likely to be motivated to become qualified, and this can be synonymous with experiencing a high level of pressure to succeed. Furthermore, the financial and time commitment involved can place additional pressure, leading to feelings of anxiety that may become difficult to manage. One of the lecturer's roles is to 'contain' this anxiety through information, boundaries and support. Lecturers are usually given specific personal tutoring support time to do this. While this is not therapeutic support, the relationship that builds can result in the lecturer gaining insight into the trainee's personal and professional development needs. Trainees will often disclose personal information about themselves and care has to be taken to deal with this sensitively while abstaining from entering into a therapeutic role. A good knowledge of institutional student support services for onward referral is vital.

Research

It is our duty as lecturers to lead by example and being an active researcher and scientific practitioner is important. Research can add value to the work we do as counselling psychologists, and also contributes to our research-informed teaching.

Working as lecturer on a doctorate in counselling psychology will usually mean that you either become a director of studies (lead supervisor) or part of a research supervisory team supporting the trainees. This is different from clinical supervision as the focus is upon the creation and completion of a research project.

Research supervision should help emphasise the trainees' role as autonomous learners and contributors while encouraging them towards topics that are relevant to counselling psychology. Topics need to be original and outward-looking, with, ideally, broad, international impact. The Research Excellence Framework (REF, 2021) emphasises the importance of research having 'impact beyond academia', and counselling psychology research is well placed to deliver this. Developing research ideas should be collaborative and trainees should feel adequately challenged so that they develop their research question and methodology with confidence, sufficiently to defend in a viva voce examination.

One of the challenges of working in an HE environment is the expectation that lecturers hold all of the knowledge on all of the topics. It is important to only teach or support research that is within your own area of specialism/experience, and to be comfortable enough to acknowledge what you don't know. Conversely, resource limitations may require you to teach topics and modules that you are less familiar with, but this can be managed with good planning, transparency regarding your limitations and direction to further reading.

Assessment

Trainees' work is continuously assessed throughout the programme, and often we are first or second markers/moderators for other modules. Trainees will be guided by the assessment criteria and learning outcomes or objectives as we are when marking. We will also have doctoral-level criteria outlined by our institution to follow, which helps us understand what a trainee needs to include to achieve a specific mark. This provides a structure for marking and enables us to ascertain the most appropriate mark to be awarded for each piece of work.

Internal and external moderation processes ensure quality assurance; however, failing a student is never easy and can be difficult for all concerned. Clear feedback that helps trainees understand what they did well and how they can improve in the future is always helpful in terms of facilitating their understanding and improving confidence. There have been occasions in my experience where there is evidence that a trainee would be an excellent therapist but does not have the capability to reach the academic level required. None of us want to fail a trainee, but neither do we want to pass someone who hasn't met the required competencies as our duty is to protect the public. Support from the team can be helpful here.

Throughout the programme, trainees are also being assessed for their suitability for the profession while on placements. Programmes engage in placement visits to assess the trainees' engagement and to ensure the placement is meeting the trainees' development needs. It is also important that we are aware of any potential fitness to practice issues – such as plagiarism, falsifying information or breaching confidentiality – that may have arisen on placement or are evident via other assessments (HCPC, 2009).

HE institutions are usually supportive of our involvement as an external examiner for other HE institutions. This is viewed favourably as it is seen as a way to exchange knowledge and identify areas of good practice. Universities pay external examiners directly, and this is generally viewed as acceptable practice even if carried out in work time.

Employability and knowledge exchange

It is anticipated that trainees of professional counselling psychology programmes will automatically apply for work as counselling psychologists once they graduate. However, it is the responsibility of programmes to support trainees to consider their future careers when identifying, for example, placements and research topics. In addition, preparation for their future career should include a focus upon professionalism and ethics and trainees should be made aware of the HCPC (2009) guidance. Employability can be enhanced with exposure to guest lecturers who work as counselling psychologists in a range of contexts and consideration of other job roles such as supervision of others, leadership and audit/evaluation.

It is a lecturers' role to be involved in the promotion of the counselling psychology profession to undergraduates at applicant open days or undergraduate psychology programme events that focus upon employability.

Universities have a commitment as part of the Knowledge Exchange Framework (KEF) (UK Research Innovation, 2021) to provide consultancy or training to external organisations in order to increase income for the institution and engage with the public and community. Counselling psychology trainees are very well suited to this and programmes could contribute to this within their institutions.

Administration

Perhaps one of the most time-consuming aspects of the role of lecturer is the administration involved, which includes an abundance of emails. Trainees will mostly communicate via this method and all emails and any other notes are subject to the same UK General Data Protection Regulation (UK GDPR) that pertains in any psychology role. It is good practice to respond in a timely way to emails, keep secure records of meetings with trainees and clearly outline where such records will be kept. Administrative time will also be used to design the curriculum, develop teaching materials and write references for trainees' placement providers or employers.

Leadership

There are many leadership opportunities within HE. Aside from the various committees within the institution where we may represent a department/faculty – for example, an ethics committee or academic board – there are other day-to day-opportunities.

Lecturers are likely to be involved in the recruitment and selection of trainees and with training other staff members. Training in recruitment, selection and staff induction is required alongside a comprehensive understanding of the importance of diversity being reflected in the cohort of trainees and the staff team who teach them (McIntosh, Nicholas & Huq, 2019).

Most programmes will provide opportunities to lead on specific aspects – for example, research and placements. This will involve liaison with organisations external to the institution, enabling the promotion of counselling psychology and enhancing our knowledge and teaching. Networking with other applied psychologists and allied health practitioners can bring richness to the programme as they can directly support our trainees' learning and development.

Research grants or research projects require leadership skills as you may recruit research assistants or lead research projects. I secured a BPS grant for a research project and employed a research assistant. In addition, we offered trainees the opportunity to carry out research for their thesis on the theme of our research project but with different client groups in order to ensure a broader impact. As a lead on research projects, we may manage budgets and people, liaise with external agencies and develop quality, impactful outputs including dissemination via conferences and peer-reviewed publications.

Module leadership requires the lecturer to ensure that there is constructive alignment between the teaching activities, what students are expected to learn (learning outcomes) and how students demonstrate this learning (assessment). Module leaders also have responsibility for developing the module guide or equivalent, responding to queries about the module content and assessment.

Some fundamental differences between lecturing and therapy as a counselling psychologist

Boundaries within our therapeutic work such as session times, the environment and confidentiality are important. Supervision enables us to reflect upon our own issues and experiences in relation to the client. As a lecturer, boundaries are still important, and we need to avoid dual and multi-relationships. We need to assert clear boundaries in terms of submission dates for assessments and time keeping, yet we do not have a formal space in which to discuss our relationships with trainees and how these impact on us. Discussions of this sort are likely to take place informally with colleagues.

The relationship is hugely important in our therapeutic encounters for the client to feel safe, and we know that at some point the relationship will come to an end. As a lecturer, the relationships develop in a different way because we know we are working towards becoming future colleagues, so the aim is something more equal – post-graduation, the relationship may even become a friendship. I have made some wonderful friendships with trainees once they became colleagues. Also, when I work therapeutically, I limit the amount of personal disclosure that I offer verbally to my clients and consider carefully the benefits to them. With trainees, I have disclosed much more about my values, experiences and how I work as I believe it is important for them to be able to engage in an open dialogue. I have always viewed myself as a role model, whose duty is to be transparent.

Confidentiality is different for a lecturer compared to working with a client, where information shared remains confidential (with some exceptions such as risk, for example). Information about the development of trainees on the programme is not usually shared with external organisations but will be shared with colleagues within the institution, specifically those who are involved in the programme.

It would be considered to be of therapeutic benefit to challenge a client's patterns of behaviour in the interest of increasing their self-awareness. It may not always be appropriate to challenge the behaviours of trainees unless we believe that their behaviour is compromising their fitness to practice or ability to complete assessments in some way. Trainees may not be ready to be challenged outright so we have to consider sensitive ways to communicate, for example, unprofessional behaviour. In addition, the dynamics within each cohort can be challenging for individual trainees and may require some support and management. Group processing opportunities can be a useful way to address any difficulties.

Entering the profession

If you haven't already gained experience teaching in an HE environment, I would suggest that you begin to make links with your local doctorate in counselling psychology. You could offer to deliver a session on your area of research or clinical specialism in person or online as a way to develop a relationship with the programme director and team. Find out from the team what it is like to work on that specific programme and let people know that you are interested in working there. If you don't have a local doctorate in your region, considering offering some guest lectures to undergraduate or postgraduate psychology programmes in order to gain some experience.

Consider working with your research supervisor to publish the findings from your own thesis, if you haven't already, and present your findings at a conference. Conference papers can be listed with publications and presenting can be enjoyable, particularly at the BPS Division of Counselling Psychology conference where you can also network with colleagues from across the UK and beyond. Perhaps you could contact a local counselling psychology programme and offer to be a 'field research supervisor' for a trainee who is interested in carrying out research in your area of special interest. I was director of studies for a trainee alongside a colleague who was the second supervisor. As the student's research focused on clients who had experienced a stroke, we made links with a colleague of ours (a graduate from the programme) who worked in an NHS stroke service. She was able to advise on where the trainee could recruit participants, help with writing documents that were suitable for stroke survivors and recommend policies and guidelines related to this clinical area. The student gained from the academic and clinical input of all supervisors and produced a high-quality, impactful piece of work.

Identify the transferable skills you have gained in your work as a counselling psychologist in the NHS, for example. Relevant here would be the clinical supervision of trainees, the delivery of training to and recruitment of staff and any projects you have undertaken that could be considered as enterprising (for example, audits, evaluations or service development).

In terms of confidence and being able to make links between theory and practice in your teaching and research supervision of trainees, I would recommend the following. Gain at least two years' post-qualifying experience as a counselling psychologist before you apply for a lecturing post. It is likely to be beneficial for your own confidence and the confidence that trainees have in you that you have sufficient experience to draw upon from your own clinical practice. Consider how you can continue engaging in clinical work while working as a lecturer so that your teaching is informed by some of your practice.

In preparation for a lecturing interview, familiarise yourself with the institution's mission/vision and strategies for the present/future. Universities operate as businesses so be aware of the national/international influencers on HE such as the TEFs and KEFs. WONKHE is a good resource for current issues in the sector.

Be mindful that the role of a lecturer requires flexibility. At times you may be required to cover for the absence of colleagues, teach undergraduates or teach a subject that you need to learn. Demonstrating your understanding of the role of a lecturer, knowledge of the wider and local context including the programme you are applying to teach on, ability to work as part of a team and flexibility in approach is likely to benefit you when being interviewed for a post.

Benefits of the role

Working in this role for 12 years, every day was a 'school day' as I constantly learned from my psychology colleagues, who brought different experiences and expertise. I learned from discussions with trainees in class, in one-to-one meetings with them and from their written work. There were many other opportunities within the university for continuing professional development including leadership and enterprise programmes, teaching qualifications, and opportunities to contribute to different committees and work with others to undertake research. Universities are filled with inspiring, educated and motivated people who are keen to share knowledge and ideas, so the development opportunities are usually continuous and complimentary. I have certainly grown in personal and professional confidence since becoming a lecturer.

The role of lecturer can be very fulfilling as we contribute to the education of the next generation of counselling psychologists. My favourite day was graduation day as, like their proud 'university mum', I applauded each trainee for their hard work, enthusiasm, determination and competence. Knowing I made a difference to the trainees I taught made the challenging times worthwhile. And, of course, teaching can be really good fun too – for example, I frequently used humour as a way to engage students and to facilitate their learning (Bakar & Kumar, 2019).

There are other perks of the role, including the ability to request 'inspection copies' of books from publishers who do not charge a fee but request feedback for the book and your opinion on its suitability for your trainees. I have a bookshelf full of 'free' books, which I appreciate. University holidays are usually aligned with school holidays and are considered to be generous in comparison to other psychology positions.

Challenges of the role

There are some challenges attached to the role of being a lecturer, as I've learnt from my own experience. The role is very exposing of our knowledge and limitations: there is nowhere to hide. This exposure can be acknowledged and overcome, or it can become all-consuming. Managing the tension between knowing and not knowing is a constant for psychologists, but when in a position of 'teacher' there is often an expectation from others (and maybe ourselves) that we are always the expert. Coping with this requires tenacity, self-care, acceptance and the energy to continue learning.

Consistent across institutions from conversations I have had with other colleagues is that the workload as a lecturer is often very demanding and at any one time there are often a lot of competing demands (researcher, teacher, entrepreneur, administrator and recruiter, to name but a few). This requires the capacity to be organised and to tolerate a never-ending 'to do' list. As there is always something we could be doing, knowing when to stop and when to say 'no' takes practice and requires good self-care and clear boundaries. My personal life allowed me the flexibility to work long days, but this was to ensure that I didn't ever work weekends. I also stayed true to my 'out of office' message, avoided looking at work emails when not at work and resisted putting my university emails on my personal mobile phone. However, the demands are high, and although the BPS specify one staff member to ten trainees, institutions interpret this in a variable fashion. Added to this is the way in which institutions base their measure of performance on national data-gathering processes. It has been argued that over-reliance on performance measurement 'undermines the professional autonomy or collegiality, which used to be the hallmark of academic life' (Graham, 2015, p. 671), and this can add to workload demands and pressure.

As with any job, there are often a number of stakeholders. As a lecturer, the stakeholders are trainees and their clients/colleagues, department/faculty colleagues, managers, placement providers and external regulators. Balancing their needs is often tricky as a lot of people need to be pleased, often simultaneously. It is helpful if the institution appreciates the distinction between a professional doctorate and a PhD as this can equate with support for the numerous roles that a lecturer might undertake compared to a lecturer of a purely academic course.

Reflection

You have just started working as lecturer teaching on the doctorate in counselling psychology. You have been asked to teach a two-hour session on ethics to the first-year trainees. Taking into account different learning styles, design a lesson plan for a workshop-style (interactive) lecture that you could deliver. Consider what skills and experience you have to deliver this lecture.

Conclusion

Working as a university lecturer on a doctorate in counselling psychology course can enrich our knowledge, understanding and provide us with the satisfaction of teaching our future colleagues. There are numerous opportunities for development and leadership as well as engagement with colleagues within and beyond the institution. It is a demanding role and is as extensive in the range of roles and opportunities as the amount of work required. For those who have never considered lecturing, guest lecturing is a great way to experience at least the teaching aspect of the role. A combination of lecturing and clinical work can provide counselling psychologists with a varied career that suits their interests and development. Of equal importance, it provides another avenue towards facilitating the growth and development of others.

References

Bakar, F. & Kumar, V. (2019). The use of humour in teaching and learning in higher education classrooms: Lecturers' perspectives. *Journal of English for Academic Purposes, 40*, 15–25.

British Psychological Society (2019). Standards for the accreditation of doctoral programmes in counselling psychology. BPS.

Graham, A.T. (2015). Academic staff performance and workload in higher education in the UK: The conceptual dichotomy. *Journal of Further and Higher Education, 39* (5), 665–679. doi:10.1080/0309877X.2014.971110.

Grand, I.J. (2006). Ascending to the concrete: Teaching complexity in a counselling psychology program. *Journal of Transformative Education, 4*(2), 157–174. doi:10.1177/1541344605283143.

HCPC (2009). Guidance on Conduct and Ethics for Students. hcpc-uk.org/globala ssets/resources/guidance/guidance-on-conduct-and-ethics-for-students.pdf.

HCPC (2015). Standards of Proficiency: Practitioner Psychologists. www.hcpc-uk.org/resources/standards/standards-of-proficiency-practitioner-psychologists/.

HCPC (2017). Standards of Education and Training. hcpc-uk.org/globalassets/resour ces/standards/standards-of-education-and-training.pdf.

HCPC. Approved programmes. www.hcpc-uk.org/education/approved-programmes/.

McIntosh, M., Nicholas, H. & Huq, A.H. (2019). *Leadership and Diversity in Psychology: Moving Beyond the Limits.* Routledge.

OfS (The Office for Students) (2019). The Teaching Excellence and Student Outcomes Framework (TEF): A short guide to the awards. www.officeforstudents.org.uk/m edia/0c6bd23e-57b8-4f22-a236-fb27346cde6e/tef_short_guide_-june_2019_final.pdf.

QQA (The Quality Assurance Agency) (2018a). The Revised UK Quality Code for Higher Education. www.qaa.ac.uk/docs/qaa/quality-code/revised-uk-quality-code-for-higher-education.pdf?sfvrsn=4c19f781_8.

QQA (The Quality Assurance Agency) (2018b). The UK Quality Code for Higher Education. Advice and Guidance. Research Degrees. www.qaa.ac.uk/quality-code/a dvice-and-guidance/research-degrees.

Research Excellence Framework (REF). www.ref.ac.uk/about.

UK Research Innovation (2021). Knowledge Exchange Framework: Decisions for the first iteration (KEF). https://re.ukri.org/sector-guidance/publications/knowledge-exchange-framework-decisions-for-the-first-iteration/.

WONKHE. www.wonkhe.com.

Wood, M. & Su, F. (2017). What makes an excellent lecturer? Academics' perspectives on the discourse of 'teaching excellence' in higher education. *Teaching in Higher Education, 22*(*4*), 451–466. doi:10.1080/13562517.2017.1301911.

Conclusion

Helen Nicholas, Daisy Best and Mark Bradley

This book illustrates the diverse and varied contexts and roles that counselling psychologists choose to work within. The chapters outlined in the three parts provide the reader with a glimpse into some of the areas where counselling psychologist are engaged in excellent work. As editors we are very aware that we have not been able to include all the areas of specialism and settings. There are many more settings within which counselling psychologists continue to provide their specialist knowledge and research expertise. Furthermore, psychology is an evolving field and as new services are formed, different ways of working are discovered and new presenting concerns and challenges arise. Therefore, counselling psychologists will find innovative, new and exciting ways to work with clients and services will continue to emerge and develop. We would love to hear more about these roles, so if you are working in an area that is not included in this first edition, please get in touch.

Each of our authors has openly and willingly invited us into their working lives and provided us with a balanced view of the opportunities and challenges associated with their roles. Some authors work within the constraints of an organisation, others have more freedom to work in ways that suit their client groups. Counselling psychologists worldwide have many therapeutic approaches and skills in common despite the broad range of contexts and experiences.

While authors have attempted to consider the economic, social and political environments that inform and inhibit different contexts, it is important to acknowledge here that all settings are influenced by wider government policies and agendas. For example, therapeutic models may be based upon broad usage rather than reflecting the most effective ways of working. They may be considered most effective because they are perceived to be more time efficient and, therefore, more cost effective. This does not always equate to individual need or choice. Therefore, a critical stance is always encouraged when reflecting on why we work the way we do and how political convenience may override clinician and client choice.

Being ethical practitioners, it is vital that we counselling psychologists work with an awareness of difference and diversity and experiences associated with

DOI: 10.4324/9781003159339-19

'power, privilege and oppression' (Winter, 2019, p. 86). In particular, how socio-political histories influence safety and trust and, therefore, engagement in and benefit from whatever service we are providing. For example, Black, Asian and Minority Ethnic (BAME) people have been subject to being 'categorised' with 'social consequences', and the social (including the 'virus' of racism), economic, educational, environmental and psychological inequalities place them at higher risk of poor health outcomes (BPS, 2020, pp. 3–4). We have a duty to ensure that we are aware of any disparities in privilege and power and that we provide 'inclusive, culturally sensitive mental health services' (BPS, 2020, p. 6). It is important to be aware that clients from 'minority' backgrounds are more likely than not to have been subject to overt and covert oppression and discrimination at some point in their lifetime (BPS, 2020).

We would hope to include chapters that explore minority groups' experiences and needs within therapeutic contexts and settings in future editions of this book. New chapters could focus on the impact that counselling psychologists have on the field of neuropsychology, and how they serve to help those in distress due to anxiety around the COVID-19 pandemic; governmental lockdowns; isolation; and reopening anxiety. Changes implemented in the UK and internationally, such as Brexit; environmental and climate issues; and the benefits of ecopsychology may also be introduced in future editions of this book.

We hope that this book will encourage skilled professionals into this wonderful career, qualified practitioner psychologists into new settings and qualified counselling psychologists to consider working with different client groups. We also hope that it helps dispel some of the myths around where counselling psychologists work and the type of work they undertake.

We have proudly illustrated how counselling psychology is a lifelong career in which we work across the lifespan, within the private and the public sector and as independent practitioners. As we have shown, the work of counselling psychologists is varied and diverse, with a broad range of opportunities to make a difference to the lives of individuals and communities.

References

BPS (British Psychology Society) (2020). Racial and social inequalities: Taking the conversations forward. DCP Racial and Social Inequalities in the Times of Covid-19 Working Group. www.bps.org.uk/sites/www.bps.org.uk/files/Member%20Networks/Divisions/DCP/Racial%20and%20Social%20Inequalities%20in%20the%20times%20of%20Covid-19.pdf.

Winter, L. (2019). Power and privilege in psychology: Can we have egalitarian leadership? In M. McIntosh, H. Nicholas & A. Husain Huq (eds), *Leadership and Diversity in Psychology: Moving beyond the Limits* (pp. 85–93). Routledge. https://doi.org/10.4324/9780429432606.

Index

Entries in **bold** denote tables; entries in *italics* denote figures.

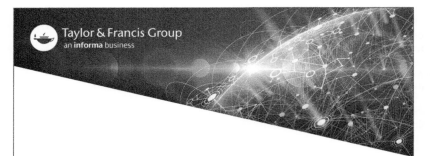